ROUTLEDGE LIBRARY EDITIONS: SOUTH AFRICA

Volume 2

APARTHEID

APARTHEID

A Documentary Study of Modern South Africa

EDGAR H. BROOKES

LONDON AND NEW YORK

First published in 1968 by Routledge & Kegan Paul Ltd.

This edition first published in 2023
by Routledge
4 Park Square, Milton Park, Abingdon, Oxon OX14 4RN

and by Routledge
605 Third Avenue, New York, NY 10158

Routledge is an imprint of the Taylor & Francis Group, an informa business

© 1968 Edgar H. Brookes

All rights reserved. No part of this book may be reprinted or reproduced or utilised in any form or by any electronic, mechanical, or other means, now known or hereafter invented, including photocopying and recording, or in any information storage or retrieval system, without permission in writing from the publishers.

Trademark notice: Product or corporate names may be trademarks or registered trademarks, and are used only for identification and explanation without intent to infringe.

British Library Cataloguing in Publication Data
A catalogue record for this book is available from the British Library

ISBN: 978-1-032-30347-5 (Set)
ISBN: 978-1-032-31041-1 (Volume 2) (hbk)
ISBN: 978-1-032-31055-8 (Volume 2) (pbk)
ISBN: 978-1-003-30779-2 (Volume 2) (ebk)

DOI: 10.4324/9781003307792

Publisher's Note
The publisher has gone to great lengths to ensure the quality of this reprint but points out that some imperfections in the original copies may be apparent.

Disclaimer
The publisher has made every effort to trace copyright holders and would welcome correspondence from those they have been unable to trace.

This is a reissue of a previously published book. The language is reflective of the time in which this book was published. In reissuing this book, no offence is intended by the Publishers to any reader.

APARTHEID
A DOCUMENTARY STUDY OF MODERN SOUTH AFRICA

Edgar H. Brookes
M.A., D.Litt. (S. Africa), Hon. LL.D.
(Cape Town & Queen's)

LONDON
ROUTLEDGE & KEGAN PAUL

*First published 1968
by Routledge & Kegan Paul Limited
Broadway House, 68–74, Carter Lane
London, E.C.4*

*Printed in Great Britain
by C. Tinling & Co. Ltd.
Liverpool, London and Prescot*

© *Edgar H. Brookes 1968*

*No part of this book may be reproduced
in any form without permission from
the publisher, except for the quotation
of brief passages in criticism*

*SBN 7100 2994 2 (c)
SBN 7100 6101 3 (p)*

Contents

GENERAL EDITOR'S PREFACE	page	ix
VOLUME EDITOR'S PREFACE		xi
ACKNOWLEDGMENTS		xiii
INTRODUCTION		xv
SUGGESTIONS FOR FURTHER STUDY		xxxiv

SELECT DOCUMENTS
PART I: APARTHEID—THE WORD AND ITS MEANING

1. The Origin of the Use of the Term 'Apartheid'. From *Dawie 1946–64* by Louis Louw, 1965   1
2. Speech by Dr. Verwoerd, 3 September 1948   2

PART II: THE POPULATION REGISTRATION ACT

3. Extracts from the Population Registration Act, No. 30 of 1950   19
4. Extracts from a speech by the Minister of the Interior, Dr. T. E. Dönges, introducing the Population Registration Act, 8 March 1950   21
5. The working of the Population Registration Act. From *Survey of Race Relations 1955–66*, by South African Institute of Race Relations   23

PART III: OPPOSITION POLICIES

6. The United Party. From *Handbook for Better Race Relations*   27
7. The Progressive Party. From *Safeguard Your Future, the Principles of the Progressive Party of South Africa*   34
8. The Liberal Party. Statement by Alan Paton, National President of the Liberal Party   37

CONTENTS

PART IV: BANTU EDUCATION

9. From the *Report of the Commission on Native Education 1945–51*, presided over by Dr. W. W. M. Eiselen   41
10. From the Bantu Education Act, No. 47 of 1953   47
11. From a speech by the Minister of Native Affairs, 17 September 1953   48
12. The closing of Adams College
    (a) From *Iso Lomuzi*, letter of the Principal, 17 September 1956   52
    (b) From the *Natal Mercury*, Durban, 3 December 1956   54
13. From an article in the *Natal Daily News*, by Dr. W. G. McConkey, December 1962   55

PART V: UNIVERSITY EDUCATION

14. From the Extension of University Education Act, No. 45 of 1959   61
15. From a speech by the Minister of Education, Arts and Science, on the Second Reading of the Extension of University Education Bill, 8 April 1959   63
16. From *A Digest of Protest against the University Apartheid Legislation*, National Union of South African Students, 1957   68

PART VI: THE CHURCHES

17. From the Native Laws Amendment Act, No. 36 of 1957   73
18. Letter by Archbishop Clayton to the Prime Minister, 6 March 1957. From *Where We Stand, Archbishop Clayton's Charges 1948–57*   74
19. From *The Churches and Race Relations in South Africa* by Lesley Cawood
    (a) The Nederduitse Gereformeerde Kerk   76
    (b) The Methodist Church   79
    (c) The Roman Catholic Church   81
    (d) The Presbyterian Church   83
    (e) The Congregational Church   85

CONTENTS

PART VII:
APARTHEID IN PRACTICE—WORK AND VOTING

20. From the Separate Amenities Act, No. 49 of 1953   87
21. Debate on influx control, House of Assembly, 11 and 13 February 1952   91
22. Labour regulations from the *Government Gazette Extraordinary*, 3 December 1965   98
23. Trade Unions. From *A Survey of Race Relations in South Africa*, 1965, by Muriel Horrell for the South African Institute of Race Relations   112
24. Coloured disfranchisement. From *South Africa*, by Professor H. M. Robertson, Duke University Commonwealth-Studies Centre, 1957   116
25. From the Promotion of Bantu Self-Government Act, No. 46 of 1959   126
26. From the Asiatic Laws Amendment Act, No. 47 of 1948   128

PART VIII: THE GROUP AREAS ACT

27. From the Group Areas Act, No. 41 of 1950   131
28. From a speech by the Minister of the Interior, introducing the Group Areas Act, 14 June 1950   137
29. The case against
    (a) From a speech on the Group Areas Act in the Senate, by Dr. Edgar H. Brookes, 14 June 1950   155
    (b) From a speech on an amendment to the Group Areas Act in the House of Assembly by Mrs. Helen Suzman, 23 February 1961   166

PART IX:
APARTHEID IN PRACTICE—SOCIAL CONSEQUENCES

30. Marriage and Immorality Laws. From *The Politics of Inequality*, by Gwendolen M. Carter, 1958   179
31. Petty Apartheid
    (a) Debate between Mrs. H. Suzman and the Minister of Community Development, 2 June 1965   187
    (b) From the *Cape Times*, 15 October 1965   191

vii

CONTENTS

32. From the Prohibition of Improper Interference Bill, 1966 — 194
33. Banning, banishment and other restrictive measures. A summary by Dr. Edgar H. Brookes — 204

POSTSCRIPTA
 (a) Intimidation — 209
 (b) U.D.I. and Rhodesia—the South African reaction — 209

SELECT BIBLIOGRAPHY — 211

SUBJECT INDEX — 215

General Editor's Preface

The World Studies Series is designed to make a new and important contribution to the study of modern history. Each volume in the Series will provide students in sixth forms, Colleges of Education and Universities with a range of contemporary material drawn from many sources, not only from official and semi-official records, but also from contemporary historical writing and from reliable journals. The material is selected and introduced by a scholar who establishes the context of his subject and suggests possible lines of discussion and enquiry that can accompany a study of the documents.

Through these volumes the student can learn how to read and assess historical documents. He will see how the contemporary historian works and how historical judgements are formed. He will learn to discriminate among a number of sources and to weigh evidence. He is confronted with recent instances of what Professor Butterfield has called 'the human predicament' revealed by history; evidence concerning the national, racial and ideological factors which at present hinder or advance man's progress towards some form of world society.

Dr. Brookes has compiled a carefully documented explanation of the doctrine of Apartheid. From inside South Africa, yet with admirable fairness, he has exposed the complex amalgam of racial, religious and economic tensions, which constitute the political scene of that country today. From such evidence the reader can begin to get the feel of what it means to be English, Afrikaans, Bantu and 'Coloured' in a state where the policy of 'Separate but Equal' results in stabbingly sharp antitheses and discords tragically unresolved.

JAMES HENDERSON

Volume Editor's Preface

The contents of this selection of documents fall into three divisions: Parts I, II and III deal with the meaning of *apartheid* for South Africa as a whole: Parts IV, V and VI concentrate on its implications for education and for the churches: Parts VII, VIII and IX demonstrate the social consequences of *apartheid* doctrine. Care has been taken to make use of quotations, not only from official sources but also from the press (e.g. Part IV, Document 13) and from reputable monographs (e.g. Part IX, Document 30). It is intended that the material should speak for itself, thus defining the complexity of the *apartheid* problem without seeking to disguise its grave moral implications.

Acknowledgments

All quotations from South African Parliamentary publications, (Hansard and Statutes) are reproduced under the Government Printer's copyright authority No. 3676 of 7 April 1966. Our thanks are also due to *Die Tafelberg Uitgewers*, Cape Town, in respect of Document 1; the South African Institute of Race Relations in respect of Documents 5, 19 and 23; the National Union of South African Students in respect of Document 16; the United Party in respect of Document 6; the Progressive Party in respect of Document 7; the Liberal Party in respect of Document 8; the Oxford University Press in respect of Document 18; Professor H. M. Robertson and the Duke University Press in respect of Document 24; Messrs. Thames and Hudson Ltd., in respect of Document 30.

E. H. B.

Introduction

1. POINTS OF VIEW ADOPTED

It would be idle to pretend that the compiler of these documents is himself impartial on the issue of Apartheid. Indeed, as reference to Documents Nos. 12 and 29 will show, he has been one of its strongest opponents. He has, however, tried to present the case fairly, so that his readers may form their own conclusions. He has done this, firstly, by quoting the actual words of the apartheid laws, secondly, by giving the case for them as well as the case against, and thirdly by letting responsible persons like the Ministers responsible for particular Bills, present the pro-apartheid case. In the necessary selection and condensation demanded by the size of this book he has not at any time been consciously unfair, and he earnestly hopes not unconsciously so. Opposed though he is to apartheid as being in his judgement irreconcilable with Christian ethics, and ultimately unwise, impracticable and against the best interests of South Africa, he has tried to carry out the principle of presenting the other side fully and fairly.

But there is more to a study of apartheid than this. We can understand a thing without necessarily approving it, but it is necessary to understand the facts which make it possible for many good and kind men in South Africa to approve apartheid, and let that understanding play its full part in influencing our own final decisions. This we shall now proceed to do.

2. THE BACKGROUND OF COLONIALISM

The great event in the history of South Africa as understood by most South Africans is the settlement of the Cape by Jan van Riebeeck in 1652. Van Riebeeck's head appears on the obverse of most South African coins and is the central figure on South Africa's bank notes. The year 1652 is significant. Earlier than

INTRODUCTION

the British colonisation of Pennsylvania and New York, of Australia and New Zealand, it is not much later than the British settlements in Virginia and New England or the French settlement in Canada. For various reasons neither Australia nor New Zealand, neither Canada nor the United States, has to face the position of a large aboriginal majority, and therefore all can more easily emancipate themselves from the prejudices and modes of thought of the colonial era. The closest analogy to South Africa would be the state of Mississippi with its present population structure detached from the United States and flung out into the ocean as an independent republic.

In the history syllabuses of most South African universities the history of colonisation occupied a prominent place until very recently. In South African schools the movement of history stressed is mainly that of the development of the three mother nations of South Africa—Holland, France and Britain —their colonising activities and the culmination of these in the South African settlement. While the world as a whole fully understands that the era of colonisation and imperialism has, after four centuries, come to an end, South Africa is still living in the atmosphere of that era, and cannot readily understand the reasoning of those who have emerged from it. The dialogue between South Africa and the rest of the world in the 1960s is thus something like the duel between the whale and the elephant.

Whatever is wrong in South African attitudes on these matters, one thing is surely an arguable point to make—that a population of some millions of White people whose ancestors were in the Cape before William Penn set foot in Pennsylvania ought not to be treated as a mere unfortunate incident, and is not rightly to be compared with very small and very recent White minorities in West or even in East Africa. Pan-Africanism over-simplifies the picture, nor, as it seems to many South Africans, has pan-Africanism a moral case. It is only another form of racial dominance.

'You call the chess-board white, you call it black', as Browning says, but it remains chequered none the less, despite Afrikaner nationalists and pan-African nationalists.

INTRODUCTION

When van Riebeeck landed at the Cape, twelve years before the British seized New York, he brought with him not a carefully selected band of cultured immigrants, but only soldiers and petty officials of the Dutch East India Company, mainly Dutch but partly German in nationality. They had the prejudices of their class and age. The local aborigines spoke a language which seemed extremely queer to the settlers. They therefore, with the half-unconscious superiority of the white man, named it 'Hotnot' or 'Hottentot', to indicate its stammering nature. The speakers of this tongue were soon called the 'stinking Hotnots' with all the olfactory arrogance of the European, and the 'lazy Hotnots' because they saw no special advantage in working for the new settlers. In these circumstances the arrival of one hundred and seventy Negro slaves mainly from Angola on the *Amersfoort* in 1658 seemed providential. South African agriculture in the very earliest days thus came to depend on Coloured slave labour, and colour, as in every slave state, became identified with inferiority.

There is nothing in all this which could not be paralleled from the history of Virginia or the Carolinas, Jamaica or Trinidad. It is not in its origins, but in its long and uncritical continuance, that the South African way of life is so specially open to criticism.

3. THE GRENSBOERE (FRONTIER FARMERS)

During the eighteenth century, the White settlers of South Africa, spread out over what is now the Western and Central Cape Province. Once they had crossed the great mountain barriers and reached the central plateau of the Karroo, most South Africans became *trekkers* (sheep and cattle ranchers). The extensive rather than intensive nature of their farming called for Hottentot or slave labour. Over the mountains they came into touch with an even earlier population group—the so-called 'Bushmen', nomadic hunters who could not understand the pastoral farming habits of the *trekkers*, and who loosed their poisoned arrows against both the farmer and his

INTRODUCTION

flocks and herds. Thus began the only war of extermination in South African history. The Bushmen were not so unfortunate as the Tasmanian 'blackfellows': some survived, some are with us still, but they suffered greatly. Against no other people of colour has a similar war of extermination been waged.

The *trekkers*, moving away from civilisation and from such centres of culture as there were in the country, forsook the world of books and of changing thought. Many of them had the old Dutch Bible as their only book. But, poor and backward as they were, it was they who went furthest in the building of a new Afrikaner nation, increasingly free from the trammels of distant Cape Town and still more distant Holland; and it was they who were the first to speak the new language, Afrikaans, which was first written in 1861 and only given official recognition in 1927, but was beginning to be a living vernacular in the late eighteenth century. Thus it was these hardy pioneers who were in the forefront of national and linguistic development, those in other words least influenced by changes of thought, new theories or humanitarian sentiments. The fact that in 1966 the Transvaal Nationalists are the most influential group in the National Party is an interesting analogy, for though they today include Masters of Arts and Doctors of Philosophy their political outlook was in its turn formed when their fathers were the isolated and embattled frontiersmen of South Africa.

4. THE COMING OF THE BRITISH

Late in the eighteenth century two new developments took place. The first was the occupation of the Cape by the British (to be renewed finally in 1806). The second was the meeting of the *trekkers* advancing northward and eastward with the advance guard of the Bantu or African tribes moving southward and westward. Here were people much more formidable in every way than the Hottentots and Bushmen—greater in numbers, more advanced in organisation, law and government, and doughty fighters.

The frontier farmers had become used to fending for them-

INTRODUCTION

selves: the Dutch East India Company had done little to help them. The British were prepared to extend a measure of military protection to the frontier, but as a corollary of this they claimed the right to pass judgement on frontier disputes and to the fury and amazement of the farmers they took the line that the Africans were not always in the wrong and the farmers not always in the right. Thus began the 'war on two fronts' of the Afrikaner—the struggle against the British and the struggle against the Africans—which has provided much of the emotional force of Afrikaner nationalism even up to the present day.

British administrators from 1795 to 1803 and from 1806 onwards were fairly conservative—some of the Governors, like Lord Charles Somerset were high Tories—but they believed in the rule of law and in the accepted norms of administrative action. They demurred at a wholesale condemnation of Xhosa (African) cattle-lifters without adequate evidence, sometimes in the face of such evidence as was available. They met something of the same problems as were found in the 'wild west' of the United States when the law caught up with the frontier.

Moreover British missionaries had appeared on the scene, and many of them were valiant fighters for what they felt to be justice. The tendency among many Africans today is to accuse missionaries of being agents of imperialism. When the smoke of present-day controversies has died away, a better estimate of missionary work will be possible. Certainly many missionaries loved the people among whom they worked, and many believed in a Christian version of the rights of man. Though the *trekkers* were also Christians, and sometimes even devout Christians, there was little in common between them and the British missionaries.

In the secular sphere doctrines of 'philanthropy' were widespread in Britain as on the Continent. Tory Governors and Tory ministers could not turn their backs on this. Indeed it was the most vilified Tory of all—Castlereagh—who took up so much of the time of the Congress of Vienna in 1814 on the issue of condemning the slave trade.

INTRODUCTION

5. THE GREAT TREK

The effect of these influences on frontier life was, from the point of view of the *trekker*, catastrophic. After three decades (1806-36) they decided to turn their backs on the British Government and go into the interior to found new states for themselves. This process in South African history is described as the Great Trek.

About the Great Trek there are one or two errors to be discussed before we come to what really happened. One of these is that the Trek was only an extension on a larger scale of the process of 'trekking' (migration) that had been going on for a century and a half. This is not true, for the Great Trek was an organised, politically-motivated movement, very different in character from the previous placid and unorganised steady movement. The second error is that the Great Trek was the result of the Slave Emancipation Act of 1833. With regard to this it is probably sufficient to point out that over 90 per cent of the Trekkers were from the eastern Cape, and over 90 per cent of the slaves were in the western Cape. The third error is that the Trekkers set out to establish slave states. It is true that some of the acts of the Trekkers were equivocal—captured children after a raid on the tribes were 'apprenticed' to farmers—but this was never on so large a scale or so systematically done as to constitute a system of slavery.

The reaction of the Afrikaner frontiersman was not against slavery, but against British race policies on the frontier. It was really the frontiersman's reaction against civil servants, or even more fundamentally a reaction of the eighteenth against the nineteenth century.

In a short introduction of this kind, it is impossible to give a balanced picture of South African history throughout the nineteenth century. Our purpose is, however, not so much to give a complete picture, impartially distributing praise and blame, as to help readers to understand what they might otherwise find difficulty in understanding—how intelligent and not unkindly men who profess Christianity can come to support apartheid.

INTRODUCTION

6. APARTHEID IN THE TREKKER STATES

From this point of view let us consider the three inland Provinces of the Republic in turn. The *Voortrekkers* (as one must now begin to call them) penetrated into the beautiful, largely depopulated area of Natal in 1837. In February 1838 their leader, Piet Retief, with sixty-seven men, was treacherously murdered by the Zulu monarch, Dingane. Immediately afterwards the Zulu armies set out and massacred family after family in their scattered encampments. On the 16 December 1838 the Voortrekkers inflicted a severe defeat on the Zulu army at Blood River. Twelve days before this battle a small British force occupied the Port of Durban. It was soon afterwards withdrawn. In 1840 the Trekkers completed the subjection of the Zulu nation as a vassal state under their new prince, Mpande, and less than two years later a new British force arrived, never to leave until all British garrisons were withdrawn in 1914. In 1843 the Voortrekkers submitted and in 1845 Natal became a British Crown Colony.

7. THE BRITISH SOUTH AFRICAN ATTITUDE: SHEPSTONE

Similarly the Voortrekkers who went into what is now the Orange Free State were annexed in 1848, and although their independence was restored in 1854, they suffered two great blows—one when the Governor of the Cape stepped in and annexed Basutoland in 1868 just as the Orange Free State seemed likely to defeat the Basuto, and the other in 1871 when the British stepped in as the allies of the Griqua chief, Andries Waterboer, and snatched away the Kimberley diamond mines, to which the Orange Free State laid claim.

The Transvaal was allowed to develop in its own remote and anarchical way until 1877, but in that year the Natal statesman, Sir Theophilus Shepstone, took advantage of its disturbed and divided condition to annex it. Even though a limited independence was restored to it in 1881, the bitterness of the annexation rankled.

INTRODUCTION

Thus, from the point of view of the Afrikaner Nationalists who form the core of the supporters of apartheid in the Republic, the Voortrekkers, moving away from the British officials and missionaries, were persistently followed up. They tried in Natal to regulate their relations with the Zulu monarch by treaty, but Dingane massacred them. They seized tribal lands without consideration or legal process in the Transvaal, but however they faced their problems, the British were there to reproach—and annex—them. There was no opportunity in the three northern States for the growth of an atmosphere like that of the Cape, in which, with general goodwill, Afrikaner as well as British, black, white and coloured men if they reached a certain not very exacting educational and financial level were registered as voters on a common electoral roll.

It must not be assumed, as it often has been in the past, that South Africans of British descent have been better than Afrikaners in these matters. Two illustrations will make this clear. Natal, as it developed after 1845, was an overwhelmingly British settlement, but there was very little liberalism in it. The mass of the colonists wanted White supremacy and cheap labour. The alternative policy—that of Sir Theophilus Shepstone—was one of maintaining the Africans in Reserves and not forcing them out to work. But it was none the less a policy of apartheid—'homelands', tribal rule, political separation—in all essentials. The franchise was obtainable by Africans but under such stringent conditions that it amounted to nothing.

8. THE BRITISH SOUTH AFRICAN ATTITUDES: MILNER

The second illustration is supplied by a study of the Milner régime from 1902 to 1906. These four years form the only period of South African history in which Britain and British South Africans were in power in all four parts of South Africa. This artificial position was the result of the Jameson Raid of 1895–96 and the War of 1899–1902. Preceded by the squalid mixture of trickery and force which overcame Lobengula and created modern Rhodesia, they were examples of imperialism at its strongest and least attractive period, touched indeed by the decadence which generally follows an imperial zenith. Britain again became, more deeply than ever before, the enemy of the Afrikaner, but it did not become the friend of the African. Milner had not been above exploiting the grievances of Coloured and Indian British subjects in the Transvaal, but when he came into power he did nothing for them or the Africans. It could have been urged with some force that the Republics were holding their non-White populations in a position of permanent inferiority, but nothing was done to alter this in any material way. The South African Native Affairs Commission of 1903–05 illustrated the weakness of the Milner rule in this field very clearly. Appointed by Milner, having only two 'tame' Afrikaners among a large majority of British South Africans, it advocated policies of separation in the field of land and of Parliamentary representation which were duly embodied in the Natives Land Act of 1913 and the Hertzog legislation of 1936. In short it stood for a policy of apartheid, a little more moderate and 'civilised' than is sometimes the case, but apartheid none the less.

Even in 1968 it is very misleading to present the English-speaking population as liberals and the Afrikaans-speaking as supporters of apartheid. The only measure of truth in this contention is that the British South African if he supports apartheid (as the majority do) finds himself in opposition to the academic and ecclesiastical leadership of his group, while the liberal Afrikaner minority—and there certainly is such a minority—faces with great moral courage the strictures of the Afrikaans Churches and universities.

We must thus dispose clearly and finally of the incorrect theory that British South Africanism is liberal and Afrikanerdom pro-apartheid. Nevertheless the point of the dedication of Afrikaans culture and religion to the ideal of apartheid is important and will be taken up again later.

9. SOUTH AFRICA 1902–10

We return to our brief survey of South African history. When the Peace Treaty was signed on 31 May 1902 it promised

INTRODUCTION

inter alia that no franchise would be given to 'Natives' in the former Republics until after the introduction of self-government. This was the Conservatives' reaction to the situation. But in 1906 the Liberal Party came into office with a larger Parliamentary majority than they had ever had before or were ever to have again, brimfull of humanitarianism and good intentions. The Liberal ministry under Campbell-Bannerman gave back self-government to the Transvaal in 1906 and to the Orange Free State in 1907, but in neither case was this coupled with any franchise of any kind for the Africans, Indians or Coloured people. This was merely a failure to advance, for there had been no such franchise before, but in 1910 the South Africa Act, passed under the aegis of the same Liberal ministry, actually took retrograde action and, by imposing a clear colour-bar on membership of the Union Parliament, took away an existing right—prized if not used—in the Cape Colony.

It is of course not wholly fair to criticise the men of 1910 by the international standards of the 1960s, or by the principles of a United Nations filled with independent African states, but, even allowing for this, it seems right to point out how the opportunity of modifying apartheid was three times lost—in 1906, in 1907 and in 1910. The British Liberal Party at the time of Union was deeply influenced by the desire to end the British-Afrikaans struggle and was inexcusably optimistic as to the course white South African politics would take. It could not foresee that General Botha and General Smuts, who did most surely respond to the Liberal Party's generosity, would in the course of time be overwhelmed by the more exclusively-minded Nationalists, and moreover even Botha was for apartheid and Smuts never, up to his last years, took up an unequivocal position against it.

10. BOTHA AND THE NATIVES' LAND ACT

Botha's first important legislation affecting 'Native Affairs' was the Natives' Land Act of 1913. This is too complicated a measure to be considered here in all its details, but the main

INTRODUCTION

principle was clear enough. Africans were thenceforth forbidden to purchase land outside the reserves and a few other special areas except by special permission of the Head of the State. Since the areas thus reserved to Africans constituted then only some 13 per cent of the area of the Union—the proportion has since been slightly extended—it meant that over three-quarters of the population were limited to a little more than one-eighth of the land. Botha, indeed, recognised the need for the extension of the so-called 'Native' areas, and the Act provided for the appointment of a Commission to demarcate new areas. When the Commission reported, a storm of opposition broke out in Parliament, for most of those who advocated separation, even while supporting new areas, were unwilling to have these areas demarcated within their own constituencies. Even if all the recommendations of the Commission had been accepted, however, there would have remained two objections—the first, that the total amount of land set apart was utterly inadequate, the second, that the principle of separation was a harsh and invalid one, especially as Africans at the time that the Bill was passed had the right to purchase freely in large areas of the Cape, Natal and the Transvaal.

A *modus vivendi* was arrived at which made it possible for some additional land to be bought, but the land question was not seriously taken up again until General Hertzog's well-known Bills of 1936.

II. THE HERTZOG LEGISLATION

General Hertzog is honoured by those who knew him as a gentleman, an honourable man, who in his own way had the interests of the Africans and the Coloured people at heart. As has been said, within the blinkers which he had put on himself, he moved forward with integrity. But those blinkers proved very serious limitations, and in effect they amounted to an uncritical acceptance of apartheid as the main principle of South African life. His Natives Trust and Land Act and Representation of Natives Act, both of 1936, represent apartheid of the old type, touched by such humanity and consideration

INTRODUCTION

as a convinced conservative could summon to his aid. Thus the Trust and Land Act, though its basis was territorial separation, did extend slightly the area for Africans, especially in the Transvaal where this was most needed, and even make some provision for individual purchase. Similarly the Representation Act, though it was a knock-out blow to the older liberalism in its abolition of the Cape franchise on the common roll, did provide for a minimum representation of the Cape in the House of Assembly on a separate roll, for a token representation of all four Provinces in the Senate, and for the creation of an advisory Natives' Representative Council.

The passing of this legislation in 1936 was made possible by the fusion of General Hertzog's party with that of General Smuts. When the outbreak of war destroyed this new union, General Smuts became Prime Minister. This great man, so outstanding in the international field, could never bring himself really to look the issues of race in his own country fully in the face. Under his premiership the members of the Natives Representative Council refused to function, describing their advisory body as a 'toy telephone'. Dissatisfaction increased. At the very end of his premiership General Smuts took a few tentative and timid steps in the direction of reform, but the election of 1948 swept him out of office and since then the Nationalist Party has had an uninterrupted tenure of power.

12. THE SIGNIFICANCE OF THE YEAR 1948

From Document 1 in this collection it will be seen that the term 'apartheid' was only coined in the Afrikaans language in the years 1943–44. It was widely used as a slogan in the election of 1948 and undoubtedly helped to bring the Nationalists into power. The Documents in this collection are drawn from the years 1948 to 1966.

There are good reasons for this limitation. To include all the documents bearing on apartheid would have taken us back to the days of Jan van Riebeeck's hedge of wild almonds planted in 1659 to mark the boundary between Dutchmen and Hottentots, and this would have necessitated four or five volumes rather than one.

Apart from this argument of convenience there are good reasons for commencing an intensive study of apartheid from the year 1948, but this introduction will have been written in vain if it does not make clear to the reader that the policy of separation goes far back into South African history and does not begin in 1948. At all times up to and including 1968 the great majority of white South Africans, whatever their political affiliations, have accepted it as the basis of policy. It was least accepted in the Cape between 1852 and 1910, most accepted in the Transvaal at all times, and in the country as a whole after 1948. It is specially bound up with the emotional life of the Afrikaner. The war on two fronts—against Britain and against the black man—has become almost part of his make-up. It requires a decisive and persistent change of heart to force him from it—an experience comparable with religious conversion. Freedom from belief in apartheid in the South Africa of today is for the few. Intellectual liberation, deep religious conviction, passionate rebellion against the trammels of the past—all these play their part in the slow but steady liberation of white South Africans from their instinctive faith in apartheid. This radical reappraisal is at the moment for the few.

It is therefore unfair to speak or to write as if one accused the Nationalists of having suddenly sprung a new theory of race on South Africa in 1948, and unjust to place the whole responsibility for South Africa's present condition on them. Apartheid, let us repeat it, springs from the life and experience of South Africa and goes back almost to 1652.

But there are, notwithstanding all this, cogent reasons for regarding 1948 as a watershed in South African political history. Apartheid after 1948 is different, not only in degree but even in some measure in kind, from pre-1948 policies of separation.

In the first place, it represents a philosophy of life rather than a mere conservative emotion. The men of 1948 set out to rationalise the prejudices of their fathers and to present apartheid as a moral principle. The doctrine of national self-

INTRODUCTION

preservation took on the overtones of a religious dogma. The ensuring of the racial integrity of the Whites became not merely a regrettable necessity, but a categorical imperative of ethics. Modern apartheid is thus something more than the older separation or 'segregation'; the question is much more than one of semantics.

South African Nationalists were sympathetic to Germany in both World Wars. Doubtless, particularly in the case of the First World War, their motivation was hostility to England and the desire to achieve South African independence rather than admiration for Germany as such. In the Second World War, which immediately preceded the election of 1948, the position was somewhat different. To accuse the Nationalists of being Nazis is an exaggeration and an affront—an election slogan rather than a reasoned judgement. All South African Nazis were Nationalists, but few Nationalists were Nazis. Nevertheless the philosophy of National Socialism did arouse a response in many Nationalists. Authoritarian ideals received a greater welcome than ever before among Afrikaners, and this is significant since independence of Government and dislike of central control had been during generations part of the Afrikaner heritage. While few Nationalists have been convinced or insistent anti-Semites, Hitler's doctrine of a master race could easily be applied, not indeed to Jews, but to the non-White races of South Africa. A philosophy of force, endemic in nineteenth and early twentieth-century German thinking, could thus take root in Afrikaner soil, particularly since the great protagonist of liberal and democratic thought had been the national enemy, England.

A second feature of post-1948 apartheid has been its terrible consistency. Whatever faults the British have had, no one has ventured to accuse them of having been too logical. But Dr. Verwoerd, although a psychologist, was logical to a fault. His reported speeches read strangely to English ears for this reason. This terrible consistency showed itself, for example, in banning a handful of African music lovers from hearing Handel's 'Messiah' in one South African city because their presence in a predominantly White audience was an infringement on the

INTRODUCTION

principle of apartheid. Unavailing were the arguments that this had been going on for decades, that the White people concerned had no objections to it, that it did not perceptibly modify the political or economic pattern of the city. These arguments would have been decisive to British minds. They would have convinced General Smuts. They might—though this is less certain—have convinced General Hertzog. But they did not convince the post-1948 Nationalists.

Modern Nationalist policies have also been bound up with an increasing belief in centralisation. This is not part of the older Afrikaner tradition: a centrifugal formation of little republics was a feature of early Transvaal history. It is only in this century, and particularly since 1948, that Afrikaner sentiment has swung to the support of a strong central authority. Since that authority is now committed to the support of apartheid, modern Nationalism sees no objection to using it.

13. APARTHEID IN LAW

Afrikaners have a great and sincere respect for the letter of the law, but the part played by conventions which is so important to Englishmen means little in their political theory and practice. Thus they accepted, however reluctantly, the decisions of the Supreme Court as to the illegality of interfering with the Cape Coloured franchise without the requisite two-thirds majority prescribed by the Constitution, but at the same time had no scruple in resorting to the clever trick of increasing the size and altering the constitution of the Senate in order to provide the two-thirds majority, a step which the Supreme Court, reluctant in its turn, had to accept. Respect for law has been modified since 1910 by the acceptance of the British doctrine of parliamentary sovereignty, which in fact makes the law the creation of the Nationalist caucus in Parliament. A highly centralised government backed by a safe parliamentary majority ruled by a highly disciplined caucus leads to something very much like party dictatorship under the forms of democracy.

INTRODUCTION

14. APARTHEID AND RELIGION

Since the Christian Church in general is opposed to apartheid, it might be expected that this would form a check on the Afrikaners. On the contrary the Dutch Reformed Church is one of the strongest influences in South Africa favouring the apartheid policy. The relation of the Afrikaner to his Church is a significant part of South African life. One speaks of 'his Church' and of 'the Dutch Reformed Church'. There are three Afrikaans-speaking churches in the Republic—the Nederduits Gereformeerde Kerk, the Nederduits Hervormde Kerk and the Gereformeerde Kerk. All three are Calvinist in doctrine and Presbyterian in discipline and church order. All are loosely translated into English as 'Dutch Reformed Church', but this term is perhaps best reserved for the Nederduits Gereformeerde Kerk, which is very considerably larger than the other two combined. All three hold essentially the same view about apartheid with only minor nuances of difference.

There are of course Afrikaners who are Methodists, Presbyterians, Anglicans, Roman Catholics, members of the Apostolic Church, Seventh Day Adventists and the like, but the great mass of them are members of the Dutch Reformed Church and its two sister churches, and it is of these that we must speak.

The Church during a great deal of its history has been 'the Afrikaner people at prayer'. The national cause through many a vicissitude has been the subject of the prayers, tears and thanksgivings of the Church. The Church can never be described merely as 'the Nationalist Party at prayer', but there has undoubtedly been a close link between the two entities. It has done much to build up the morality and the family life of the people. The Afrikaner people are a believing and a churchgoing people to a greater extent than British South Africans. It is all the more significant then that, except for a few heroic men who have had to suffer greatly for their opinions, the Church as a whole has supported apartheid. To the Afrikaner himself this has been a great factor in leading

INTRODUCTION

him to feel that his national policy is deeply rooted in morality and religion. To the world outside, and to the wider Christian Church, it has been something almost inexplicable, widening the gap between the Dutch Reformed Church and the world-wide Christian community. To many Africans it has been a scandal and a stumbling block, reinforcing the Communist and African Nationalist denigration of religion and of Christian missionaries.

If the attitude of the Church leaders in question were to change, the whole South African situation would be transformed. In the meantime when one considers the facts of the Afrikaner's history and realises that his Church and his cultural leaders have encouraged his feelings and not challenged them, it is not difficult to understand why apartheid has taken such a hold on the South African white electorate.

For Afrikaans cultural leadership has gone in the same direction. The Afrikaans universities have for years encouraged uniformity rather than enquiry or revolt in all those branches of learning which impinge on the national political life.

15. IS APARTHEID PRACTICABLE?

This brief survey should explain to readers how it comes about that so many white South Africans are supporters of apartheid in a world which considers race distinction as obsolete, discredited and wrong. We now leave the question of whether apartheid is moral and go on to consider its practicability.

One of the difficulties in assessing apartheid is that so many of its supporters refuse to face its full implications. Most practical apartheid schemes assume that the white man will still remain in control, holding the greater part of the land and possessing the greater part of the national income. Dr. Verwoerd used to speak of a commonwealth of South African Nations analagous to the British Commonwealth, but he showed no signs of conceding to the Transkei the complete self-government which South Africa demanded from Great Britain. Certainly the fairest form of apartheid would be a division of the land more or less in proportion to the population

INTRODUCTION

of the different racial groups. This would mean vast sacrifices on the part of the White population, but if it ever did take place, is there any guarantee that pan-Africanism would not try to sweep the resulting enfeebled White state out of the continent? Moreover considerable Indian and Coloured minorities would probably neither be willing to fall under the African state nor to remain in the European state without full equal rights.

A federation of racially separated states would have to meet in the end in a more or less integrated federal parliament. Many supporters of apartheid imagine that African leaders would be satisfied with self-government in their own provinces or states without any real voice in federal legislature or in the affairs of the 'South African Commonwealth', but this is surely wholly unrealistic thinking.

The fact is that for most supporters of apartheid, even those who would like to be described as enlightened supporters, apartheid is an uneasy attempt at a synthesis between White self-interest and justice. Awkward facts are evaded. Difficult reasonings are not pursued to the end. The lie in the soul remains to bedevil South African life. Few people are ready to think apartheid right through.

16. APARTHEID DEMANDS SACRIFICE

It was part of the greatness of Dr. Verwoerd that he saw clearly the necessity for immense sacrifice if the Afrikaner race was to preserve its identity, and that he helped many others to see it. It was part of his weakness that he never faced all the implications of his doctrine, and particularly that he introduced new and stringent apartheid restrictions before his policy of 'positive apartheid' had gone very far.

His 'Bantustans' were to be mainly rural paradises—his critics would prefer to use the term 'rural slums'—without any heavy industries and depending on the wages of the men of the area to be earned in 'border industries', near but not in the homelands. Economically, the Transkei is not a viable proposition.

INTRODUCTION

17. THE TRAGIC DILEMMA OF THE AFRIKANER

Once justice has been invited in to take a part in the argument, the unwilling but honest Afrikaner is bound to see the South Africa that he has known and loved, on which he has lavished the riches of his emotional life, disintegrating before his eyes. It is a fair question to ask whether the final result will be any more favourable to Afrikanerdom than an integrated State with equal rights. This dilemma can only be avoided by bowing justice out again as an embarrassing intruder.

To expect the Afrikaner, whose past and present we have been studying, to accept the liberal policy of integration and equal rights is to expect a very big thing. For over a century and a half he has been striving for independence from Britain. In 1899–1902 he was beaten to his knees. Valiant with a stubborn valour in war, he was equally persistent and equally courageous after the surrender. Certainly he lost the war. With equal certainty he won the peace. In 1914 the last British garrisons left South Africa. In 1961 the last Governor-General laid down his office. The Government is overwhelmingly Afrikaans-speaking, so is the Civil Service, so is the police force. The ideals of Nationalism have triumphed after decades of disaster, disappointment and suffering, all along the line. And just at this point of long-deferred triumph, the Afrikaner is asked to assent to political and ethical doctrines which will leave him in even worse case—not under the British this time, but under the despised Africans. This is more than flesh and blood can stand, and so the Afrikaner finds himself in 1968 hesitating between an incomplete and inadequate apartheid, and a pugnacious defiance of the whole outside world and indeed of the whole nature of things.

This frightful situation is not made easier by the propaganda of pan-Africanism, which desires not only democratic rule but African rule as such. Sooner or later, if democratic principles prevail, Africans will of course form a decided majority of the South African electorate, but it makes a difference whether this is attained by consent with mutual goodwill or is merely the triumph of African nationalism. Most white South Africans

INTRODUCTION

are afraid of the latter, and highly-coloured accounts of what has happened to White minorities in the Congo and elsewhere have made them still more afraid. But there are strong forces making for sanity and goodwill if they could only be marshalled. The Indian and Coloured communities stand to suffer from triumphant African nationalism and are much more attracted to a non-racial liberalism. Many Africans would welcome moderation. Will the Whites learn to work with those or will they persist in lumping them all together as 'the enemy' and spend their energies in trying to hold them back as long as possible? The theory of apartheid helps to strengthen this tendency to dig one's self in and resist to the end.

This is the South African dilemma. It is poignant and painful in the extreme. A peaceful way out of it is not clear. To the majority of white South Africans apartheid presents itself as the least painful solution. The object of this Introduction has been to enable the reader to see the circumstances in which the documents which follow have been possible. You, the reader, must now read them and come to your own conclusions.

SUGGESTIONS FOR FURTHER STUDY

Readers who would like to make a still further study of this complicated subject are advised to consider the following questions:

1. *How is the European minority in South Africa to be forced to concede equal rights to the African, Coloured and Indian majority?*
The operative word here is 'forced'. It is force that we must consider under this head, not persuasion. Even to raise the question in South Africa is to be suspected of treason against the existing state, yet raised it must be if our study of the subject is to be thorough.

There is little comfort for the impatient radical who tries to answer this question. South Africa is a strong country with a terrain to which its soldiers are accustomed and the soldiers of its invaders are not—a country moreover of great distances. Fighting against overwhelming numbers, with no financial resources and inadequate equipment, it kept the whole British Empire at bay for two and a half years at the turn of the century. The united forces of the great powers would undoubtedly prevail if they could remain united and vigorous, but the country would be a shambles, its survivors the survivors, in the words of Tacitus, 'not only of the others but also of themselves'. No one can say what might befall the African, Coloured and Indian population whom the outer world would be fighting to release. No one can say that the explosive situation created would not divide the attackers and even lead to a third world war.

2. *Can the situation be met by the imposition of economic sanctions?* At the time of writing (early in 1967) this seems problematical even in Rhodesia, much more so—even should Rhodesia finally succumb to sanctions—when applied to the much larger, richer and more self-contained economy of South Africa.

3. *If sanctions will not work, two questions arise.*
First, has the world not to admit in that case that it cannot solve the problems of South Africa by force, military or economic? Second—and from the world point of view this is tremendously important—how can a world organisation coerce a recalcitrant state of any size or strength? In this case as well as in others which we shall consider later, have we not perhaps undervalued and insufficiently studied the educational and spiritual resources of humanity?

4. *What is to become of the European minority in South Africa?*
If it is a question of a group of survivors beaten to their knees and compelled to accept an African government rendered hostile by the passions of war, can any effective protection be given to the human rights and property of these people? If it is desired to negotiate a settlement with the White minority before this last dread moment, what terms could be offered which would reassure them and at the same time be acceptable to the African, Indian and Coloured majority?

5. *Is complete partition possible or desirable?*
In the view of the writer it is neither. But what is your view? Could a boundary line be drawn by consent under international

INTRODUCTION

supervision? On which side of the boundary line would the Coloured and Indian groups desire to fall? If a small all-White state is thus constituted would this silence the pan-African demand for the ending of all White rule in Africa? Would the international organisation be able and willing to protect a state which, weakened financially and militarily, might not be able to protect itself?

The reader might none the less be led to the conclusion that out of many doubtfully acceptable solutions this would be the least bad. If so he should endeavour to give concrete form to his ideas by drawing the boundary of the new reduced White state.

6. *Is democracy the only solution?*
The world thinks so. The writer has no wish to argue otherwise. But a conscientious student of the South African situation cannot leave this question unstudied. Can we say that the democratic solution has been an unqualified success in Africa and in parts of Latin America? Does democracy necessarily involve the principle of 'one man, one vote'? And is this the whole of democracy? The writer would himself answer 'Yes', to the first question and 'No' to the second. What would the reader's view be? The principle of 'one man, one vote' led to the installation of Hitler in Germany. Will a majority government based on universal franchise protect individual freedom and ensure human rights better than Hitler did? The experience of the world is not such that we can answer this question in the affirmative without serious reservations. Is it important to give such guarantees? How, if at all, can they be given effectively?

7. *What, then, are the possibilities of the situation?*
Whatever path we take seems to lead to disaster and failure. Yet can the world leave the situation as it stands? Can the world say to the African, Coloured and Indian majority of South Africa: 'We are sorry, but the situation is too much for us, and we cannot help you'? The question answers itself. To the writer, as to many others the colour bar is morally wrong—a denial of the essential human qualities in every man. This consideration is decisive against making terms with apartheid.

INTRODUCTION

Students using this book have thus the herculean task of trying to see if there are any remedies which have yet to be considered. Certainly the world has given inadequate attention to the educational and spiritual forces which are to be found among men. In a country where forces of this kind are subjected to severe restrictions, this too may possibly turn out to be a will o' the wisp, but it must certainly be given more attention than has yet been devoted to it.

By whatever way we tread, all of us inside and outside South Africa who value human rights and respect all men, white men included, must keep on trying, must continue to hope and work for better things. If every reader of this book puts his mind and heart into this effort, solutions may come in unexpected ways, ways hitherto inadequately explored. The temptation is to take one of the extreme views—either that the white man must maintain his predominance, or that he must be handed over, by force and bloodshed if need be, to the African majority. We must advocate neither of these unless (a) we can satisfy our consciences that it is right; (b) we can satisfy our minds that we can find a practicable and effective way of carrying out our principle. As one who has grown old in this struggle without (he hopes) wholly losing faith, hope or charity, the writer hands the issue to his readers for their honest consideration.

PART I

Apartheid—the Word and its Meaning

The following extracts are taken from *Dawie 1946–64*, an Anthology selected from the writings of *Die Burger*'s political correspondent by Louis Louw.

'Dawie' (pronounced Dah-vee) is the political correspondent of *Die Burger* the oldest and perhaps the most moderate Nationalist newspaper in South Africa. 'Dawie' is liked and respected even by his opponents. This extract is translated from Afrikaans and quoted by permission of the publishers, Tafelberg-Uitgewers.

DOCUMENT 1. THE ORIGIN OF THE USE OF THE TERM 'APARTHEID'. FROM *Dawie 1946–64* BY LOUIS LOUW, (TAFELBERG-UITGEWERS, CAPE TOWN, 1965).

The origin of 'apartheid'

From London comes an enquiry about the coming into use of the word 'apartheid'. Who first used it and when?

I have done a little research in the matter and so far as I can determine the word was used for the first time in a leading article in *Die Burger* on 26 March 1943. In this reference was made to the 'Nationalists' policy of apartheid'. The next use of the term was again in a leading article in *Die Burger* on the 9 September 1943, in which mention was made of 'the recognised Afrikaner standpoint of apartheid'. The first use of the term in Parliament, as far as I can determine, was on the 25 January 1944 when Dr. Malan in his republican motion described the nature of the republic which he envisaged *inter alia* as follows: 'To ensure the safety of the white race and of Christian civilisation by the honest maintenance of the principles of apartheid and guardianship.'

APARTHEID—THE WORD AND ITS MEANING

If there are readers who know of an earlier use of the word I shall be obliged if they will write to me. . . .

In English

The word 'apartheid', although already used early in 1943, gained currency only slowly, perhaps among other reasons because political attention was focused more on the war than on colour policy.

Shortly after the war the word became generally used, especially because it was taken over untranslated into English political terminology. Naturally this created a stir. There is no reason why a translation such as, e.g. 'separation' could not have been used, but the intention was most probably to suggest, by the use of a foreign word in the English language something foreign and ominous, something so bad that there was no word at all in English for it!

AN EARLY EXPLANATION OF THE MEANING OF APARTHEID

What follows is a series of extracts from a very long speech by Dr. Verwoerd, at that time Senator, made on the 3 September 1948. It constitutes Dr. Verwoerd's first public exposition of the meaning of 'Apartheid'. It arose out of a motion moved by Senator Edgar H. Brookes on the 1 September 1948, reading:

> That this House would welcome an elucidation of the policy of 'apartheid' by the Government insofar as it affects (i) the purchase of land for Native occupation and (ii) the extension of opportunities for Natives to serve their own community in administrative and professional positions.

This motion was rejected by 20 votes to 19 and an amendment supporting the Government policy of apartheid was carried by the same majority.

DOCUMENT 2. SPEECH BY DR. VERWOERD, 3 SEPTEMBER 1948.

It is a matter for regret that when one is engaged in discussing a point of view with great earnestness, one gets only a repetition of words which are really not fit to be used in this Place. I am referring to the allegation that the attitude of this side of the House is 'political fraud', that it is 'scandalous'. Those are the terms of one of the pamphlets of the chief organiser of the United Party.[1] These words are to be found there. Here is another pamphlet issued by the chief organiser of the United Party, namely *Election News*, and these words are there: 'The Nationalist Party's Great Political Fraud'. 'Apartheid is Political Fraud.' So I could go on quoting example after example of instances where the ideas which have been put up here as new criticism of the Government's policy are nothing else than political propaganda. That, then, is the first reason why we so greatly regret the attitude of the Opposition towards the policy of this side of the House. We are anxious, moreover, that everything that can be said against the attitude which we take up should be said, but then it must not be said in terms of vague, general charges; that is scarcely fitting under the circumstances in which we find ourselves today. Then, in the second place, we must regret the fact that (quite apart from the mistake that the Hon. Senator [Conroy] has made in this regard) he has made an effort to bring to the front once more an atmosphere created in an election of years ago. He referred, in fact, to a certain poster, which he called the 'halfbreed' poster. If I heard him aright, he referred to that as a poster which was used in connection with the election of 1929, in connection with the black peril, as he calls it. That was naturally a mistake, the poster was used in 1938, and not in 1929. What were the true facts in connection with that poster? They were that at that period a comprehensive inquiry was being made into the question of mixed marriages, and that during that period things had been said on the part of leading members of that side of the House against which the party on this side of the House had raised objections. On 5 May 1938, Mr. Hofmeyr addressed a meeting at Ceres in the Cape Province, and a question was put to him. The question was: 'Assuming now that the Commission of Inquiry into the question of mixed marriages recommended that legislation

[1] For the policy of the United Party regarding apartheid see Document 6.

prohibiting mixed marriages was essential, on which side would you vote?' Then his answer was that if the Commission recommended that, the Government would have to decide what it was going to do, but that he would not remain a member of a government which introduced legislation of that sort. In the light of a point of view such as that a poster was then drawn up in which an appeal was made to the mothers of South Africa to see that legislation prohibiting mixed marriages really was introduced. Figures were produced which placed before the public the unhappy and regrettable extent to which mixed marriages had taken place. On that there followed an atmosphere of recriminations and suspicion, to which I do not want to refer at any greater length now, except to say that one should like to discuss the matter of mixed marriages on this occasion, but not again in an atmosphere which everybody regrets; after all, it is wrong and unnecessary to create such an atmosphere once again. In similar manner, more or less, it is stated on the opposite side of the House that incalculable damage had been done by the fight as to what we are said to have called the 'black peril'. The Hon. Senator Conroy condemned us in the strongest terms. But has he forgotten that his own leader, the former Prime Minister, also referred to the black peril? I want to quote here what he said on the 29 January 1947. It is recorded in Hansard. He was then speaking about immigration and on the need for increasing the European population, and on that occasion he said, among other things, the following: 'We had before us certain facts which the Government had at this stage to take into account. In addition we were aware of the fear of the people that unless special steps were taken the small forces of European civilisation would be in danger.' But he did not leave the matter there, at his statements on the fears of the people, of which he was aware. He associated himself with those words, by going on a little bit further: 'We have come face to face with the fact that something has happened here, that there is a red light which shows us that there is danger' (Hansard 1947; No. 24, Col. 11843). Mr. President, if the former Prime Minister was able to talk about the phenomenon as a danger, then we at least are also entitled to do so, and if it is a fact that there is a danger to European civilisation in South Africa, then surely we are allowed to say that as well. I remember that the former Prime Minister six months later in his customary way went back on his words and attacked us. He then also spoke about the terrible position we were in and that we were driving the whites and the non-Europeans into conflict with one another, just as the Leader of the Opposition in this House has done at present. He also made the mistake of saying that for that reason the Native will be regarding us as a white peril. But, Mr. President, that will only happen if matters were to go on as they went on under the policy of members on the other side of the House, and then I should not blame any Native for talking about a white peril. With the disorder and chaos that were arising in the country under the administration of the previous Government we were becoming a mutual danger to one another. That is really the object of the whole apartheid policy —the whole object of the policy adopted by this side of the House is to try to ensure that neither of the two will become a danger to the other. The Hon. the Leader of the Opposition in this House went on to say that we had created enmity between white and white, that our policy of apartheid is not any worse than the state of enmity between European and European in South Africa. But, Mr. President, has there ever been anything during the more recent period of South Africa's history, which has brought about so much unanimity among people who formerly found their views clashing as just that apartheid policy for which we stand? Even the Free State and Natal have extended their hands towards one another on the apartheid policy. Hands have been extended to one another between the English-speaking and the Afrikaans-speaking sections. Those who stood for the policy of apartheid won an election in circumstances which the other side of the House did not expect. Is that the result of creating greater enmity between white and white? Or does it mean that by at last bringing a bit of clarity into the muddy waters in one field we are gaining an opportunity of getting a little closer together in other aspects of life as well. My contention is that so far from our setting up whites against whites by this, we are engaged in getting the whites to stand together shoulder to shoulder. Where he then said further that we were creating enmity between Europeans and non-Europeans there I contend too, that the opposite is the case. Europeans and non-Europeans in recent years have been working up to a crisis. Ten, twenty, thirty years ago we did not know points of dispute in every field of life as we know them now. It was under the policy of the previous Government that we saw more and more trouble blowing up, clashes in the towns, crimes, the creation of all sorts of hamlets on the borders of the towns full of poverty and misery, clashes on the trains, assaults on women. Wherever you go, and in every field, you find an increase in the tension between Europeans and non-Europeans. That was the result of the policy of the other side. In this policy of ours we are seeking to achieve, and to take steps for the achievement, of a condition of greater peace. We want to get rid of these points of friction and these clashes themselves in so far as that is humanly possible. . . .

The question is, therefore: What is apartheid? And now I hope that hon. members on the opposite side of the House really want to know and will genuinely accept it if I try to explain to them by quotation from several documents what it is —in other words, what they want to know. The impression that has been created up to now is that on this side we can simply say what we please, but that all they do is to stop up their ears and prove that they really want to know nothing. I want to say in the first place that there is nothing new in what we are propagating, nor have we made any claim that there is anything new in it. The claim that we have made is that we are propagating the traditional policy of Afrikanerdom, the traditional policy of South Africa and of all those who have made South Africa their home—that we want to apply that traditional policy to the full; that is our claim. Our claim is that, whether it is called segregation or by the clear Afrikaans name 'apartheid', our claim is that the traditional policy must be put into effect, otherwise South Africa will really land in a position which not we, but members on the other side of the

House apparently want. And when they come along with their allegation that we do not know what our policy is, and that the Prime Minister is supposed to have said that he first wanted to go and work out the policy and that the Minister of Native Affairs is supposed to have said that he first wanted to have a policy sought by a commission, then I say: 'That really is not true.' There is a difference between the two things: to indicate unequivocally your line of policy, and the working out in detail the administration or effecting of your policy. It is one thing, if you are the Minister of Lands, to say that you intend to build large dams or to build small dams that will be scattered throughout the length and breadth of the country. That is a question of policy. But surely it is not expected of him, when he gives information in that way about the matter, that he should at the same time be in a position to come along with all the specifications, for example with the estimated quantities of cement and sand he will require. There is a difference between the investigation that you can have made into the application of a policy and the stating of a policy that is unequivocal and clear. When the Minister of Native Affairs now says that he is going to institute an investigation as to how to apply the policy which the Government has, and which it stands for very clearly and in very specific terms in many directions—now that he wants to appoint commissions to work out the application in detail (for example, exactly where industries can be set up in those reserves, etc.)—then surely it is in the highest degree unreasonable for a man to come along and say: 'You do not know what your policy is.' . . .

Nobody has ever contended that the policy of apartheid should be identified with 'total segregation'. The apartheid policy has been described as what one can do in the direction of what you regard as ideal. Nobody will deny that for the Native as well as for the European complete separation would have been the ideal if it had developed that way historically. If we had had here a white South Africa in the sense in which you have a white England and a white Holland and a white France, and if there had been a Native state somewhere for the Natives, and if this white state could have developed to a self-supporting condition as those European states have developed by themselves, then we should certainly not have had the friction and the difficulties which we have today. Surely it would have been an ideal state of affairs if we had not had these problems. If the Native had not had anything to do with the whites, if he were capable of managing his own affairs, it would also have been an ideal state of affairs for him. And if that is the case, then surely it cannot do any harm to see it and to state it; it can do only good. If you appreciate that you are saddled with a complicated situation, a highly complicated situation, you must have the direction in which you wish to move to solve your problems clearly in mind. In every field of life one has to fix one's eyes on the stars, to see how close one can come to achieving the very best, to achieving perfection. For that reason I say this: keep in view what promises to be best for your country and try to approach it within the realm of what is practical. . . .

This is what the Minister of Lands, the leader of the National Party in the Transvaal, wrote, among other things:

> As far as territorial segregation is concerned, 'total segregation', as you call it in your letter of 31/10/42 addressed to the secretary of our party on the Rand, would have been the ideal solution, but in practice it is incapable of being carried out, because quite apart from all the other difficulties, our own people, our farmers and thousands and tens of thousands of others, who use the services of the Natives and coloured people as labour, would never agree to it. For that reason, as far as 'territorial segregation' is concerned, we have adopted as a policy mainly the following:
>
> (1) That Natives should not be allowed to own land among white people, but that so far as the ownership of land is concerned they should be confined to the various Native reserves;
>
> (2) that Natives and coloured people in our towns and villages should not live in European residential areas, but that there should be separate residential areas for them, that is to say, separate Native and coloured villages; and
>
> (3) that in our factories, etc., Europeans and non-Europeans should not be allowed to work among one another, but

separately, and that certain sorts of work should be reserved for the Europeans.

In connection with that I myself have stated up to now, I want to draw attention to the fact that he says in it precisely what was said above, total segregation may be the ideal but that that is not practicable, and that what can be put into effect are these forms of territorial segregation, among other things. (Naturally, political segregation as well.) That is what Mr. Strydom wrote in 1942. He went on to refer to hospital and medical services for Natives, and then he wrote *inter alia* of:

... the fact that we use the Natives as labourers in our businesses, in our industries and in many cases in our homes ....

The fact that he used that sentence serves to prove further that having the Native everywhere was within the scheme which he envisaged. Then he went on and remarked:

Now so far as trading activities and so on in the Native areas and also in the Native residential areas of our cities are concerned. It is clear to me that if segregation is to mean anything we Europeans, except for necessary officials, should stay out of the Native areas. Shops and so on should in my opinion be in the hands of Natives in those areas. For the same reasons we Europeans will have to keep out of the Native residential areas in our cities, just as we want to keep the Natives out of the European residential areas, except for those who have to come in there daily to work.

We are therefore applying the same principle on both sides, and it is indicated here how the Natives will be everywhere and how they will be separated from the whites. Now I ask in the light of such a clear statement, which must have been known to the Hon. the Leader of the Opposition in this House, because he referred to this self-same letter, how can one in the light of such a clear and unequivocal statement say: 'You do not know what apartheid is' and in the second place 'those people want total apartheid'? I understand further that his contention is that during this last election we pleaded for apartheid as if it meant total segregation, and that the fact that the Minister of Lands had said earlier that such a thing was impracticable should be taken as proof that we had tried to defraud the public. Has he tried yet to analyse the logic of that argument? What does it really mean? It means in the first place that a person who is, surely, a responsible and thinking person addressed his whole party openly in 1942 and took up the attitude that while total segregation might well be an ideal, it could not be carried out in practice, and furthermore it was a thing that would be rejected by tens of thousands of people, farmers and who knows who else. Then, a few years after that, in the course of an important election, he is supposed to have gone to the country to plead for what he had said would be both impracticable and unpopular! Then, when he had in spite of that won the election he would then suddenly turn round and refuse to carry out the policy for which he had gained unexpected support. Surely it is foolish in the highest degree for any person to make such an accusation. One simply cannot believe that anybody could think so illogically. The second point is that this correspondence was addressed to a person who opposed the idea that apartheid should not be the same thing as total segregation. The Minister should have seen that he was going to lose supporters if he pleaded for territorial and other forms of segregation as being practicable and capable of being applied instead of for total segregation. And the leader, with a full sense of his responsibility, made that clear to that person who then also left the party and formed his own party at that stage. 'I cannot agree with you that apartheid can in practice simply boil down to total segregation.' There are all the various reasons that I have mentioned for that. He was prepared rather to see his party weakened than to give up the point of view on which he had taken his stand. Yet this attitude is being raised here today as evidence that we have committed a political fraud, whereas it is in fact a proof of the highest degree of political honesty; in which one suffers harm for one's faith. Mr. President, I also have here in my possession a number of documents which are general knowledge. They have been spread far and wide. In them is set out the colour policy of this side of the House in unequivocal terms. In the first place the basis on which it is founded is to be found in the programme of principles of the party. Here it is as it appeared in the Transvaal as the programme of principles of the party. In each of the provinces the relevant clause is exactly the same:

> The party accepts the Christian trusteeship of the European race as the basic principle of its policy in regard to the non-European races. In accordance with this it desires to afford the non-European races the opportunity of developing themselves in their own fields, according to their natural ability and capacity, and it desires to assure them of fair and just treatment in the administration of the country, but it is emphatically opposed to any mixture of blood between the European and the non-European races.
>
> It further declares itself in favour of the territorial and political segregation of the Natives, as well as in favour of the separation between Europeans and non-Europeans in general in the residential and, in so far as it may be practicable, also in the industrial field.
>
> Further, it desires to protect all sections of the population against Asiatic immigration and competition, among other things by prohibiting further intrusions into their fields of activity, as well as by an effective scheme of Asiatic segregation. . . .

Two things again emerge very clearly everywhere, that the non-European worker will be there to assist in the economic progress of the country; and that there will be protection for one group as well as for the other. It has also been stated, and we are propagating it, that there must be a worthwhile wage for European labour. It has also been stated that there must be enough non-European labour for the country districts. That has been propagated openly. When we come to 'Social Welfare and Public Health', you find that it is stated here:

> There must be separate residential areas for Europeans and non-Europeans, and as far as possible this principle of apartheid must also be applied to the various non-European racial groups in their relationships towards one another, such as coloured people, Indians and Natives.

They must also as far as possible be separated from one another: the Indian, the coloured people and the Natives. The Natives must be separate, the Indians and the coloured people each separate too. Now that almost tens of thousands of these documents have been spread throughout the country it is still said that our apartheid policy has never been defined and is not clear. That is an unimaginable idea. There is another pamphlet which was distributed in tens of thousands through the country. All in all close on 100,000 must have been circulated throughout the country. In regard to the first one might say: There is the economic scheme, and to read no further, but here he cannot say that he has not read anything more, that he therefore has an excuse for not knowing. Here you have clearly 'The Colour Policy of the Nationalist Party', 'Maintenance of European Civilisation as the Prime Task'. In it the various aspects of the matter are worked out extensively. The United Party must know of them. I am only going to make a few quotations. Under the heading 'General Basis' you find:

> The party believes that a determined policy of separation between the European race and the non-European racial groups, and the application of the principle of separation between the non-European racial groups as well, is the only basis on which the character and the future of each race can be protected and made secure and enabled to develop in accordance with its own national character, abilities and destiny.
>
> In their own areas the non-European racial groups will be afforded a full opportunity of development and they will be able to develop their own institutions and social services, and in that way the abilities of the more progressive non-Europeans will be enlisted in the advancement of their own people.

Under 'Policy towards the Natives' we find the following:

> The policy will aim at concentrating in so far as it is possible the main ethnical groups and sub-groups of the Bantu in their own separate territories, where each group will be able to develop into a self-sufficient unit.

That is not an effort to exploit differences between the races, this is not an effort to stir them up to hostility towards one another—an effort to divide and rule! As the nations of the world each in its own territory accomplishes its own national development, so also the opportunity will be given here to the various Native groups each to accomplish its own development each in its own territory. To each of them, from the tribal chief to the ordinary Native, the chance is being given to accomplish a fair and reasonable development within his own national group. That has come from those who are stigmatised by the other side as oppressors of the Natives.

Senator Jackson: Will the Natives be entitled to eat bread?

Senator Dr. Verwoerd: I shall counter that by another question: does the Hon. Senator think that we shall not give the Natives the right to drink water? If the Hon. Senator answers that question for himself he will realise how nonsensical his question is. Under 'Native Land' we find here:

> The principle of territorial segregation between Europeans and Natives is generally accepted. Further, land will only be allocated under the 1936 Act in a sensible way and after a careful investigation, while a determined policy for the rehabilitation of the land and a campaign against overcropping, in which the assistance of the Natives themselves will be enlisted, will be carried out.

A body of experts to bring about the proper use of land in the Native territories will be brought into being. Then further, and, indeed, under the heading 'Native Reserves', it is stated:

> The Native reserves must become the true fatherland of the Natives. It is there that his educational institutions should be, and it is there that these improved services for the Natives should be made available, in contrast to the present policy which is to make them available in urban locations. Prestige and respect must be accorded to the Natives in all fields in the reserves, so that they may set a standard and act as the mouthpiece of the Bantu.

Is that oppression?

A greater variety of economic activities will gradually be brought into being so as to bring about greater productivity and stability for the Native reserves, and for this purpose planning committees will be instituted.

Is that oppression? Then, under the heading '*Natives in Towns*':

The Party appreciates the danger of the influx of Natives into the towns and undertakes to preserve the European character of our towns, and to take energetic and effective measures for the safety of persons as well as of property and for the peaceful life of urban residents.

All Natives must be placed in separate residential areas, and their concentration in our urban areas must be counteracted. The Native in our urban areas must be regarded as a 'visitor', who will never have the right to claim any political rights or equal social rights with the Europeans in the European areas.

Let me just interpolate something here and make a statement to Hon. Senators as to what, for example, happens in other countries where a great trek of workers from one country to another takes place. It is known that so far as France is concerned about three million labourers come in there from Italy every year; they are seasonal workers. Those three million seasonal workers who come from Italy do not obtain any civil rights in France; they are regarded as visitors. And the same thing will apply to the Native in the European areas, though, at the same time we are now going to give him civil rights in his own territories such as he enjoys nowhere at present. That will be the place in which to achieve his ideals. The Native who becomes a lawyer, or the Native girl who becomes a nurse or teacher or whatever the case might be, will in the first place be able to provide his services there in his own community. However, as soon as the Native comes into an area of a European community, then he will have no such political rights there, there in the white man's country. But the reverse is also true. If there are Europeans who have to go into the Native territories, and they will only go there because they have to in order to help the Natives, they will not enjoy any political rights there. Then I read on further:

The number of detribalised Natives must be frozen. After that the coming of the Natives into the towns and their regular departure will be taken under control by the State on a country-wide basis, in co-operation with the urban authorities. The Native territories must be placed under effective efflux policy and the towns under an influx policy. All surplus Natives in the towns will have to be sent back to the country districts or to the Native reserves or to wherever they came from.

The Hon. the Leader of the Opposition became so worried yesterday about the use of the word 'frozen', as if one were dealing with people who became bodily frozen so tight in the plains of the South Pole that they could not get away again, for he asked whether it meant that the Natives would be placed in concentration camps.

Senator Conroy: He may not go home to the reserves. In other words, it is a sort of slavery.

Senator Dr. Verwoerd: On the contrary, we hope that some of those Natives who become able to serve their own people actually will migrate to the reserves. They should be dealt with in such manner that they will go there. What will happen is that in that sense the numbers in the cities will be frozen to such an extent that no more Natives will be allowed to come in from outside other than the Natives who have the full residential right to stay there; let only those who are there retain that right. That is not unreasonable. Freezing therefore means that we are not going to permit any new influx as happened under the previous Government, and, indeed, to such an extent that Johannesburg and the Witwatersrand and the whole of that neighbourhood has become one vast breeding-place of injustice and crime, of unemployment and all sorts of misery, of poverty and of mutual oppression. Within and outside that city the position has become impossible. It is also stated here that all surplus Natives in the towns should be sent back to the country districts or to the reserves from which they came. They must be away from the misery of those hovels, away from those sacking villages, away from starvation, of little boys who run about and perish and degenerate, and go back to places where some care can be taken of them again. So 'freezing' in this case has not the meaning as in the interpolation of the Hon. Senator. I am reading further:

APARTHEID—THE WORD AND ITS MEANING

Natives from the country districts and the reserves will in the future be allowed to enter the white towns and villages only as temporary workers, and on the termination of their service contracts they will regularly have to go back to their homes.

That must also be well understood. The Natives who remain behind in the towns are one group. But a further influx into the towns will be allowed only in the form of such temporary labour. That is very fair, and it is very important that it should be carried out if we want to ensure them, too, the happiness to which they are just as much entitled as we are, namely to be linked to their own community and their liberties. The pamphlet also says:

> The principle of apartheid will be carried out so far as it is possible in practice in factories, industries and workshops. The Natives must be induced to build up his own social, health and welfare services in his own reserves. His own capabilities must be enlisted for that purpose.

Social and welfare services take place within the perspective and policy of this side of the House and best by providing for the Native through the Native himself. The hand that gives must be drawn from the people to whom the services are given. That is the first principle of all welfare services. The same applies to self-management. As to its own management I read the following:

> The party is in favour of an individual system of local government, more or less on the basis of the Bunga[1] system, in which the Native chiefs will be completely incorporated and which will at the same time present the educated Native with an opportunity of enlisting himself in the service of his own people. Such a council will be brought into being for every reserve, and they will be able to develop into separate central councils for the various ethnic groups and sub-groups.
> The Native Representative Council will be abolished. In the urban locations councils will be instituted which will, however, never be able to develop into independent bodies.

[1] The 'Bunga' was the Transkeian Territories General Council.

Those two points must be clearly understood. Even the Natives who are going to get their residential areas within or rather near the towns and who will be able to achieve a great deal of local government within those residential areas, those Natives will not be able to go any further within the European area than the obtaining of local government. If they have ambitions in the direction of full citizenship, then they have to go back to the areas that are theirs; but if for their own selfish interests and their own economic gain they want to stay in the Native residential areas within the European areas, then the greatest share in government which they can achieve will be local government. That is giving them more than what for instance those Italians are able to achieve in France.

PART II

The Population Registration Act

The extracts following are the essential points of the Population Registration Act No. 30 of 1950. It has been amended in detail since, but the essential principles remain unchanged.

DOCUMENT 3. EXTRACTS FROM THE POPULATION REGISTRATION ACT, NO. 30 OF 1950.

2. There shall, as soon as practicable after the fixed date, be compiled by the Director and thereafter maintained by him, a register of the population of the Union.

* * *

5. (1) Every person whose name is included in the register shall be classified by the Director as a white person, a coloured person or a native, as the case may be, and every coloured person and every native whose name is so included shall be classified by the Director according to the ethnic or other group to which he belongs.

(2) The Governor-General may by proclamation in the Gazette prescribe and define the ethnic or other groups into which coloured persons and natives shall be classified in terms of sub-section (1), and may in like manner amend or withdraw any such proclamation.

(3) If at any time it appears to the Director that the classification of a person in terms of sub-section (1) is incorrect, he may, subject to the provisions of sub-section (7) of section *eleven* and after giving notice to that person and, if he is a minor, also to his guardian, specifying in which respect the classification is incorrect, and affording such person and such guardian (if any)

an opportunity of being heard, alter the classification of that person in the register.

6. The Director shall assign an identity number to every person whose name is included in the register.

7. (1) There shall, in respect of every person whose name is included in the register, other than a native, be included in the register the following particulars and no other particulars whatsoever namely:

(a) his full name, sex and ordinary place of residence;
(b) his classification in terms of section *five*;
(c) the date and place of his birth;
(d) his citizenship or nationality, and in the case of an alien, an indication of the fact that he is an alien;
(e) his marital status;
(f) in the case of a registered voter, the electoral division and polling district in which he is registered as a voter under the Electoral Consolidation Act, 1946 (Act No. 46 of 1946);
(g) the date of his arrival in the Union, if not born in a part of South Africa included in the Union;
(h) a recent photograph of himself, except in the case of a person who has not yet attained the age of sixteen years, or who has been admitted to the Union for a temporary purpose; and
(i) his identity number.

(2) There shall in respect of every native whose name is included in the register, be included in the register the following particulars and no other particulars whatsoever, namely:

(a) his full name, sex and the district in which he is ordinarily resident;
(b) his citizenship or nationality, the ethnic or other group and the tribe to which he belongs;
(c) the date, or if the date is not known, the year or reputed year, and the place, or if the place is not known, the district of his birth;

(d) his marital status;
(e) the year of his arrival in the Union, if not born in a part of South Africa included in the Union;
(f) a recent photograph of himself in the case of a native who has not yet attained the age of sixteen years, and, in the case of a native who is not a South African citizen, his fingerprints; and
(g) his identity number.

(3) Upon the death or permanent departure from the Union of a person whose name is included in the register, the date of his death or departure from the Union, as the case may be, shall be recorded in the register.

DOCUMENT 4. EXTRACTS FROM THE SPEECH OF THE MINISTER OF THE INTERIOR, DR. T. E. DÖNGES, INTRODUCING THE POPULATION REGISTRATION ACT AND TAKEN FROM THE HOUSE OF ASSEMBLY HANSARD 8 MARCH 1950, COLUMNS 2498–2501.

This Bill makes provision for the introduction of a population register, and I deem it essential that we know at the outset what the basic principles of a population register are. A population register is actually a book containing the life-story of every individual whose name is recorded on that register. It contains the most important facts relating to such a person. In some cases the life-story of the individual is very short. In the case of a stillborn baby it contains only one entry and one page. In other cases a long life-history has to be recorded in that book. All those important facts regarding the life of every individual will be combined in this book and recorded under the name of a specific person, who can never change his identity. It is only when the last page in that book of life is written by an entry recording the death of such a person that the book is closed and taken out of the gallery of the living and placed in the gallery of the dead.

That is the basic principle. I may just say that although it is very important to collate and to keep together all the important

THE POPULATION REGISTRATION ACT

facts pertaining to the life of the individual, this book of life will only be of historical value, if it is not also a living book. If it only contains a series of facts and names on a specific date, it might perhaps be of importance to posterity, but if it is not kept up to date so that it could rightly be said that it is also a living book, it loses a great deal of its value as an important contribution to the social life or the political administration of the present. Provision, therefore, is made to record the address of the individual concerned in this book of life, in this register, and when such a person changes his address, the new address will also be recorded, in order to keep the register up to date.

I may perhaps mention one more example. The determination of a person's race is of the greatest importance in the enforcement of any existing or future laws in connection with separate residential areas—and here I specifically have in mind the Group Areas Bill,[1] which I promised to introduce in this House and which was also announced in this year's Speech from the Throne. Members who would like to see those laws enforced, must remember that this Bill is one of the instruments which will not only enable us to enforce such legislation, but which will also cause that legislation to function as smoothly as possible, without any unnecessary friction.

THE WORKING OF THE POPULATION REGISTRATION ACT

The following extract gives instances of the abuses and difficulties arising from this legislation.

The term 'Coloured' in South Africa is in general confined to persons of mixed race, not as in the United States, to all who are not white. The exact legal definition of a Coloured person is an extremely complex point, but for all practical purposes it may be taken as anyone who is not African, Indian or European.

[1] See Documents 27–29.

THE POPULATION REGISTRATION ACT

DOCUMENT 5. FROM THE *Survey of Race Relations 1955–66*, PUBLISHED BY THE SOUTH AFRICAN INSTITUTE OF RACE RELATIONS (PAGES 36–38).

Classification of Coloured People

There has been considerable pressure on Coloured people in the Transvaal and elsewhere to present themselves to census officials for race classification. According to evidence given before the special Appeal Board on 7 and 29 May 1956, the police are still rounding up dark-skinned people who claim to be Coloured but have the appearance of Africans, and are ordering them to report for official classification. Towards the end of 1955 the Transvaal Provincial Administration ruled that in 1956 all those wishing to enter institutions for the training of Coloured teachers would have to produce population registration certificates showing that they were Coloured.

The Minister of the Interior said during May[1] that officials had already dealt with 18,469 cases in which objection had been raised to the classification claimed by the person concerned. Of these, 1,182 had been classified as White, 9,642 as Coloured, and 7,645 as African. (No information was given as to the racial groups claimed by these individuals.)

Persons dissatisfied with rulings by officials of the Bureau of Census and Statistics may appeal, in the first place, to the special Board and thereafter to the courts of law. The Board sat in Pretoria in December 1955 and early in 1956, moved to Johannesburg in April, where some 200 appeals were heard, and then went on to other major centres. Some appeals were allowed and others dismissed; it was difficult to gain any idea of the proportions in either case as a majority of the appellants elected to be heard behind closed doors. At its Executive Committee meeting in January, the Institute of Race Relations noted with appreciation the assistance that Legal Aid Bureaux were giving to persons experiencing difficulty in presenting their cases.

Coloured people have maintained that race classification was

[1] Assembly 9 May 1956. Hansard 15, cols. 5259/60.

THE POPULATION REGISTRATION ACT

introduced 300 years too late. The Minister of the Interior said in the speech quoted above that 90,000 borderline cases had already been encountered: each of these involves individual suffering, and there is often much doubt as to the correct classification. As was mentioned in our last *Survey*, the S.A. National Council for Child Welfare was informed by the Director of Census during 1955 that children born from parents one of whom is an African were to be classified as Africans; but in May 1955 the Appeal Board ruled that a man whose father is a European and whose mother an African, is officially Coloured. A full bench of the Supreme Court, Pretoria, held during June 1956 that a woman with an Asiatic father and Malay mother could not be classified as Asiatic, as the Department of the Interior had maintained in a prosecution brought in terms of the Group Areas Act.

In its original statement on the Population Registration Act[1] the Institute of Race Relations pointed out that the system was open to abuse, and that encouragement would be given to 'informers'. The truth of this was borne out in a prosecution under the Group Areas Act, heard in the Johannesburg Magistrates' Courts in March 1956. During 1951 a family moved into a house previously occupied by Whites. As some doubt was subsequently raised as to whether the family was White, an inspector of the Group Areas Board visited them. A letter dated 18 January 1954 was then sent by the chief inspector to the householder's attorney, reading:[2] 'Your client would appear to be a member of the White group. Under the circumstances, your client's occupation is lawful. . . . This opinion is given without prejudice to any action I may deem necessary in future.' A Coloured school principal admitted in evidence, later, that he informed the Board that the family was not White, but Coloured; and the householder was then charged with unlawful occupation of the property. It transpired that he had lived all his life as a European, as had two of his brothers, one of whom was serving in the Royal Navy. A sister of his was, however, living as a Coloured person. His wife's

[1] RR 45/1950.
[2] *Rand Daily Mail* report, 21 March 1956.

employer accepted her as White, one of his children attended a prominent high school for White children; but two others, being darker-skinned, had been sent to a Coloured school to save them from embarrassment. Although names were suppressed in press reports the family's associates must obviously have known of the case—the stigma that resulted needs no underlining.

Some cases of great hardship have been remedied by the Appeal Board. There was the case, for example, of an old man aged 81 who had been married for 25 years. When census officials classified him as African and his wife as Coloured, they contemplated divorce proceedings, for she could not face having to live in an African location. His appeal was allowed. An 18-year-old lad, too, won his appeal and was reclassified as Coloured. He had passed his Junior Certificate in a Coloured school and wished to become a teacher after completing his general education. At this stage census officials declared that he was an African; but his brother was classified as Coloured. Not only was a family split threatened, but the lad concerned found it impossible to continue with his education since, knowing no African languages, he could not gain admission to any school for Africans.

But as members of the Opposition pointed out in the debate on the Population Registration Amendment Act, there are thousands of cases in which permanent hardship and heartbreak have been caused.

PART III
Opposition Policies

The following documents were obtained from the three main opposition parties as current expressions of their views in 1966.

DOCUMENT 6. THE UNITED PARTY. FROM *Handbook for Better Race Relations*.

United Party policy meets the challenger

First and foremost, our programme provides for:
  (a) The maintenance of South Africa as one State where the practice of fair and just policies will earn and deserve the loyalty of all;
  (b) Immediate action to relax internal tensions and promote international goodwill;
  (c) The establishment of firm foundations on which to build, acceptable to the electorate and indicative of a change in direction;
  (d) Long-term objectives which will have as their aims:
    (i) the promotion of a sense of security among the Whites;
    (ii) hope and proof of a fair deal for the non-White, and the re-establishment of his confidence in the White;
    (iii) the approval and support of responsible opinion, irrespective of race, both at home and abroad.

This programme will be advanced in three phases which will inevitably overlap.

A. First phase:
Immediate reforms and action

1. Immediately on return to power the Party will examine and review all legislation which is discriminatory, offends the rule

of law, or impinges on the dignity of the individual, to determine which laws should be amended or repealed. Some of these are:

The Pass Laws;
The Population Registration Act;
The Natives (Prohibition of Interdicts) Act;
The Separate Universities Act;
The Group Areas Act;
The Suppression of Communism Act;
The General Law Amendment Act;
The Immorality Act;
The Industrial Conciliation Act, especially those portions dealing with job reservation and the splitting of trade unions.

2. The United Party will establish machinery for consultation with the non-White peoples at all levels to promote an understanding of the issues facing the country and co-operation between the people of all races.

3. Immediate steps will be taken to promote a dynamic, state-aided immigration scheme, together with social planning, to increase the White population, so that the White man's influence will be supported by his numbers, and the fear of political and economic swamping reduced.

4. The Party will create a climate favourable to industrial expansion and by means of active planning and state assistance, it will promote economic growth and raise living standards among all sections. It is the lesson of history that revolution and Communism do not thrive where people are contented.

B. Second Phase:
Orderly advance to a federation of the races

1. While bearing in mind the pillars upon which our policy rests, we shall in this phase begin firmly to carry out a policy which will enable us to share our civilisation, without sacrificing it. It will be a difficult road requiring courage and a united effort by all our people.

2. Interim constitutional reforms to provide proper machinery for consultation with the non-Whites at all levels will be immediately instituted.

3. As consultation will also be necessary at Parliamentary level, these interim reforms will include the restoration of the Coloured voters to the common roll in the Cape and Natal. Bantu from all Provinces will be represented in Parliament by not more than EIGHT White representatives in the House of Assembly and SIX in the Senate. These representatives will be elected on a separate roll.

4. The Cape Coloureds will be recognised as Westernised people. They will not only have their former political rights to vote on the common roll in the Cape and Natal restored to them, but in addition, will be allowed to sit in Parliament if elected.

The Coloured people in the Transvaal and Orange Free State, who have had no previous political experience—except the right to vote for Senators representing the Bantu people if they were prepared to be treated as Bantu for the purpose of the 1936 Act—will have representation on a separate roll in the Senate, and by their own people if they so wish.

5. Official Government policy from 1948 was that the Indians should be repatriated. Subsequently the Group Areas Act has been applied to them in such a manner that there is a risk of their being deprived of their traditional and vested means of livelihood.

Today it is generally agreed that repatriation is impossible, and the South African Indian community is accepted as a permanent part of the population. Accordingly, it is absurd that their means of livelihood should be attacked under the guise of residential separation. On the contrary, they must achieve higher standards, especially the poor who are still in the majority among them. Consultation with them must determine their future political status in South Africa.

6. The Bantu permanently settled in our urban and industrial areas who have broken their tribal affiliations pose an entirely different problem from the Bantu who live in the Reserves or still have their roots there.

OPPOSITION POLICIES

The number of Bantu who are permanently settled in the urban areas was estimated at 1½ million in 1951 and was of the order of 3.1 million in 1962.

For indisputable reasons, these Bantu will never all find permanent homes and jobs in the Reserves. Their presence in the Republic outside the Reserves must be accepted as a fact.

In respect of the urban Bantu therefore:

(i) Steps will be taken immediately for more humane administration of the pass laws and influx control. The emphasis will be upon bringing opportunities of employment to those in search of jobs.

Women will be freed from the pass laws and the United Party's system of pass exemptions for certain categories of men re-introduced and extended.

(Under the United Party about 50,000 Bantu were exempted by 1948 and the number was steadily growing. Exemptions were granted to:

(a) Bantu holding letters of exemption granted under any law;
(b) enrolled Parliamentary voters in the Cape;
(c) registered owners of immovable property etc.;
(d) chiefs and headmen appointed under the Native Administration Act of 1927 and officials of Government, Provincial Administration and certain local authorities;
(e) professional men like advocates, attorneys, medical practitioners; and
(f) the wives and minor children of those exempted.)

(ii) Urban Bantu will be given a stake in the maintenance of law and order by:

(a) making it possible for deserving Bantu to gain controlled freehold title to their homes in the big urban locations;
(b) ensuring his enjoyment of undisturbed family life;
(c) actively fostering the emergence of a responsible middle-class as a bulwark against agitators;
(d) the abandonment of job reservation, which in the

interest of racialism arbitrarily denies to human beings the right to use their talents, and its replacement by the principle of 'the rate for the job' which will ensure that non-White labour is not used to replace White labour at lower rates of pay;
(e) providing for a measure of local self-government on an elective basis in Bantu urban locations and a measure of participation in the government of the country by representation on a separate roll in Parliament.

Bantu in the Reserves wage a never-ending war against extreme poverty. This war can only be won by:
(a) active steps to rehabilitate the soil and conserve water with Government assistance;
(b) changing the system of land tenure to make it possible for individuals to own land;
(c) developing the Reserves industrially with the aid of White skill, White capital and White enterprise from private as well as State sources.

C. *Third phase*: *A race federation*

Under United Party policy a Federation of the Races will be established as the future constitutional form of the Republic of South Africa. Such a Race Federation will be based on three cardinal principles:

First: That the Protection of White leadership is in the best interests of South Africans of all races;

Second: That each race group (the White and the Coloureds being associated with each other for the purpose) will have a pre-determined share in the government of the country;

Third: That, by introducing federal elements into the Constitution, a real measure of protection will be given to the rights of each individual, each race group, and, where appropriate, the people living in certain geographical units in the State.

By recognising these principles the United Party will seek to give each race as much say in its own affairs as possible. By seeking that in the development of a Federation of peoples, it will not be necessary to break up and dismember the Republic of South Africa. The races will remain in one South Africa, but the one will not interfere unduly in the affairs of the other.

It should be noted that a Race Federation is not a federation made up of geographical units like that of the United States of America or that attempted in Rhodesia and Nyasaland. It is a different idea altogether. The emphasis in the United Party's plan is on the race group and not on geographic units.

The most important thing about the United Party's plan for Race Federation is that there will be room for different ways of life. All people like freedom to manage their own affairs as much as possible. For that reason we believe this plan will work in practice.

Under the United Party's plan a Central Government, representative of all the races, will exercise general control over the affairs of the Republic. It will retain general control over the Republic and will specifically control such matters as Central Finance, Defence in War and Peace, Foreign Policy, International Trade Agreements, Communications, Inter-Race Relations and so on. Generally speaking it will be entrusted with the keys to the safety of the State.

Subject to this over-riding consideration the race groups which make up the population of the Republic will have the widest possible measure of communal government, especially in such matters as education, cultural affairs, local government and certain matters of public health.

Communal Councils for each race will control those affairs (detailed above) which intimately affect that race. A Communal Council will also be established for an area like the Transkei or for a grouping of smaller Bantu Reserves.

Matters which cannot be separately controlled by each race, such as making roads and bridges, or the supply of electricity and water, will be the responsibility of a Joint Board representative of the Communal Councils concerned, or directly by the Central Government.

The powers given to each Communal Council will not

necessarily all be the same. They will depend on the stage of development reached by each race.

Each race will have the chance to be represented in the Central Government.

For a country like South Africa, where the races cannot be geographically separated, a federation of the races is obviously the right thing and it is eminently practicable.

One may consider how each church, like the Anglican or the Dutch Reformed or the Methodist Church, controls its own affairs and serves its own people without interference from others and without interfering in the freedom of others. If the rights enjoyed by the various churches as the result of custom were to be given the force of law and written into the Constitution, one would have a federation of churches. By writing into the Constitution the rights which each race should enjoy, and the powers which each should exercise over its people, one similarly creates a race federation.

Mr. Marais Steyn, M.P., has defined *Race Federation in one sentence*. He said: '*Race Federation is a system of government primarily designed for multi-racial states under which the power of self-government devolves on each race in those matters which intimately concern itself, while a central parliament retains control over matters of over-riding common concern; each race is represented in the central parliament in accordance with that state of civilisation it has reached so that the most advanced groups will retain political power although sharing it with the less-advanced.*'

The United Party's policy for a Federation of the Races offers a new approach to the problems of South Africa. It was first raised, although not under its present name, by the late General Smuts in May 1947, when he proposed to reform the Native Representative Council in order to give it administrative and executive powers over South Africa's Bantu population, not only in the Reserves, but also in other parts of South Africa where Bantu lived, despite the fact that the Bantu were already represented in Parliament. General Smuts realised that the fragmentation of South Africa would bring new dangers to our complicated land; he also saw that mere representation on public bodies without participation in the executive functions of government and in the administration of affairs did not give satisfaction to the people concerned, but merely intensified their sense of frustration.

This view of General Smuts the United Party supports. That is why it has developed the General's idea into the firm concept of a Federation of the Races.

*Tensions will decrease in a Federation of Races because defined executive and administrative powers will vest in each race. As a result it will be possible to retain wise conventions like social and residential separation without these being symbols of oppression to any race.
*In the Federation of the Races, the destiny of the Republic of South Africa will be controlled by civilised people.
*A Federation of the Races will prove to the world that South Africans are willing to share their civilisation, but not to sacrifice it.
*A Federation of the Races will regain for South Africa respected membership of the Western community of nations.

DOCUMENT 7. THE PROGRESSIVE PARTY. FROM *Safeguard Your Future, the Principles of the Progressive Party of South Africa.*

Government of all races—By all races for all races

In any multi-racial society there is likely to be a deep-seated fear in every community that it may be selfishly dominated by another. Today the non-White communities deeply resent the fact that they have no effective say in the government and are dominated by the Whites. The White people, conversely, fear that one day the superior numbers of the Africans will give them effective political control, and that the non-African communities may suffer in the same way.

It is this fear which, today, makes so many White people determined to cling to their dominant position even though they know it is morally indefensible and, in the long run, impossible to maintain. It is the converse fear which drives the African political organisations to insist on immediate universal suffrage as their best method of ensuring that the Whites do not retain the power to dominate and oppress other groups.

OPPOSITION POLICIES

But fear is a bad master, and neither of these two attitudes, both born of fear, can bring peace. Either will mean a power struggle for domination, with incalculable consequences. What is needed is a parliament so constituted that government by racial domination is impossible, no matter which community may be in the majority on the voters' roll. In a measure, the common roll, non-racial, qualified franchise contributes to such a state of affairs, because a candidate with a policy acceptable to all groups will always be at an advantage, and a qualified electorate will tend to vote for moderation; but by itself it is not sufficient.

Franchise Policy—merit the measure

Broadly speaking, there are three approaches to the question of the qualification which should entitle a man to have the vote in South Africa. The reactionary White parties would award rights on the basis of race—it would be easier for a White man to get the vote than for others. Both Nationalist and United Party policies would give the vote to any White person even if illiterate. Yet the United Party would require high qualification for a Coloured man to vote and would not allow his wife to vote at all. The Nationalists, even worse, would let the Coloured man vote only on a separate roll. Both these policies are manifestly unjust, designed simply to retain White racial domination.

Second, there is the universal suffrage policy advocated by the Liberal Party, the Congress Alliance and certain other groups: the system of one man, one vote. In South African circumstances, this system would lead inevitably to the exploitation of illiterate voters and probably to the triumph of a purely sectional Black nationalism.

Third, there is the concept of the qualified franchise. On the one hand, it gives absolute equality of opportunity to all South Africans regardless of race, creed or sex. On the other, it keeps the responsibility of the vote in the hands of people who, according to objective criteria, are qualified to exercise it.

The Progressive Party, at its inauguration, chose the third way—the qualified franchise for justice and stability. Dr. Jan

Steytler appointed the expert Molteno Commission to examine this and other questions, and after prolonged study, the Commission gave the nation the Molteno Report. After consideration of the report, the Progressive Party decided on the following franchise qualifications:

The full franchise on the ordinary roll will be made available by the Progressive Government to all South Africans who are sufficiently educated to have an understanding of politics, and who have a sufficient economic stake in the country to make them desire its stability.

Thus the Party will extend full franchise rights to any South African citizen of 21 years or over who:

has passed STANDARD VIII;
has passed STANDARD VI and either
had an income of R600 per year for two consecutive years; OR occupied property worth R1,000 for two consecutive years;
OWNS unencumbered property to the value of R1,000, and is literate.

A married person may claim the economic, but not the educational qualifications of the husband or wife, and any person who at any time has been a voter for the House of Assembly will be entitled to the ordinary franchise. The financial qualifications will be adjusted to meet proved fluctuations in the value of money.

The Unqualified People

The qualifications for the ordinary roll were fixed by the Party as representing a reliable standard of responsibility that can endure. Yet it would be wrong to ignore the large part of our people who cannot initially meet these. To lower the general standard in order to enfranchise more people immediately would be to depart from our determination to confine the control of the government to the civilized; yet an unduly restrictive franchise might leave South Africa deaf to the claims of the underprivileged.

There is one sensible solution: a special roll. This roll will be open to all South Africans who are literate and who are not registered on the ordinary roll. They will have the right to elect 10 per cent of the members of Parliament unless and until their numbers fall below 20 per cent of the number registered on the ordinary roll, when the number of special roll seats will be correspondingly reduced.

Our education and economic programmes will gradually eliminate the special roll. Until this happens the control of the government will be in the hands of the ordinary roll voters, with at least 90 per cent of the seats: but the voice of our temporarily unqualified citizens will also be heard.

Qualifications for the special roll will be:

21 years; South African citizenship; and literacy.

THIS IS JUSTICE

So equal rights will be given to all civilized men: and equal opportunity to become civilised will be ensured through the Progressive policies of extension of free compulsory education and the raising of wages.

THE WHITES will know that they are making allies instead of enemies of their fellow South Africans of other races.

THE NON-WHITES will know that the stigma of inferiority has been removed from them.

ALL SOUTH AFRICANS will share a common patriotism, and join in the building of a greater South Africa.

DOCUMENT 8. THE LIBERAL PARTY. FROM AN INTRODUCTION TO LIBERAL PARTY POLICY BY ALAN PATON, NATIONAL PRESIDENT OF THE LIBERAL PARTY, AND THE SECTION ON FRANCHISE AND CONSTITUTIONAL POLICY.

The Liberal Party is a non-racial Party. All its policies are non-racial. It believes that non-racialism is the only sure foundation for a multi-racial society of such complexity as ours, and that our problem can only be dealt with by people of all groups working together.

The policies of the Liberal Party accord full political, social and individual rights to all adult South Africans. This is done not only because it is a non-racial party, but because it seems to us to be unrealistic to suggest anything else in Africa today. We reject the qualified franchise, not only because we believe it to be absurd to suggest the re-introduction of a franchise whose previous record was one of continuous retreat, but also because we believe that every adult person is entitled to a voice in the election of his government.

All colour bars must go. The damage they have done to race relations in Africa is incomputable. But they must not only be removed; strong measures must be taken to redress the imbalance of privilege which we have inherited. This Handbook contains policies on land, taxation and education which are designed for this purpose.

The Liberal Party believes that any Government would need tremendous powers to carry out such reforms, but it is opposed to any form of authoritarian society. The provision of work, security and opportunity for all people is of the highest priority, but they must not be attained at the expense of fundamental civil liberties. Therefore the Party aims to secure the consent of the people to the setting up of a controlled constitution, in which their rights will be entrenched, and to which all authorities, national and local, as well as the citizens themselves, will be subject.

Franchise and Constitutional Policy

In the opinion of the Liberal Party, the present constitution of South Africa suffers from two fundamental defects: it limits political rights to white people and it fails to protect individual rights against arbitrary curtailment.

The Liberal Party aims to achieve the responsible participation of all South Africans in the Government and Democratic processes of the country and, to this end, to extend the right of franchise on the common roll to all adult persons.

It is not possible at this stage to forsee the precise circumstances under which the change will occur, but the Party aims to have the idea of a universal franchise accepted by the people of South Africa and to bring about the changes with the minimum possible dislocation.

Such an extension of the franchise will remedy the first of the fundamental defects of the present constitution, but by itself it will not remedy the second. Liberalism does not concede to the majority any more than to the minority the right to rule tyrannically and without due regard to the rights of the individual. A constitution based upon universal franchise and the unlimited sovereignty of the central legislature leaves the way open for tyranny by the majority. In countries with a long tradition of democracy and a homogeneous population, purely conventional safeguards may suffice to prevent the abuse of majority rule. In a country such as South Africa, more substantial safeguards are required.

The Liberal Party therefore advocates a controlled constitution, in which a Bill of Rights will be entrenched. The Bill of Rights will be based upon the Universal Declaration of Human Rights, and the rights enshrined in it will be placed outside the powers of an ordinary parliamentary majority.

In order further to limit the power concentrated in the hands of the central legislature, and to enable those provinces or regions which have special language, cultural or other interests to safeguard their interests, the Liberal Party advocates a decentralised form of constitution. The powers of the provincial authorities should be defined in the constitution and should not be subject to alteration by an ordinary parliamentary majority.

If constitutional guarantees are to be effective, it is essential that the power to enforce them should be vested in an independent judiciary. The right of the Supreme Court to declare legislation invalid if it offends against the provisions of the constitution must be recognised, and the independence of the judiciary must be fully guaranteed.

The future constitution of South Africa must be established by the consent of the people as a whole, and this consent can best be expressed by a National Convention, representative of every section of the people.

PART IV
Bantu Education

THE EISELEN REPORT

It should be noted that the education of Africans was begun by missionary bodies early in the nineteenth century. Before 1910 the Colonies, and after 1910 the Provincial Administration, supervised and subsidised this education and in a few cases conducted schools of their own. By 1925 the total amount paid for by all four Provinces for this service was £340,000 per annum. In that year the Union Government undertook the responsibility of subsidising this education, taking the £340,000 as a minimum and adding to it out of a fund consisting of 4s in every £1 of Native Poll Tax. Due mainly to the influence of J. H. Hofmeyr this amount was raised to 8/-, 12/-, 13/4, 16/8 and then 20/- in the £. By 1945 expenditure totalled over £2,200,000. In that year, by Act 29, the administration of the subsidy was transferred from the Native Affairs Department to that of the Union Education Department, and the cost was met by grants from the Consolidated Revenue Fund not depending on the Native Poll Tax. Large sums beyond these subsidies were spent by churches and missionary bodies, and they conducted many large and flourishing schools.

The Eiselen Report, from which the following extracts are taken, suggests that these developments were none the less on the wrong lines.

DOCUMENT 9. FROM THE *Report of the Commission on Native Education 1945–51*, PRESIDED OVER BY DR. W. W. M. EISELEN.

1051. Your Commission is of the opinion that education must be broadly conceived as a vital social service concerned not only with the intellectual, moral and emotional development of the individual but also with the socio-economic development of the Bantu as a people. Education, as one of a number of social services, must be integrated organically with all other State efforts designed to raise the level of Bantu life, and this integration should be effected both at the local and the national levels.

1052. With the above considerations in mind the Commission has made a number of recommendations which may be summarised as follows:

(a) Since we conceive education not as an end in itself but as a means to the general development of the Bantu, it is essential that both a general development plan, and the necessary governmental machinery to carry it out, should be called into being as soon as possible.

(b) It is essential that the carrying out of this development plan should be entrusted to a department of the Union Government with Union-wide jurisdiction; and it is equally essential that, in order to ensure the necessary co-ordination, the administration of Bantu education should be placed in the hands of a special section of that same Department.

(c) The recommendation is therefore made that a Division of Bantu Affairs should be called into being, consisting of a Department of Bantu Administration, a Department of Bantu Technical Services, a Department of Bantu Education and a Bantu Development Authority; the latter body to be served by a Research Organization.

(d) In order to secure the active participation of the Bantu in the solution of local problems it is recommended that Bantu Local Authorities be set up in the Reserves and in the urban areas. The intention is that these bodies should in course of time evolve into local government units charged with the administration of all local services, including education. Their funds would be drawn from local and national taxation.

(e) Recommendations are made for the establishment of a number of bodies designed to effect close co-ordination of effort between the three proposed Departments of the Division of Native Affairs at all levels.

(f) It is proposed that the Department of Bantu Education should be divided into six regional units each with its own Regional Director and Educational Advisory Council. These regions have been proposed in order to secure adequate administrative de-centralization and to group together as far as possible homogenous elements of the population.

(g) The general approach of the Commission to problems of curricula is that as soon as the general development plan has been satisfactorily drawn up the educational authorities will have a clear picture of the types of individuals they will be called upon to produce. The great dilemma of Bantu education at present is that it lacks clear and definite aims, stated in terms of what children will do when they leave school (if they do not become teachers).

(h) In connection with school organization it is recommended that there should be instituted the following types of schools:
  (i) A lower primary school with a four year course.
  (ii) A higher primary school with a four year course.
  (iii) Secondary and Technical schools with courses lasting four or five years.
  (iv) Post-matriculation and university education.

The Commission regards the lower primary school as being particularly important as it is at this stage of the educational process that the present very high wastage of pupils occurs and a low standard of work is found which handicaps the work of the rest of the school system. It is hoped that in the not too distant future attendance at a lower primary school for four years will be made compulsory. Since only a small proportion of Bantu pupils at present complete the primary course it is recommended that the lower primary syllabus should be a rounded-off course, complete and worthwhile in itself, but also making provision for those children who wish and have the ability to proceed to higher stages in the school system. To emphasize their fundamental importance it is recommended that lower primary schools should have their own principals and should be inspected by Bantu sub-inspectors fully conversant with the mother-tongue of the pupils.

(i) With 75.2 of all Bantu pupils in the first four classes of the primary school and only 2.5 per cent in classes above Std. VI it is obvious that not to use to the fullest the mother-tongue as the medium of instruction is to impose a very heavy burden on both pupil and teacher. Accordingly your Commission has made recommendations designed to promote the increased use of mother-tongue instruction. At the same time the importance of a knowledge of both official languages to the Bantu is not ignored.

(j) In consonance with our recommendations designed to secure the active participation of the Bantu in local government and the control of schools, we have recommended the increased use of Bantu teaching personnel in post-primary schools and the appointment of Bantu sub-inspectors of schools. With such a large percentage of pupils in the two lowest classes of the schools the importance of inspection by persons thoroughly at home in the language of the pupils needs no further demonstration.

(k) Concerning the financing of Bantu schools your Commission recommends the adoption of the following principles:
  (i) Educational expenditure should be correlated with the development plan and attention given to the problem of using education to improve the economic situation.

(ii) The responsibility for financing education must be shared by the State and the Bantu Local Authorities or communities.

(iii) As the development plans take effect it is expected that Bantu Local Authorities will be able to shoulder a proportionately heavier share. In the earlier stages, however, the share of the State will be heavier and must be regarded as an investment or 'pump-priming' device.

* * *

772. We now turn to the question why it should be *Bantu Education*. A number of witnesses laid it down as axiomatic that education was one and indivisible; others maintained that all education to be efficient should be expressed in terms of the needs of a particular people, situated in a particular environment, at a particular stage of their development.

773. The Bantu child comes to school with a basic physical and psychological endowment which differs, so far as your Commissioners have been able to determine from the evidence set before them, so slightly, if at all, from that of the European child that no special provision has to be made in educational theory or basic aims. The now universally accepted principle of leading the child in his education from the known and familiar to the unknown and the unfamiliar has to be applied equally in the case of the Bantu child as with children of any other social group. But educational practice must recognize that it has to deal with a Bantu child, i.e. a child trained and conditioned in Bantu culture, endowed with a knowledge of a Bantu language and imbued with values, interests and behaviour patterns learned at the knee of a Bantu mother. These facts must dictate to a very large extent the content and methods of his early education.

774. The schools must also give due regard to the fact that out of school hours the young Bantu child develops and lives in a Bantu community, and when he reaches maturity he will be concerned with sharing and developing the life and culture of that community.

775. When we come to the more advanced stages of schooling a more difficult set of considerations has to be met. Here the problem is largely to find an answer to the question: What type of individual should the school produce that will function to the best advantage in Bantu society?

776. The educational theorist is compelled to guess at future development whether or not he desires to play the part of prophet. What will be the most likely features of Bantu society in, say, 1970? Or to simplify the problem: What are the qualities, attitudes and skills which the Bantu are most likely to need in 1970 under the existing circumstances of life at that time? Very briefly, and without entering into details as to why certain items are included, it is suggested that the following are among the needs for which provision should be made:—

(a) Religious knowledge and attitudes.
(b) Literacy in a Bantu language both as a means of communication and of calculation, and as a vehicle for the preservation of pride in national traditions.
(c) Literacy in one, or preferably, both European official languages to serve as a means of communication with Europeans, as a help in economic matters and as a means of securing contact with the knowledge of the wider world.
(d) Knowledge of hygiene for the preservation of health.
(e) Knowledge of technical skills in agriculture, and the whole gamut of professions and trades which have grown up as the result of the development of the worldwide phenomena of industrialization.
(f) Social patterns and values which make a man a good member of his community, a good parent and a useful member of society. (He should, for example, possess such qualities as punctuality, initiative, self-confidence, sense of duty, persistence, sociability, mannerliness, neatness, reliability, power to concentrate, etc.)
(g) Knowledge of and sympathy for the development and well-being of the Bantu people, as well as other groups in South Africa.

777. The above list is not exhaustive but has been given to show that Bantu education does have a separate existence just as, for example, French education, Chinese education or even European education in South Africa, because it exists and can function only in and for a particular social setting, namely, Bantu society.

The extracts which follow are from Act No. 47 of 1953, under which African education was transferred from the Provinces to the control of the Bantu Affairs Department of the Union.

DOCUMENT 10. FROM THE BANTU EDUCATION ACT, NO. 47 OF 1953.

2. As from the date of commencement of this Act:
(a) the control of native education shall vest in the Government of the Union subject to the provisions of this Act;
(b) there shall cease to be vested in the executive committee of a province any powers, authorities and functions, and the provincial council of a province shall cease to be competent to make ordinances, in relation to native education: Provided that, subject to the provisions of section *eleven*:
 (i) a provincial administration shall continue to administer any pension, retirement or provident fund established or conducted by such administration in connection with native education;
 (ii) a provincial council shall continue to be competent to make ordinances for the proper administration of any such fund.

3. (1) It shall be the function of the Department under the direction and control of the Minister, to perform all the work necessary for or incidental to the general administration of native education.

(2) The Minister may, subject to the laws governing the

public service, from time to time appoint such officers and employees as he may deem necessary for the proper performance by the Department of its functions under this Act.

* * *

9. (1) As from a date to be fixed by the Minister by notice in the *Gazette*, no person shall establish, conduct, or maintain any Bantu or native school, other than a Government Bantu school, unless it is registered as prescribed.

(2) The registration of any such school shall be refused or cancelled if the Minister, acting on the advice and recommendation of the Native Affairs Commission constituted under the Native Affairs Act, 1920 (Act No. 23 of 1920), given after due enquiry by the said Commission is of opinion that its establishment or continued existence is not in the interests of the Bantu people or any section of such people or is likely to be detrimental to the physical, mental or moral welfare of the pupils or students attending or likely to attend such school.

(3) Any person who, after the date fixed under sub-section (1), admits any Bantu child or person to, or establishes, conducts or maintains, any Bantu or native school which is not registered in terms of this Act, shall be guilty of an offence and liable on conviction to a fine not exceeding fifty pounds, or, in default of payment, to imprisonment for a period not exceeding six months.

THE CASE FOR THE ACT

The quotations which follow are taken from the speech of the Minister of Native Affairs on the 17 September 1953 moving the second reading of the Act in the House of Assembly.

DOCUMENT 11. FROM A SPEECH BY THE MINISTER OF NATIVE AFFAIRS, 17 SEPTEMBER 1953.

I shall proceed from the premise that members have knowledge of the contents of the report of the recent Native Education Commission, which has already been mentioned in this House.

From that report they will know how, notwithstanding the fact that education has for all these years been controlled by the provincial authorities, there has been continual confusion, confusion of control, various methods applied to the financing of education, and how often in the course of the history of the matter the possibility was considered of making a change in regard to provincial control. I just want to remind hon. members of one incident in the history of the matter, namely that in 1936 an Inter-Departmental Committee was appointed to investigate Native education, which also came to the conclusion that the Central Government should control Native education, but the hon. member for East London (City) [Dr. D. L. Smit], who at that time was Secretary for Native Affairs and who give [sic] evidence before that committee, was not in favour of having Native education under the control of his Department, the Department of Native Affairs, and the findings of that Committee were probably influenced by the evidence given by him to that effect. That was in 1936, but in the years following there were also other influences at work within the then Government which judged otherwise than he did and also otherwise than the Inter-Departmental Committee, namely, the Native Affairs Commission which at that time issued a report expressing the opinion that Native education ought to resort under the Department of Native Affairs, and if I am not mistaken, Senator Nicholls was one of the important figures in that move. If my information is correct, it is as the result of the memorandum framed by him, or rather, as the result of the report of his Commission, that finally it was decided that Native education should be brought under the control of the Department of Native Affairs. Thereafter, certain provinces raised objections and the war clouds started rolling up and the matter was not continued with, but under the régime of the then Government, in about 1939, a Bill was actually drafted to bring Native education under the control of the Union Government in general and the Department of Native Affairs in particular. Therefore, what we are dealing with now is not without historical background, even in regard to certain hon. members on that side of the House, on whose part I can therefore take it that there will still be a reasonable measure of sympathy for that point of view. . . .

Then I still want to add that it is sometimes said that there is no difference between European and Native education. Of course there are certain fundamental educational principles which are common to all types of education, but forgetting for a moment those principles, when you come to practical teaching, there are definitely differences with which one has to reckon. What is the use of subjecting a Native child to a curriculum which in the first instance is traditionally European, in which one learns of the Kings of England and how much wheat Canada has exported and through which our children are taught these general facts as a means of building up a fount of knowledge? What is the use of teaching the Bantu child mathematics when it cannot use it in practice? That is quite absurd. In other words your teaching should begin where all education should begin, namely with the known facts or common knowledge. The common knowledge of the white child is different from that of the Bantu child. Everybody who has had anything to do with intelligence tests knows that when you try to apply an intelligence test based on the common knowledge of children of a certain community, the test can be a complete failure and give entirely wrong results in respect of children not falling within the same group of common knowledge. If the contents of that intelligence test is based on the knowledge of an urban child, you cannot apply that same test to the rural child. He possesses a different fund of common knowledge. The same applies to education. It is therefore also correct to say that Bantu education must of necessity be different, because it has as its starting point other sources and other kinds of knowledge. One should therefore not confuse fundamental principles of education which may be similar for all people, with the practical form which positively differs for different people.

A further point is that education is after all not something that hangs in the air. Education must train and teach people in accordance with their opportunities in life, according to the sphere in which they live. Certain of the Natives have to be trained to be able to serve their own people in the higher professions; we all know that. It is well known that especially my Department has available professional possibilities for Natives, for which we cannot find adequately trained Natives. I just want to add that if my Department controls Native education it will know for which type of higher profession the Native can be trained, where he will be able to make a living with his knowledge, instead of choosing his own path in a direction where he cannot find a sphere of activity, thus turning him into a frustrated and dissatisfied being. But apart from these persons who can serve their own people, there is the much greater number of Natives who have to find a future in other forms of work. The latter should have a training in accordance with their opportunities in life, and no department will know better where and how great the opportunities are for the Bantu child in various directions than the Department of Native Affairs. For that reason it will be wise to entrust that Department with this type of education which will prepare the people for the battle of life.

Then I want to add—and this is very important—that their education should not clash with Government policy. I suppose hon. members will at once say that we want to give ideological education.

Mr. Lawrence: That is indoctrination.

The Minister of Native Affairs: I just want to remind hon. members that if the Native in South Africa today in any kind of school in existence is being taught to expect that he will live his adult life under a policy of equal rights, he is making a big mistake. Hon. members always profess not to be in favour of equal rights, and therefore they should now support me in principle in what I am saying. If they, like we on this side, are not in favour of equal rights, and if they are, like we are, in favour of the Native's development within his own sphere and in the service of his own people, then such a person should be reared in that idea right from the start. Should the South African government spend money in order to send into the world an ever increasing number of dissatisfied persons, or should we look for a way of improving racial relations by giving them the chance of development; the government's policy is that their opportunity for development should be to serve their own people in the higher spheres as well as in the more humble positions. That is what I mean when I say that education should be in accordance with government policy as seen in its broadest sense. Consequently, I say that as my Department is principally responsible in the sphere of government policy as far as the Bantu is concerned, it is also the most suitable to give guidance in regard to the education that should be supplied.

THE CLOSING OF ADAMS COLLEGE

The following extracts refer to the closing down under the Bantu Education Act of a school which had rendered yeoman service to South Africa. Adams College, founded by the American Board of Missions in 1853, had in 1956 an enrolment of approximately 400 students divided between the Training College, High School and Industrial School. Its teachers included Chief Luthuli, Dr. Z. K. Matthews and Dr. D. G. S. M'Timkulu, and its students, Sir Seretse Khama, Mr. Joshua Nkomo and Chief Gasha Buthelezi.

The first extract is from *Iso Lomuzi*, the magazine of the College, and is the farewell letter of the last Principal. The second is a description of the farewell ceremony, reported by the *Natal Mercury* of Durban, on 3 December 1956.

DOCUMENT 12a. FROM *Iso Lomuzi*, LETTER OF THE PRINCIPAL, 17 SEPTEMBER 1956.

Adams College,
17th September, 1956.
Dear Friends,
This is my eighth annual letter for our *Iso Lomuzi*; and, alas, it is my last. It is not that I have reached the age limit or been incapacitated in any way. Rather, the reason is that the Minister of Native Affairs has refused to give Adams College permission to continue after the end of this year.

The decision of the Minister is grievous, yet not surprising. When a person thinks as he does and glorifies APARTHEID, then the generally accepted basic standards of justice, mercy, and truth have to take second place. Make no mistake, as long as Apartheid remains the Minister's chief end then we must expect such a decision. It matters not that the record of service of the College is long and honourable; it matters not that many Africans wish it to remain open; it matters not that there are those who are willing to give their time and talents to the College. No, in order that the cause of Apartheid may be advanced, Adams College must be liquidated. Indeed, in the eyes of the Minister there can be no place in Bantu Education for any institution which does not bow its knee before the Apartheid Idol.

For our part, we have, I verily believe, fought a good fight. Now we are about to finish our course. We know that we have acted in obedience to our vision of Christian discipleship. Therefore, we have the joy of men and women who have stood for something in which they believe. That joy no man can take from us. Though our line of action has ended in apparent defeat, yet in God's good time the outcome will be quite different. That is our faith.

As this is my last letter as Principal I must now do two things. The first is to thank you for the support which you have given my wife and me, and the financial support which you have given to the College. Without this personal and financial support we and the College would have ceased long ere this. So I pray you please accept our most grateful thanks.

Secondly, on behalf of my wife and myself, I have to bid you good-bye, may be for good. In this new order there is unlikely to be any suitable opening for us in African Education in South Africa. It is hard to believe that in a so-called Christian country in this year of grace 1956 we who take our stand on Christian principles are now about to be debarred from making our contribution through the medium of a Christian School, and all because we stand for an education which is Christian and liberal rather than for one which is Christian and National.

BANTU EDUCATION

DOCUMENT 12b. FROM *The Natal Mercury*, DURBAN, 3 DECEMBER 1956.

Century-old Adams College Era Ending

As scores of rich, meaningful Bantu voices rose to the crescendo of the last Amen in the Adams College Mission Church yesterday afternoon, more than a century of Christian endeavour came to an end and the political era of the Bantu Education Act came to the college.

Yesterday was the closing service at the college and on Thursday the final word in its history will be written when the doors close on the last day of the 1956 academic year.

Next year when the old building reopens it will probably be as the Amanzimtoti Zulu College, a name that will have no meaning to generations of Africans who received the benefit of a liberal Christian education which enabled them to go out as teachers and ministers to their people.

The closing address yesterday was delivered by a former Senator and principal of the college, Dr. Edgar Brookes, and the whole tone throughout was one of regret rather than of recrimination.

He said: 'We should not end these 103 years on an air of righteous indignation but on one of penitence.' He said that nothing would ever persuade him that the policy which was to be implemented was just or right in forcing out of existence an independent school with a century's tradition and history behind it.

During the address a rainstorm broke and the old mission church thundered to the roar of the rain on the high corrugated iron roof and a sea of faces, European and non-European, strained forward to hear every word Dr. Brookes was uttering with obvious feeling and sincerity.

Dr. Brookes told those of the staff and students who would not be returning next year to go out and preach love and faith. Saying that missionary work in Africa was under judgment, he added that it was not easy not to feel resentment at what had happened. They should, however, ask God's blessing for those who were to take over, that He should be asked to guide them and that there should be prayer that those in authority would meet with success.

It would not be possible, he said, to ask for God's blessing for all that would be wrong. African education could not be different from the education of free men. There were those who said that African education should be taken back to the old Zulu tradition but there could not be the belief that what was suitable for others was not suitable for Africans.

Writing in the last college magazine which appeared yesterday, Dr. Brookes said: 'Whatever takes the place of the college it will not be the same school, actuated by the same ideals of liberal education, and educational freedom. It would be foolish to pretend that those of us who knew the old Adams do not feel deeply hurt by the compulsory changes that have been made. But we do not and must not cherish bitterness.'

Brief addresses during the service were made by Mr. D. C. Macdonald, chairman of the Council of Governors, the Rev. B. G. M. Nomvete, chairman of the Bantu Congregational Church of South Africa, and a former student; the Rev. A. F. Christoforsen, resident senior missionary, and Mr. G. C. Grant, the college's last principal.

Mr. Justice E. S. Henochsberg, a former chairman of the Governing Council, was also present at the service.

A REASONED CASE AGAINST IT

The article which follows appeared in the *Natal Daily News* in December 1962 and was written by Dr. W. G. McConkey, former Director of Education of the Natal Province.

DOCUMENT 13. FROM AN ARTICLE IN THE *Natal Daily News* BY DR. W. G. MCCONKEY, DECEMBER 1962.

A great industrial economy requires a highly developed system of education, turning out well-trained people at all levels for the ever-increasing number of skilled and responsible tasks.

The most highly industrialised countries in the world— America, Britain, Western Europe, Russia, Japan—are all vigorously expanding their education services, lengthening and diversifying secondary education, doubling facilities for university and higher technological education. Moreover they realise that direct vocational training is not the main need. A high degree of general education is necessary to provide the flexibility and adaptability required in days when new jobs arise and old jobs become obsolete with increasing rapidity. The United States is rapidly reaching a stage when unskilled workpeople are increasingly difficult to employ at all.

'In the most practical sense,' said the United States Ambassador to South Africa in Johannesburg last month, 'it can be demonstrated that investment in education and training directly yields at least as high a rate of return as direct investment in industry or agriculture, and this quite aside from its indirect benefits to a society and the ensuing enrichment of the life of the individual.'

The American Ambassador's words do not represent only American policy. They express the current outlook on education of all civilised governments.

Now this outlook is not completely strange in South Africa. It is commonly accepted by Nationalist educational theorists—for the White group. For that group the accepted formula has been 'equal educational opportunities for all, with something extra for the backward'. As a 'group' policy, that has worked wonders. What is wrong with it nationally is that it excludes most of the nation. If South Africa had been a racially homogeneous country, we should long ago have had a system of universal compulsory education geared to our vigorously expanding economy. Instead we have, for the majority of our population, 'Bantu education' geared to the perpetuation of tribalism and the pre-industrial way of life in which tribalism flourishes.

The restrictive philosophy which inspires 'Bantu education' is an inheritance from the days of widespread White poverty and rural under-employment, when the African was seen as a competitor for the limited number of jobs available. 'Native education' was attacked in those days, and has continued to be attacked, as 'teaching Natives to compete with Europeans', and therefore as a 'danger to White civilisation'. The good Native was the tribal Native who did not compete and so was not a 'danger'. Therefore 'the Natives should learn to be good Natives as tribal Natives, and should not be imitators of the White man'.

'My Department's policy,' said Dr. Verwoerd, 'is that Bantu education should stand with both feet in the reserves. What is the use of teaching the Bantu child mathematics when it cannot use it in practice? That is absurd. ... There is no place for the Native in the European community above the level of certain forms of labour. ... It is of no avail for him to receive a training which has as its aim absorption in the European community.'

In the narrow context of poor Whitism a generation or two ago talk like that may have sounded sensible. It was certainly good electioneering tactics. There was no excuse for it in 1954, and there has been none since. In the Africa of 1962 it is madness.

Bantu education is a unique system—the only education system in the world designed to restrict the productivity of its pupils in the national economy to lowly and subservient tasks, to render them non-competitive in that economy, to fix them mentally in a tribal world and to 'teach them', in Dr. Verwoerd's phrase, 'that equality is not for them'.

Behind a façade of increasing enrolments it has systematically degraded the quality of the education given. I mention some of its sorry triumphs:

Expenditure

Financial Starvation: Expenditure per child per annum has been forced down from over R17 in 1954 to about R12 in 1962 (compare with R158.15 per child in Natal European schools in 1960). The vote from general revenue has been frozen at the 1954 level and the entire burden of increased enrolments placed on special African taxation. An incredible niggardliness governs supplies of equipment, stores, buildings and the apparatus of education generally.

Despite widespread malnutrition and vast 'surpluses' of

agricultural products, the school meal system has been practically eliminated.

Teaching

Teachers: The pupil load per teacher has risen from 42 to 59. In most lower primary schools (schools for the first four school years) the teachers work double shifts, taking one class in the early session and another in the late. This reduces the school day for the pupils to less than three hours—instead of the normal four hours for the two sub-standards and five hours for standards I and II. After standard II most pupils leave school. Those who go on do so heavily handicapped by their inferior preparation.

In spite of classes so large that sound schooling is impossible, the number of teachers in training has been deliberately reduced and bursaries theoretically available for training courses have been withheld and the funds diverted. Teacher training has been kept at a low level. Less than a quarter of high-school teachers are graduates. Of 136 high-school teacher-trainees this year only 27 are graduates. Most African children receive their entire schooling from teachers who have had two years of training after Form 1 (equal to Standard VI in non-Bantu schools).

Morale

Service conditions of teachers are deplorable. Morale has been depressed by intimidation, loss of security of tenure, low salaries and the persistent denial of pensions. At high-school and university level the predominantly English-speaking teachers who built the service have been very largely replaced by Christian-Nationalists. Teachers other than citizens of the Republic are barred from permanent appointment.

Isolation: Education to end at university-college level has been tribalised, the pupils and students of each major tribe being systematically isolated from outside contacts.

Language Policy: In countries whose language has local currency only, education normally rests on two supports: the vernacular plus a world language. This recipe was followed in most African schools in pre-Bantu-education days. The world language used was English, which became the medium of instruction from about Standard V.

New Policy

Nationalists have opposed this use of English and under Bantu education the place of English has been systematically reduced. The new policy is that three languages—the vernacular, English and Afrikaans—have to be learnt from the first school year; that the vernacular has to be used as medium not only in the early stages but throughout the school, and that, when this is not possible in respect of some secondary-school subjects, half of these subjects must be taught through Afrikaans and the other half through English, the less academic subjects always being taken through the vernacular.

This compulsory learning of three languages by all pupils throughout the primary school course—with a view to their use of all three as concurrent media of instruction in the secondary school—is unique in the history of popular education.

Responsible

It is extraordinary that the Nationalist Government should be responsible for it. In the early 1940s all four provinces considered and rejected the principle of dual-medium education for White children, and Nationalist educationists were particularly emphatic that it made unreasonable demands on the pupils and led to inefficient learning. The present trilingual, triple-medium policy for African schools obviously makes much more unreasonable demands. Its motivation is purely political. Educationally it is indefensible. It should be abandoned.

Syllabuses: Many of the syllabuses, taken separately, are tolerable professional jobs; but in the aggregate they compel a gross distortion of educational effort. Reference has been made to the treatment of the languages. The social studies are clearly designed to bolster up a tribalism whose economic basis has quite disappeared. Even the practical subjects show the bias against training for the modern world.

Upper Primary

Children in the upper primary school—the select minority who have survived the lower primary school and who will supply the leaders of the future—spend six hours a week on these subjects! tree planting and soil conservation (two hours), gardening (two hours) and handwork A, which in most cases boils down to planting reeds and grasses and making useless articles out of scraps of waste wire, old boxes, beads and so on. Children so trained can be guaranteed non-competitive!

Bantu education fails not only to prepare African children for life in the general economy of South Africa, but fails even to provide the technicians and artisans required by the Bantustans. There is no need, we are told, for Bantu engineers. Poor Bantustans!

PART V

University Education

THE EXTENSION OF UNIVERSITY EDUCATION ACT

The following extracts are taken from the so-called 'Extension of University Education' Act, No. 45 of 1959, which prescribed rules for the University Colleges for Africans, Indians and Coloured, set up when such students were excluded from the ordinary universities. By this Act the conditions of service of the academic staff are in the hands of the Minister and the conditions of service which make public criticism of the Government a dismissible offence are to be found in the Regulations.

DOCUMENT 14. FROM THE EXTENSION OF UNIVERSITY EDUCATION ACT, NO. 45 OF 1959.

2. (1) The Minister may, in consultation with the Minister of Finance, out of moneys appropriated by Parliament out of the Bantu Education Account for the purpose:
(a) establish;
(b) maintain and conduct,
university colleges for Bantu persons.

(2) The establishment of any such university college shall be notified by notice in the *Gazette*.

(3) The Minister may, in consultation with the Minister of Finance, out of moneys appropriated by Parliament out of the Bantu Education Account for the purpose, pay to the council of such a university college annually such amounts as are necessary for carrying out such functions as may be entrusted to it by or under this Act and subject to such conditions and on such basis as may be determined by the Minister.

3. (1) The Minister may, in consultation with the Minister

of Finance, out of moneys appropriated by Parliament for the purpose:
(a) establish;
(b) maintain and conduct,
university colleges for non-white persons other than Bantu persons.

(2) The establishment of any such university college shall be notified by notice in the *Gazette*.

(3) The Minister may, in consultation with the Minister of Finance, out of moneys appropriated by Parliament for the purpose, pay to the council of such a university college annually such amounts as are necessary for carrying out such functions as may be entrusted to it by or under this Act and subject to such conditions and on such basis as may be determined by the Minister.

* * *

14. The Minister may refuse admittance to any person who applies for admission as a student of a university college if he considers it to be in the interests of the university college concerned to do so.

* * *

17. No white person shall register with or attend any university college as a student.

* * *

31. As from a date to be fixed by the Governor-General by proclamation in the *Gazette* for the purposes of this section, no non-white person who was not registered as a student of a university established by Act of Parliament, other than the University of South Africa, on or before the said date, shall register with or attend any such university as a student without the written consent of the Minister: Provided that this section shall not apply to non-white persons in respect of their registration and attendance as students at the Medical School.

* * *

32. (1) As from a date to be fixed by the Governor-General by proclamation in the *Gazette* for the purposes of this sub-

section, no non-White person shall register with or attend any university established by Act of Parliament, other than the University of South Africa, as a student: Provided that the provisions of this sub-section shall not be construed as preventing any non-white person who is registered as a student at a university other than the University of South Africa, on the said date or who was so registered prior to the said date, from completing at that university the course of study or training for the degree, diploma or certificate for which he is or was so registered: Provided further that this sub-section shall not apply to non-white persons in respect of their registration and attendance as students at the Medical School.

(2) Different dates may be fixed under sub-section (1) in respect of:
(a) different universities;
(b) separate faculties or departments of a university;
(c) Bantu persons;
(d) non-white persons other than Bantu persons; and
(e) different ethnic or other groups of non-white persons.

* * *

40. Any person who contravenes any provision of section *seventeen, thirty-one* or *thirty-two* shall be guilty of an offence and liable on conviction to a fine not exceeding one hundred pounds or in default of payment to imprisonment for a period not exceeding six months.

DOCUMENT 15. FROM THE SPEECH OF THE MINISTER OF EDUCATION, ARTS AND SCIENCE ON THE SECOND READING OF THE EXTENSION OF UNIVERSITY EDUCATION BILL ON THE 8 APRIL 1959.

During the second reading debate on the Viljoen Bill of 1957, the Opposition, as they have done so often in the past, strongly urged the reference of this measure to a Select Committee before second reading. We knew that this Bill would be a most contentious measure. We knew that on the previous occasion the United Party had already opposed it when leave to introduce was sought. At that time the Government refused to do so and decided to refer the Bill to a Select Committee after second reading 'to investigate and submit recommendations on the details of the Separate University Education Bill with due regard to the principles contained therein, as adopted at the second reading of the Bill'. We have the results of that investigation before us today in the form of a majority report and a minority report, in the form of a proposed Bill submitted by the majority and an alternative proposed Bill submitted by the minority. These have already been in our hands since August of last year. It is unnecessary for me to say that fundamental differences exist as to how this problem should be approached. The whole history of recent years shows quite clearly that fundamental differences exist. These differences are also clearly apparent from the majority report and the minority report as signed by the Government members on the one hand and the remaining members on the other hand, as well as from the proposed Bills. These differences are also set out in paragraph 2 of the minority report.

As hon. members know, the Government have in the main accepted the majority report, and I now want to place very great emphasis on the chief points of difference between the majority report and the minority report. The chief points of difference relate to:

(a) The limitation of the admission of non-white students to certain university institutions.
(b) The nature and form of the proposed institutions and the method of control.

The Bill before us at present, proposes that initially there will be State institutions which will gradually develop towards greater independence so that eventually they can become full-fledged universities on such a basis that they will be able to serve the non-White population of this country in exactly the same way as the White universities are at present serving the Whites. The majority report emphasises this point on at least 12 occasions. If a university is to comply with all the most important requirements which it must meet during its process of growth and development, it cannot stand aloof from the people and/or the national group it serves. It is a fundamental premise that a university cannot stand aloof from the people or national group it serves because it must adjust itself to and be at one with the life of the community it serves. South Africa's universities or university institutions are no exception to this rule. They must necessarily have their own South African character. The majority report and the minority report appear to differ fundamentally from one another as regards the premise I have just laid down.

I want to make this point quite clear on the basis of the reports themselves. We have the majority report and the minority report together with the reasons for those reports, which is rather an unusual position. In the majority report it is specifically stated:

> The university college should be related to the culture and life of the nation.

An Hon. Member: Which culture?
The Minister of Education, Arts and Science: Hon. members will be given all the information they require and I think they will get more than they bargained for. I read from this report:

> The university college should be related to the culture and life of the nation. The product of the university should seek and find its highest fulfilment in the enrichment of its own social group.

This principle is embodied in paragraph 27 of the majority report, and this specifically entails legislative provision for the separation of White and non-White. . . .

Mr. Speaker, I want to lay down a further premise: As mankind and groups of people differing in nature and development have developed, various needs have arisen during this process. Thus university institutions have been established throughout the world and have developed in accordance with the needs of the times and in accordance with the particular needs of the particular people they serve. I go further and say that universities do not only train professional people. Such a university must also produce individuals who are aware of their mission in life. It is the specific aim of this Bill not to estrange people from their own national group. It is fatal, and it will always remain fatal, to try to turn a non-White into a White and conversely to try to turn a White into a non-White. Consequently we must ensure that the racial groups are separated on a racial basis and that their education fits in with their own national character. If hon. members opposite are of a different opinion, they are of course entitled to that opinion. They must tell me whether they disagree with my basic premise, and whether they wish to guide this development process along such lines that it will also eventually result in complete social intermingling. Mr. Speaker, when a university student leaves university, he should not only ask himself: 'What can I derive from the education I have enjoyed?' but he should also ask: 'After receiving this education, how much can I give to my people to whose service I am returning?'

I assume that all sides of the House have studied this legislation. Members on all sides of the House have made a thorough study of the matter. I therefore only want to refer briefly to one or two of the most important provisions. This Bill has already been the subject of a Second Reading debate. The main principles of the Bill are embodied in Clauses 2, 3, 17 and 32.

Clauses 2 and 3 provide for the establishment, the maintenance and the conduct of university colleges for non-White persons, and for the payment of subsidies, with the distinction that funds for Bantu institutions will come from the Bantu Education Account, and for the other institutions from the normal State funds. My predecessor gave the House full details of the proposed plans and sites when he moved the Second Reading of the original Bill on 27 May 1957. On that occasion he also gave full details of the curricula, the financial implications and so on. As far as the estimated costs and the curricula are concerned, the position today is essentially unaltered.

Clause 17 prohibits the admission of White persons as students to the university colleges and it has been taken over unaltered from the previous Bill. The minority report proposes that there should be a proviso saying that once the non-White university colleges have been established, the Minister concerned will be given the power in terms of the proviso to admit Whites if he so desires.

Clause 32 prohibits the registration or attendance of non-White persons as students of the eight residential universities. The University of South Africa is not included for two obvious reasons. Firstly, because it provides education by means of correspondence, and secondly because it will act as the examining body for the new university colleges.

I must now state quite specifically that the exclusion in terms of Clause 32 will be applied gradually as and when adequate separate facilities become available to the non-White population. This does not apply to the Natal Medical School. It is specifically excluded from the provisions of this legislation.

Those non-White students who are legally registered as students at the so-called 'open universities' and at Natal University on the date upon which this prohibition becomes effective, will be permitted to complete their courses.

Clause 31 links up with Clause 32. I do not want any uncertainty in this regard either. A date will be fixed after which no non-White may register with or attend an existing White university without Ministerial approval. I think it is necessary that I should say with the utmost emphasis at this stage that this House, the country and the world must understand clearly that the main principle of this measure is the establishment of the proposed separation (apartheid) and its implementation in the way which we feel convinced is in the interests of Whites and the non-Whites of South Africa. There must be no misunderstanding on this point. We therefore shall not and cannot be a party to allowing an unprecedented influx of non-White students into the open universities with the sole purpose of defeating the Government's policy. The Government does not intend enacting legislation providing for separate university institutions and then allowing anyone in the world to divert it from its purpose. We are aware of the fact that even in overseas countries organizations have been established even to collect money abroad with the specific purpose of thwarting our efforts. We are aware of that fact.

UNIVERSITY EDUCATION

By this legislation we are making the necessary provision for the needs of all the national groups in South Africa. Do hon. members on all sides of the House not agree with me that never in the history of South Africa have student organizations, students, university councils or the State attempted to interfere with the domestic affairs of other countries in so far as their domestic arrangements for the education of their youth were concerned? If there are hon. members opposite who have in fact done so, let them say so. (Laughter.) Mr. Speaker, I can understand how the Opposition feels. But on behalf of South Africa I want to lodge the strongest possible protest against the fact that organized efforts are being made, inspired moreover from *inter alia* South Africa, to tell us how we should manage our affairs in our own fatherland.

PROTEST AGAINST UNIVERSITY APARTHEID

The following are taken from *A Digest of Protest against University Apartheid Legislation*, prepared by the National Union of South African Students in 1957. The universities referred to below are:

The University of Cape Town (A and B), founded in 1829 and given its present Charter in 1918, with an enrolment in 1957 of 4,782 students, of whom 456 were non-Whites.

The University College of Fort Hare (C), founded in 1916 mainly for non-European students with an enrolment in 1957 of 378 students.

The University of Stellenbosch (D), founded in 1863 and given its present Charter in 1918, with an enrolment in 1957 of 3,335 students, all White.

The University of Witwatersrand (E), founded in 1904 and given its present Charter in 1922, with an enrolment in 1957 of 4,677 students, of whom 214 were non-Whites.

DOCUMENT 16. FROM *A Digest of Protest against the University Apartheid Legislation*, NATIONAL UNION OF SOUTH AFRICAN STUDENTS, 1957.

UNIVERSITY EDUCATION

A.

From the Chancellor of the University of Cape Town, the Hon. A. van der Sandt Centlivres, former Chief Justice of the Union of South Africa:

It is clear that a very great principle is at stake, a principle which in the Western World is regarded as sacred. That principle is that the Universities should enjoy academic freedom. Preventing the open universities from admitting non-European students would very seriously affect the status and reputation these Universities enjoyed in the world. He appealed to the Government to reconsider its decision to introduce apartheid legislation for the Universities of Cape Town and the Witwatersrand and to adopt the policy of live and let live.

It is of inestimable value to anyone to be able to continue his studies at a university institution where he can exchange his ideas with others, provided that the institution is not subject, as the Universities were in Hitler's Germany, to complete control by the State as to who should teach, what should be taught, and whom should be taught. The experiment of making all people hold the same views has been tried in some countries, but it has never succeeded. Differences of opinion are not to be deplored.

B.

From the Council of the University of Cape Town:

The University is opposed in principle to academic segregation on racial grounds. It believes that separate academic facilities for European and non-European could not be equal to those provided in an open University. The University is convinced that the policy of academic non-segregation which, as far as possible the University of Cape Town has always followed, accords with the highest University ideals and has contributed to inter-racial understanding and harmony in South Africa. It desires that the University be permitted and enabled to carry on its functions under the same conditions as hitherto, and that nothing be done to change or impede the

University's policy of academic non-segregation. (The *Senate of the University of Cape Town* had previously adopted a similar resolution.)

C.

From the staff members of the University College of Fort Hare:

We must state publicly that we are totally opposed to the nationalisation of our University and to any interference with the autonomy of any University in this land. . . . The Bill is a flagrant interference with the conduct of an autonomous University. No academic reason whatever has so far been advanced in favour of the separation of Fort Hare from Rhodes University.

D.

From a group of Stellenbosch professors and lecturers:

Legislative enforcement of complete academic segregation on racial grounds is an unwanted interference with University autonomy and academic freedom. Total educational apartheid is both impossible and unnecessary because whites and non-whites in South Africa have become so interdependent and intermingled that complete territorial segregation is beyond the bounds of possibility.

E.

From the Council of the University of the Witwatersrand:

Opposed in principle to legislative enforcement of academic segregation on racial grounds, it believes that the policy of academic non-segregation accords with the highest ideals and contributes to inter-racial understanding and harmony. It desires that the University be permitted and enabled to carry on its functions under the same conditions as hitherto and that nothing be done to change or impede the University's policy of academic non-segregation.

F.

[From a group of prominent South Africans, mainly academic and professional men]:

UNIVERSITY EDUCATION

It is of paramount importance in this country that flexibility and experimentation should be preserved and that the stultifying uniformity which the Government now declares it will impose should be avoided. . . . Segregation means discrimination and isolation. To destroy the present system of open Universities will mean the destruction of one of the last bridges leading to inter-racial understanding and respect.

PART VI
The Churches

LEGAL RESTRICTIONS

DOCUMENT 17. FROM THE NATIVE LAWS AMENDMENT ACT, NO. 36 OF 1957.

29. (b) The Minister may by notice in the *Gazette* direct that the attendance by natives at any church or other religious service or church function on premises situated within any urban area outside a native residential area shall cease from a date specified in that notice, if in his opinion:

(i) the presence of natives on such premises or in any area traversed by natives for the purpose of attending at such premises is causing a nuisance to residents in the vicinity of those premises or in such area; or

(ii) it is undesirable, having regard to the locality in which the premises are situated, that natives should be present on such premises in the numbers in which they ordinarily attend a service or function conducted thereat; and any native who in contravention of a direction issued under this paragraph attends any church or other religious service or church function, shall be guilty of an offence and liable to the penalties prescribed by section *forty-four*; Provided that no notice shall be issued under this paragraph except with the concurrence of the urban local authority concerned, and that the Minister shall, before he issues any such notice, advise the person who conducts the church or other religious service or church function of his intention to issue such notice and allow that person a reasonable time, which shall be stated in that advice, to make representations to him in regard to his proposed action; and provided further that in con-

THE CHURCHES

sidering the imposition of a direction against the attendance by natives at any such service or function, the Minister shall have due regard to the availability or otherwise of facilities for the holding of such service or function within a native residential area.

(c) Except with the approval of the Minister given with the concurrence of the urban local authority concerned, and subject to such conditions as the Minister may deem fit, which approval may at any time after consultation with the urban local authority concerned be withdrawn by the Minister, no person shall on premises situated within any urban area outside a native residential area conduct any school, hospital, club or similar institution which is attended by a native or to which a native is admitted, other than a native attending in the capacity of an employee thereat, unless such school, hospital, club or institution was being so conducted on those premises at the commencement of the Native Laws Amendment Act, 1937 (Act No. 46 of 1937), or if the number of natives attending or admitted to such school, hospital, club or institution at any time exceeds the number of natives who attended or were admitted to that school, hospital, club or institution immediately prior to the commencement of that Act: Provided that this paragraph shall not apply with reference to the admission of a native to any hospital in the event of emergency.

'DEATH COMES TO THE ARCHBISHOP'

On 6 March 1957 the Anglican Archbishop of Cape Town was found dead in his study by his Chaplain. His last act, shortly before this, was to sign the following letter to the Prime Minister. The letter was later published in *Where We Stand, Archbishop Clayton's Charges 1948–57* (Oxford University Press, 1960).

DOCUMENT 18. LETTER BY ARCHBISHOP CLAYTON TO THE PRIME MINISTER, 6 MARCH 1957.

Dear Mr. Prime Minister,
    We, Bishops of the Church of the Province of South Africa,

are approaching you rather than the Minister of Native Affairs because we believe that the issues raised in clause 29(c) of the Native Laws Amendment Bill[1] cannot be regarded merely as Native affairs. It appears to us that as far as the Anglican Church is concerned, churches and congregations in every urban area within the Union, even those mainly attended by Europeans, will be affected by this clause. Further, it is our belief that the Clause raises the issue of religious freedom and more particularly that of freedom of worship, and we venture to submit that this is a wider issue than that of Native Affairs only.

We desire to state that we regard the above-mentioned clause as an infringement of religious freedom in that it makes conditional on the permission of the Minister of Native Affairs:

(a) the continuance in existence of any church or parish constituted after 1 January 1938 in an urban area except in a location which does not exclude Native Africans from public worship;
(b) the holding of any service in any church in an urban area except in a location to which a Native African would be admitted if he presented himself;
(c) the attendance of any Native African at any synod or church assembly held in an urban area outside a location.

The Church cannot recognize the right of an official of the secular government to determine whether or where a member of the Church of any race (who is not serving a sentence which restricts his freedom of movement) shall discharge his religious duty of participation in public worship or to give instructions to the minister of any congregation as to whom he shall admit to membership of that congregation.

Further, the Constitution of the Church of the Province of South Africa provides for the synodical government of the Church. In such synods, bishops, priests and laymen are represented without distinction of race or colour. Clause 29(c)

---

[1] For a detailed examination of this Bill and the subsequent Act see Brookes and Macaulay, *Civil Liberty in South Africa*, Oxford University Press, 1958, pp. 125-30.

makes the holding of such synods dependent upon the permission of the Minister of Native Affairs.

We recognize the great gravity of disobedience to the law of the land. We believe that obedience to secular authority, even in matters about which we differ in opinion, is a command laid upon us by God. But we are commanded to render unto Caesar the things which be Caesar's, and to God the things that are God's. There are therefore some matters which are God's and not Caesar's, and we believe that the matters dealt with in clause 29(c) are among them.

It is because we believe this that we feel bound to state that if the Bill were to become law in its present form we should ourselves be unable to obey it or to counsel our clergy and people to do so.

We therefore appeal to you, Sir, not to put us in a position in which we have to choose between obeying our conscience and obeying the law of the land.

We have the honour to remain, Sir,
    Yours faithfully,
    (Signed on behalf of the Bishops of the
    Church of the Province of South Africa)
    GEOFFREY CAPETOWN
    Archbishop and Metropolitan.

OFFICIAL CHURCH STATEMENTS

The following statements of policy on behalf of different Churches are taken from *The Churches and Race Relations in South Africa* by Lesley Cawood (South African Institute of Race Relations). The numbers given after the name of each church in the text give the membership as given by the last available census figures.

DOCUMENT 19. FROM *The Churches and Race Relations in South Africa* BY LESLEY CAWOOD

A. The Nederduitse Gereformeerde Kerk (The Dutch Reformed Church)

THE CHURCHES

Membership: European *1,325,000;* African *556,000;* Indian *500;* Coloured *442,000. It is to be noted that nearly all the non-Whites are members of the D.R.C. Mission Church, a parallel body.*

In 1955 the Federal Council of the Nederduitse Gereformeerde Churches in South Africa appointed an *ad hoc* committee to follow up the findings of the Commission for Current Problems and to prepare a statement for publication overseas interpreting the viewpoint of the Nederduitse Gereformeerde Churches. This *ad hoc* committee drew up a report which was adopted by the synods of the then federated churches and was first published in 1956. In this report the Nederduitse Gereformeerde Church maintained the following as its policy:

(a) That the founding and development of independent indigenous churches for the purpose of evangelizing the Non-White races of South Africa was both necessary and in accordance with our understanding of the nature of the Church of the Lord Jesus on earth, and has been richly blessed during the many years that have passed.

(b) That since, under the pressure of circumstances, the historical development in the missionary sphere throughout the centuries showed tendencies of unchristian exclusiveness, thus impeding the realization of the true Christian fellowship between believers, this has happened not through ill-will towards the Non-Whites, nor with the approval of the official leadership of the Church, but must be seen as the result of uncontrollable circumstances and of general human weakness.

(c) That in each congregation both the mother and the indigenous daughter churches reserve the right to regulate their membership according to the realistic demand of circumstances, and in accordance with the spirit of Christ, but at the same time it is also the Christian duty of the above-mentioned churches to educate their members for and in the practice of a healthy Christian communion of believers, avoiding, however, any evil motives or annoying and wilful demonstrations.

THE CHURCHES

In the Addendum to the 1956 report there is the following statement: 'We accept the existence of separate Churches according to each indigenous group. As a matter of principle no person will be excluded from corporate worship solely on the grounds of race or colour.'

The Ecumenical Synod of the Reformed Church which met in Potchefstroom in 1958 and was attended by representatives of the five federated Nederduitse Gereformeerde Churches in South Africa adopted a report submitted by a committee on race relations which included the following statements: 'In admitting members of another race to our gatherings, we should guard against any impression of discrimination which could imply the inferiority of the other race, the members of which should be made to feel that they are being regarded as fellow-members in the body of Christ, bound to us by the closest of ties', and '... the Church by its teaching and example should guide and prepare its members for the practice of Christian communion with believers of other races. ...'

A national mission conference of the Nederduitse Gereformeerde Churches was held at Kroonstad in April 1960. This was soon after the riots which had occurred at Sharpeville, Langa and elsewhere in South Africa in March of the same year. At this conference one of the resolutions passed read as follows: 'The conference urgently requests White and Non-White members of our churches to witness earnestly, in deed, by acting in our multi-racial land with its racial tensions with Christian love, self-restraint, obedience to the law, mutual respect, and faithful prayer for each other.' An urgent appeal was made to the entire population of South Africa for mutual respect and co-operation between the races, in order that the glory of God and the extension of His Kingdom might be advanced.

The 1961 Synod of the Nederduitse Gereformeerde Church of the Cape Province adopted a resolution which read as follows: 'This Assembly has with approval taken cognisance of the attempts made in several congregations of our Church to establish closer contacts between ministers, church councils, congregations and church organizations of our mother church and its mission churches. The Synod wishes to encourage all congregations of our Church to search for ways and means by which, with due discretion in a spirit of Christian love, we as Christians and church members with a common creed can learn to know each other better, to co-operate more effectively and to pray together for what concerns the Kingdom of God.

> The Synod considers this to be an urgent matter with a view to times of increasing stress for the Church in the world which, according to the Scriptures, are at hand.

The Southern and Northern Transvaal Synods of the Church met in Pretoria during March and April 1963 respectively. The Synods felt that the present State law allowed full freedom of worship, but requested the Government to grant relief as far as frivolous objections against *bona fide* church attendance by Non-Whites living in White areas were concerned.

The Northern Transvaal Synod passed a resolution stating: 'It is in accordance with the spirit of the Scriptures that provision be made for visitors from any other Christian church who come with the *bona fide* desire to meet us and join us in worship.' (This includes Non-White visitors.) The establishment of separate churches for the sake of good order and more efficient ministry to members from different languages and cultures was, however, also in accordance with the Scriptures, said the Synod.

B. *The Methodist Church*

Membership: European *269,000*; African *1,313,000*; Indian *2,100*; Coloured *117,000*.

In 1960, the Conference accepted an outline for a programme of *Education in Race Relations* which included the following recommendations:

(b) *Circuit Study Groups and District Conference.* On the ground that the best method of educating people to associate with members of another group or race is to get them to begin associating with them, any programme of education envisaged should allow for as much discussion and free exchange of ideas as possible between the various racial groups comprising our church. The church must encourage and promote personal contacts as much as possible along the lines of district conferences. Such conferences would be multi-racial in composition, and it would be the responsibility of chairmen of districts to call and organize them. From these conferences attempts should be made to establish inter-racial study groups at circuit level.

(c) *Pulpit Exchange*. It is suggested that a great deal can be done along the line of pulpit exchanges to break down prejudice, and the circuits throughout the Connexion are urged to implement the resolution of the 1959 Conference in this connection.

(d) *Visits between Church Organisations*. The promotion of personal contacts between the various races by visits between church organizations (e.g. the Women's Auxiliaries, Women's Manyanos, Local Preachers, Guilds and Men's Leagues). The principle here is the same as that outlined in No. (c) above—to get our people to associate in Christian love and brotherhood across the racial barriers.

(f) *The Inclusive Church*. The Committee to explore the possibility of establishing in one of our City Circuits a racially inclusive Church as a pilot scheme.

Four pamphlets were drawn up and distributed on behalf of the Conference by the Committee for the Programme on Race Relations. The pamphlets dealt with the following subjects: *Biblical Principles Affecting Race Attitudes*, *The Methodist Attitude to Race*, *Why the Methodist Church Rejects Apartheid*, and *The Implications of Christian Race Attitudes*.

In 1961, the Conference resolved:

In accord with its declared policy that the Methodist Church be one and undivided, the Conference resolves to proceed with the removal of racial demarcation from its official records and legislation, and authorizes the Secretary of the Conference to consult with the Secretaries of Departments in regard to the implementation of this resolution.

In 1962, the Conference confirmed its previous resolution to encourage consultation between leaders in all fields of thought and activity and in all racial groups, and to give its full and hearty support to any national multi-racial conference which might be called for the purpose of such consultation.

One of the most important developments in the Methodist Church was that the 1963 Conference elected an African, the Rev. Seth Mokitimi, to be President.

C. *The Roman Catholic Church*

Membership: European 192,000; African 260,000; Indian 10,200; Coloured 119,000.

In the pastoral letter issued in 1957 entitled *Statement on Apartheid* the bishops condemned the principle of apartheid as something intrinsically evil and recommended a change as follows:

> There must be a gradual change: gradual, for no other kind of change is compatible with the maintenance of order, without which there is no society, no government, no justice, no common good. But change must come, for otherwise our country faces a disastrous future. That change could be initiated immediately if the ingenuity and energy now expended on apartheid were devoted to making South Africa a happy country for all its citizens. The time is short. The need is urgent. Those penalized by apartheid must be given concrete evidence of change before it is too late. This involves the elaboration of a sensible and just policy enabling any person, irrespective of race, to qualify for the enjoyment of full civil rights. . . .
>
> To our beloved Catholic people of White race, we have a special word to say. The practice of segregation, though officially not recognized in our churches, characterizes nevertheless many of our church societies, our schools, seminaries, convents, hospitals, and the social life of our people. In the light of Christ's teaching this cannot be tolerated for ever. The time has come to pursue more vigorously the change of heart and practice that the law of Christ demands. We are hypocrites if we condemn apartheid in South African society and condone it in our own institutions.

In the pastoral letter issued in 1960 the bishops expressed

their concern for the future of the country. They felt that although they had already spoken about this question in previous statements published in 1952 and 1957, the urgency of the matter required that they speak about it again. They stated that this problem had to be solved soon, and in the light of Christian principles. Otherwise there was little hope for peace and order, as antagonism would grow, prejudices harden into intolerances, and frustration would lead to outbursts of disorder and violence.

This pastoral letter was perhaps more positive than the two which preceded it. Although no less condemnatory, it placed the whole question of race relations on a broader basis. It was more positive in its approach, more particularly in its straightforward call to integration. It dealt with the dignity and rights of man and the essential unity of all men. It also dealt with practical questions such as the granting of the vote to the voteless and the conceding of economic and social opportunities to those less privileged.

The pastoral letter issued in 1962 dealt with the subject 'Christ in Our World' and under the heading 'We Dare Not Remain Silent', the bishops said:

> Since we are people of diverse racial and national origins it seems inevitable that human weakness will express itself in colour prejudice and in national misunderstandings. The fact of human frailty should not, however, constitute an insurmountable barrier to the building up of mutual trust and co-operation, if we remain faithful to the moral principles which are the foundation of Christian tradition 'where Justice joins hands with Charity'.
>
> As Christian people we dare not remain silent and passive in the face of the injustices inflicted on members of the unprivileged racial groups. Colour must never be permitted to offer an excuse or a pretext for injustice. We must use every lawful means suggested by our Christian conscience in order to counteract and overcome the injustices pressing down on underprivileged groups through the toleration of a starvation level of wages, of job reservation, of the evils which flow from compulsory migratory labour, particularly when the people who belong to these groups are denied the elementary right to organize in defence of their legitimate interests.

Let there be no doubt among us that it is a Christian duty to use every lawful means to bring about a more equitable and harmonious relationship between all the different groups of people who together form our Southern African society.

D. *The Presbyterian Church*

Membership: European *110,000;* African *204,000;* Indian *300;* Coloured *7,000.*

In 1960 the General Assembly adopted a statement on race relations which included the following paragraph:

We re-affirm the historical position of our Church. There is no barrier on the grounds of colour or race to attendance at worship or to membership in any congregation, but we follow the Reformation principle of the right to worship in one's mother-tongue and the freedom to develop forms of worship appropriate to different cultural backgrounds. Language and residence have led to the formation of separate congregations, but members of all races meet together in Presbytery and General Assembly. We believe this arrangement, for practical purposes, to be conformable to the Will of God, and acceptable to our members of all racial groups. We must nonetheless be constantly alert that this natural division does not produce real alienation between groups within the Church.

In 1962 the General Assembly passed two resolutions on race relations which read as follows:

The Assembly:

(a) strongly urges ministers and sessions to increase and strengthen multi-racial contacts, not only for the purposes of worship, but also for discussion, mutual understanding, and joint service;

(b) instructs Presbyteries to organize ministerial retreats and conferences for office-bearers and youth, on a multi-racial basis.

The following extracts were taken from reports of the Church and Nation Committee to the General Assembly. These reports do not necessarily express the feelings of the General Assembly as they were not 'deliverances' or 'resolutions' but opinions expressed within the General Assembly. They are, however, indicative of thinking among some members of the Assembly.

With a few exceptions that redound to the glory of God, contact between Black and White in the Church is so rare and superficial that there can be no understanding of one another, no desire to pray for one another, no desire to bear one another's burdens. The contact is rare because the world has infected us with its own fear and suspicion, and has stifled that perfect love which can cast out fear. What kind of spiritual insight can be granted to a church where brotherly love is so conspicuously lacking? That there is much to arouse our compassion, who can deny?

Our task in this situation is to build up, even if only in microcosm, the Christian community that lives, works, worships and witnesses without regard to the fundamentally irrelevant divisions of race. As first steps towards the manifestation of such a community, your committee suggests:

(a) Joint meetings of European and African sessions to discuss together the work of the eldership. (The same principle can, of course, be applied to boards of management and deacons' courts.) Such joint meetings have already been tried with great success in one or two congregations.

(b) The holding of occasional inter-racial services of worship as a manifestation of our fundamental unity in Christ, and an expression of our conviction that no worshipper should be excluded from any church on the grounds of colour alone.

(c) The organizing of local ministers' fraternals, including clergy from all groups for frank study of those things which cause estrangement, suspicion and bitterness.

(d) The holding of inter-racial camps and conferences, especially for young people.

(e) The inauguration of courses in the domestic arts by women members of the European Women's Associations for their African sisters.

(f) The inauguration of a literacy school for African illiterates sponsored by a congregation, or congregational organization.

In 1962 the Church and Nation Committee Report contained the following paragraph:

THE CHURCHES

A massive effort is needed to overcome the appalling ignorance of White church members concerning the sufferings and disabilities of their Non-European brothers in Christ, and to break down their even more appalling apathy. A concentrated and concerted effort is needed to increase and strengthen the contact, fellowship and understanding between White and Non-White Christians, and to awaken church members to the fact that their Christian vocation demands that they take responsibility for their society and their politics.

E. The Congregational Church

Membership: European 16,000; African 135,000; Indian 200; Coloured 137,000.

The Assembly meeting in 1961 passed the following two resolutions on race relations:

That we strongly support every effort for the holding of a multi-racial convention or a national multi-racial consultation to plan for better relationships, and happier conditions, rights, and privileges for all peoples of this land.

That this Assembly expresses its gratitude to the World Council of Churches for arranging the Cottesloe Consultation as a creative contribution to the solution of the many problems of a multi-racial society such as exists in South Africa. Though we ourselves might have made a more far-reaching statement, we are grateful to God for the measure of agreement attained and pray that the process of consultation between the churches begun at Cottesloe may continue at all levels.

In 1962 the Assembly stated: 'The Congregational Union of South Africa believes that all law-abiding inhabitants of a country have the inalienable right to freedom of movement, association and domicile within its borders.'

The Congregational Union has consistently condemned all legislation which discriminates on grounds of colour.

PART VII
Apartheid in Practice—Work and Voting

This Act (No. 49 of 1953) speaks for itself. It disposes finally of the doctrine of 'Separate but Equal' in South African life.

DOCUMENT 20. FROM THE SEPARATE AMENITIES ACT, NO. 49 OF 1953

To provide for the reservation of public premises and vehicles or portions thereof for the exclusive use of persons of a particular race or class, for the interpretation of laws which provide for such reservation, and for matters incidental thereto.

BE IT ENACTED by the Queen's Most Excellent Majesty, the Senate and the House of Assembly of the Union of South Africa, as follows:

1. In this Act, unless the context otherwise indicates:
    'public premises' includes any land, enclosure, building, structure, hall, room, office or convenience to which the public has access, whether on the payment of an admission fee or not but does not include a public road or street;
    'public vehicle' includes any train, tram, bus, vessel or aircraft used for the conveyance for reward or otherwise of members of the public.

2. (1) Any person who is in charge of or has control of any public premises or any public vehicle, whether as owner or lesee or whether by virtue of his office or otherwise, or any person acting under his control or direction may, whenever he deems it expedient and in such manner or by such means as he may consider most convenient for the purpose of informing all persons concerned, set apart or reserve such premises or such

vehicle or any portion of such premises or such vehicle or any counter, bench, seat or other amenity or contrivance in or on such premises or vehicle, for the exclusive use of persons belonging to a particular race or class.

(2) Any person who wilfully enters or uses any public premises or public vehicle or any portion thereof or any counter, bench, seat or other amenity or contrivance which has in terms of sub-section (1) been set apart or reserved for the exclusive use of persons belonging to a particular race or class, being a race or class to which he does not belong, shall be guilty of an offence and liable on conviction to a fine not exceeding fifty pounds or to imprisonment for a period not exceeding three months, or to both such fine and such imprisonment.

(3) If in any prosecution under sub-section (2) it is proved that a notice in both official languages announcing that any public premises or any public vehicle or any portion thereof or any counter, bench, seat or other amenity or contrivance has been set aside or reserved for the exclusive use of persons belonging to a particular race or class, appears at, in or on such premises or vehicle or portion thereof or such counter, bench, seat or other amenity or contrivance, it shall be presumed, unless the contrary is proved, that such setting aside or reservation was made under due and proper authority in accordance with the provisions of sub-section (1).

(4) Nothing in this section contained shall affect the provisions of the Railways and Harbours Regulation, Control, and Management Act, 1916 (Act No. 22 of 1916), or any other law which provides for the setting aside or reservation of any public premises or public vehicle or any portion thereof or any counter, bench, seat or other amenity or contrivance for the exclusive use of persons belonging to a particular race or class.

3. Whenever any person or authority has under and by virtue of the provisions of section *two* or any other law, at any time before or after the date of commencement of this Act, set apart, demarcated or reserved any public premises or any public vehicle or any portion thereof or any counter, bench, seat or other amenity or contrivance in or on any public

premises or public vehicle, for the exclusive use of persons belonging to a particular race or class, such setting apart, demarcation or reservation shall not be invalid on the ground merely that:
- (a) no such premises or vehicle or portion thereof or no such counter, bench, seat or other amenity or contrivance as the case may be, has similarly been set apart, demarcated or reserved for the exclusive use of persons belonging to any other race or class; or
- (b) any such premises or vehicle or portion thereof or any such counter, bench, seat or other amenity or contrivance, as the case may be, similarly set apart, demarcated or reserved for the use of persons belonging to any other race or class, is not substantially similar to or of the same character, standard, extent or quality as the premises, vehicle, or portion thereof or the counter, bench, seat or other amenity or contrivance, as the case may be, set apart, demarcated or reserved as aforesaid.

4. No setting apart, demarcation or reservation under section *two* or any other law of any public premises or public vehicle or portion thereof or any counter, bench, seat or other amenity or contrivance in or on such premises or vehicle shall operate to exclude from such premises, vehicle or portion thereof or such counter, bench, seat or other amenity or contrivance any person who:
- (a) is a representative in the Union of a foreign government or a member of his family; or
- (b) is a national of a foreign country travelling within or through the Union on official business; and
- (c) is in possession of a certificate issued to him by or under the authority of the Secretary for External Affairs for the purposes of this section.

5. This Act shall be called the Reservation of Separate Amenities Act, 1953.

NOTE A—Under this Act, beaches have been segregated in many parts of the Republic, e.g. for 200 miles in the Western Cape, and while some attempt has been made at equality of areas, the Coloured people obviously do not get the best areas at the expense of the Whites.

At Cape Town Railway Station there are separate entrances for Whites and non-Whites to reach, be it noted, the same platforms and different coaches of the same trains. The White approach is roofed, the Coloured approach, at the time of writing is open to the elements.

The Coloured people, who are notoriously great rugby 'fans', have only been allowed to watch rugby at B field of the famous Newlands rugby field on condition that a six-foot wire fence is built between them and the other spectators.

Scientific societies (including the South African Bird-Watchers) have been directed to exclude non-whites from their membership. (To their credit many have refused.) Coloured scientists being so few, how could their segregated scientific associations enjoy equal amenities?

A blind white girl accompanied by a Coloured maid was told by a white taxi driver in Cape Town that he was not allowed to carry White and Coloured passengers in the same car.

There has even been an enquiry to see if it is possible to enforce apartheid upon anglers fishing from the rocks in Knysna lagoon, Cape Province!

These few examples illustrate how this Act operates in practice.

NOTE B—The following extract from the *Cape Times* of 6 May 1965 illustrates an educational aspect of 'separate amenities':

Apartheid in Science: Isolation Fear

Senator de Klerk, Minister of Education, Arts and Science, said in the Assembly last night that non-Whites would not be allowed to join White scientific organisations once alternative societies had been established for them.

The Minister who was speaking during his Education vote, was replying to Mr. J. A. L. Basson (U.P., Sea Point), who earlier had made a sharp attack on the Government's plan for promoting separate non-White scientific societies.

Would this mean, asked Mr. Basson, that existing organisations would be compelled to get rid of their Coloured members and alter their constitutions so that non-Whites could not join them?

Senator de Klerk said that as soon as alternative facilities were available and the necessary liaison established, non-Whites would not be allowed to join these White organisations.

APARTHEID IN PRACTICE—WORK AND VOTING

In a lively speech Mr. Basson warned the Government that its plan for separating scientific societies could cause great harm to South Africa and might result in the isolation of the country's White scientists. Overseas bodies might take action against South Africa if *apartheid* were brought into science. Already scientists were afraid they would be unable to send students to overseas universities to follow doctorate and honours degrees because this was often done through the personal contact of professors.

When the Minister had announced his plan for separate societies last week, he had said it was because he felt sorry for Coloured scientists. Out of 12,000 White members of the Associated Scientific and Technical Societies, only eight were Coloured. But the truth was that the Minister had sent a circular to scientific organisations asking them to change their constitutions to 'kick out' non-Whites, or he would withhold their subsidies. When they took no notice of the Minister he had decided on this new step. 'It was not out of love for the Coloureds but out of pettiness because he didn't get his way. It will do unending harm to the good name of South Africa and to scientific standards.'

Why could the eight Coloured scientists not be allowed to remain members of the White organisation? They had never been any trouble, said Mr. Basson. Surely all contact between people of different races did not have to be forbidden. How was a physicist to discuss physics with a geologist or chemist? Even a Government-supporting scientist had strongly opposed this plan.

URBAN AREAS AND LABOUR: INFLUX CONTROL

What follows, taken from the House of Assembly Hansard of 1952 (Volume 77) gives a classic example of the arguments for influx control as presented by the Minister of Native Affairs and against influx control as expounded by Mrs. Margaret Ballinger, M.P.

DOCUMENT 21. DEBATE ON INFLUX CONTROL, HOUSE OF ASSEMBLY, 11 AND 13 FEBRUARY 1952.

The Minister of Native Affairs: Then there is a series of clauses, namely 27 to 32, which have reference to the so-called control. This is a form of control that already exists. According

APARTHEID IN PRACTICE—WORK AND VOTING

to the existing law a Native can be prevented from looking for employment in a city when the local authorities are convinced that there is already a labour surplus, when there is already sufficient labour. That can be controlled today but the local authorities complain that they experience great difficulties because the existing law makes it compulsory to arrest such a Native at the moment when he enters the city. If the authorities have therefore decided that there is sufficient labour in their area and that they are not going to impose further burdens on the shoulders of their ratepayers to pay for accommodation, health services and such matters, namely for even more Natives than they need for their work, then they find themselves in this difficulty, that they have to stop all the inflowing Natives at the moment they enter their area. It stands to reason that we have no police cordons around our cities to be constantly catching every Native as he crosses a certain border. The result is that it is extremely difficult to enforce this law. The result is that raids are often carried out to discover which Natives are unlawfully in the city. Another result is that often Natives who have only come into the city for a few hours (to pay a visit, or to buy or sell some vegetables, or to buy something else when they are living outside the city) are also caught during such a raid although they have no real intention of remaining there to look for employment and although it was not the intention that they should fall under the law, in other words, that they contravened the prohibition on entry for the purpose of settling there. The fact remains, however, that all such Natives are unlawfully within the city in terms of the present law. Now I feel that an improvement must be brought about in this matter, among other reasons also because the police, when arresting those who have clearly come into the city unlawfully, have no hold on them if all sorts of lies are told, for instance, that they only came in for a few hours. For that reason too it is necessary to make an alteration. It is now proposed to introduce an alteration corresponding to the periods laid down in connection with the usual registration system. We propose that such a Native may be in the city for 72 hours. Then the person who comes in to pay a short visit, to buy or sell something or who visits the city for a few hours cannot be arrested together with all the others, so that all will not have to be screened in the usual way. There will be a period of 72 hours during which such a Native may be in the city without permission. If, however, he wants to remain in that city for a longer period, if he wants to look for employment or if he wants to do anything else which he may legitimately do there, he must ask permission for that purpose. In this way he is therefore properly registered, the local authority is aware of his presence and has approved of his presence there, thereafter our Department therefore has the right to expect from the local authorities that they will properly carry out their responsibilities in respect of those persons whom they have allowed into the city. It is also clear that in such cases the onus will have to rest on the Native to prove that he has been in the city for less than 72 hours if he says that he has been there for less than that period.

An Hon. Member: That is very difficult.

The Minister of Native Affairs: It is not difficult for the Native himself to prove it. It is the easiest thing in the world for him. He only has to prove that he has been there for less than 72 hours. But if he has been there longer than that period, if he is trespassing, if he has not used his three days of grace to go to the registration office to obtain proper permission to remain, if he has committed an offence, then, in these circumstances it will be possible for the police to determine who committed the offence.

Mr. Barlow: Must he carry a watch?

The Minister of Native Affairs: The measure therefore removes the unfair position we have had in the past, namely that they must be arrested the moment they enter the city, and that large numbers are unnecessarily subjected to close scrutiny if they are found without the permit—I say that position is being done away with. It makes matters easier for the Native in this respect but it also ensures the safety of the community because it can now be ascertained very thoroughly that no one unlawfully remains behind in the city. . . .

* * *

APARTHEID IN PRACTICE—WORK AND VOTING

Mrs. Ballinger: Sir, do not let us have any doubt about the amendments to the Urban Areas Act. They are profoundly important and very wide reaching. They are extensive changes in the principle and the practice of the Act. They are, in fact, a strengthening of the original character of the Urban Areas Act in exactly the opposite direction from that recommended by the Fagan Commission. They are a facing away from the whole proposal and the findings of that commission. Their intention is and their effect must be to increase the obstacles that are already in existence to the peaceful process of urbanization which has been recognized as the essential condition for industrial progress in this country. In fact, what these amendments are going to do, as has been shown, is to make it impossible for any Native to go to a town to seek work except under the stress of restrictions which put him in contact with the police at every turn. Such liberty as remains today to the Native people to go to towns to seek work is going to be done away with. They will not be able to move to any town at all without these cumbersome provisions, and in fact, as the hon. member for Langlaagte (Mr. Robinson) has suggested, without new permits, new passes, new difficulties in their daily lives. That is the implication of this 72-hour rule, which is going to close all urban areas to all Natives. All Natives who are found without permits will now be faced with the obligation of proving that they have been in the town for less than 72 hours; in other words, from now onwards no Native in any urban area will ever at any time be free from police supervision and interference. How the authorities are going to administer this provision, Heaven alone knows. We are already hopelessly short of the necessary quota of personnel in most of our Government Departments. How we are going to find the personnel to carry on this extended inquisition I have no idea and I doubt if the Minister has.

But more than that, it is not only Clauses 16 and 27 that are so important, but in the definition clause we are importing the idea of prescribed and non-prescribed areas which means in effect that we are going to cover the whole country, not merely the urban areas with these checks upon the Native population. We are getting steadily to the stage where it will be utterly impossible for any Native to move from any one place to any other without standing on the doorstep of some official and justifying to him, whatever his knowledge may be and whatever his standing and whatever his authority, that he has a right to do it. Sir, in a country like this the whole of whose future depends upon progressive industrialization, how on earth do we think we are going to develop our manpower and use our physical resources with these barriers raised at every turn to these adjustments? Of course, it is true this is only an extension of what was happening. In the war years, I remember with regret it was the United Party which began this system of extending the area subject to permits. We fought determinedly against the provision to give divisional councils and other local authorities the powers of urban areas for the purpose of controlling the movement of the Native population. But I will say this that at the end of the war there was a recognition of the fact that that type of legislation was not sound legislation, that it did not accord with modern conceptions of how to control a labour force, and there was, I was encouraged to believe, a recognition of the fact that in a country like this in the process of urbanization, it was essential that our systems of labour control should take on a modern character, that is to say, that we should recognize not only the right, but actually the will of the Native worker to work and to help him to get into work; to help him to find work, not to block his entry into the labour market and send him round the country looking for work wherever he might be allowed to look for it. The truth of the matter is that the whole of this type of legislation is absolutely antiquated and ridiculous in a modern society. All it does is to set up an enormous range of expensive administrative machinery which is always utterly and completely ineffective. None of these checks on the movement of the Native population has ever been effective. Both employers and employees have always got round it.

An Hon. Member: Why worry about it then?

Mrs. Ballinger: I will tell the hon. member why I worry about it. The hon. member does not seem to be concerned, but

I will explain for the benefit of the people who may be concerned. It means expensive administrative machinery. Will that be of any interest to the hon. member? It means that you have to find Europeans to man offices to control Natives—Europeans who ought to be doing more constructive work in this country. It means that you have to have a large army of police. It means that you have to have a large number of gaols. It means all these costly extravagant and inefficient things. You are spending money recklessly; you are wasting money on activities which are absolutely ineffective in themselves and which are completely disastrous to the relations between Europeans and the Natives in this country. The range of these things is going to be enormously increased by this legislation. You include in the net now boys of 15 years of age, and successive Governments have refused—I cannot imagine with what justification to their consciences—to admit that people who have been born in a town have the right to be there, and that people who have become urban workers should be allowed to move from one town to another. The law still lays down, and this law lays down again, that a Native has no claim to remain in any town. He must not only have been born in the town but he must have been continually resident in it, or—the only 'or' that you are permitted—you have been in employment with the same employer for ten years. Can you imagine any more ridiculous provision in a modern industrial State than to tie a man down to an employer for ten years when the whole essence of industrialization is elasticity, so that people can move from one job to another as the jobs demand it. What we are doing in this Act is to say, 'You cannot stay in a town unless you have been born in it and unless you have remained in it continuously. If you go out of it, or if you are turned out of it, even if you have been born in it, you have no right to come back to it; and you have no right to move into a town from an outside area unless you have permission to come in for seven days or a fortnight to look for a job; and when you have found a job you can stay in the town as long as you have that job, but the moment you leave that job, even if you find another job, you may not be allowed to stay in the town in which you have taken the job.' I think any industrial community would laugh in our faces if they heard that this was the way in which we propose to organize a labour market. Imagine trying to organize a labour market in this twentieth century, in this fantastic sort of fashion.

These consolidated and very complicated labour regulations are taken from the Government Gazette Extraordinary of the 3 December 1965. Through the legal verbiage of these regulations the following points emerge:

(a) No African has the right to seek work where he wants to or of the kind which he desires. At every stage he requires a permit.

(b) As far as the Government is able to enforce the law—and it is managing to enforce it pretty generally—no white employer in an urban area may strike his own bargain with an African employee to whom he would like to give work. He must work through the local labour bureau and select his employee from among the men it sends him.

(c) An African may not, unless he falls under certain specified exemptions or has special permission from the prescribed authority, remain in an urban area for more than seventy-two hours.

(d) The wife and children of an African labourer may not reside with the husband or father, unless the latter has been born in the urban area and resided there continuously since birth or unless he has worked in the same employment for not less than ten years.

(e) An African cannot enter an urban area unless he has permission to do so from his local Commissioner, who could refuse permission if, e.g. there is a shortage of farm labour in the district. An African workseeker in town may be required to take a particular type of job (e.g. domestic service) and may be refused a permit if he refuses to do so.

(f) In general the whole life of an African worker in an urban area is hedged round by regulations and permits.

With these principles to guide him the reader may find his way through the labyrinth of regulations.

APARTHEID IN PRACTICE—WORK AND VOTING

DOCUMENT 22. LABOUR REGULATIONS FROM THE *Government Gazette Extraordinary*, 3 DECEMBER 1965.

8. The following are prescribed areas or are deemed to be prescribed areas for purposes of these regulations:
(a) Every urban area, if not already included in a prescribed area;
(b) every other area which on the first day of January 1965, was proclaimed under sub-section (1) of section *twenty-three* of the Urban Areas Act;
(c) any areas declared by the Minister by notice in the *Gazette* under sub-section (1) of section *nine bis* of the Urban Areas Act as prescribed areas.

9. (1) Every person who ordinarily employs a Bantu in a prescribed area shall have himself registered at the local labour bureau.

(2) The municipal labour officer shall keep and maintain a record card substantially in the form set out in the Thirty-fourth Schedule to these regulations of each person who employs Bantu in the prescribed area and record on such card the names of all Bantu registered in the service of such person and shall submit such returns to the Bantu Reference Bureau as may be required from time to time.

(3) Every person on whose establishment a vacancy for a Bantu has occurred, shall within fourteen days of such vacancy having occurred, advise the municipal labour office in writing of such vacancy.

10. (1) Every Bantu who under section *ten* of the Urban Areas Act qualifies to be in or is permitted to be employed in a prescribed area who is unemployed or not lawfully employed shall within three days after becoming unemployed or within fourteen days of attaining the age of fifteen years or ceasing to be a full-time pupil or student at an educational institution, have himself registered as a workseeker at the local labour bureau of the area where he resides, shall satisfy the municipal labour officer as to his identity, the types of employment for which he is suitable or eligible and furnish such further information as such officer may require.

(2) The municipal labour officer shall not refuse to register a workseeker under sub-regulation (1) in a prescribed area:

(a) if such Bantu is entitled in terms of paragraph (a), (b) or (c) of sub-section (1) of section *ten* of the Urban Areas Act to be in that prescribed area and such Bantu has not been ordered under any law to leave such area; or

(b) if such Bantu is specially authorised by the chief Bantu affairs commissioner, the regional labour commissioner or an aid centre having jurisdiction in that prescribed area, to take up employment in that prescribed area: Provided that such authority shall be granted only after consultation with the municipal labour officer and after due regard to the availability of Bantu labour in that prescribed area.

(3) The municipal labour officer shall, in respect of every Bantu who reports to him in terms of sub-regulation (1) and who is not prohibited under these regulations or any other law from taking up employment in that prescribed area but qualifies for registration:

(a) complete a record card in respect of such Bantu substantially in the form set out in the Thirty-fifth Schedule to these regulations or if such a card has already been completed in respect of such Bantu, make the appropriate entries on such card;

(b) endorse the reference book or passport of such Bantu 'Registered as a workseeker at the local labour bureau at............................';

(c) inform the Bantu of vacancies registered with him;

(d) endeavour to place such Bantu in employment;

(e) if he cannot place such Bantu in employment forthwith instruct such Bantu, should such Bantu fail to obtain employment, to report to him on such dates as he may indicate and endorse the reference book or passport of such Bantu 'To report to the local labour bureau at ....before..................'

(4) The provisions of sub-regulation (1) shall not apply in the case of a Bantu:

(a) under the age of fifteen years;
(b) female, save where such female desires to seek or take up employment or where such female is dependent on employment for her livelihood;
(c) male over the age of sixty-five years;
(d) who is in the opinion of the municipal labour officer incapable of being employed on account of physical or mental infirmity;
(e) who is a pupil or student at an educational institution or who having completed a course of study at one institution, is awaiting admission to another institution.

11. The municipal labour officer may in the case of a Bantu in a prescribed area:

(i) who is unemployed and is not registered as a workseeker in terms of regulation 10 of this Chapter;
(ii) who is not permitted under paragraph (a), (b) or (c) of sub-section (1) of section *ten* of the Urban Areas Act to be in that prescribed area; and
(iii) who is not otherwise authorised under any law to be or to take up employment in that prescribed area,

order such Bantu to leave such prescribed area forthwith or within a stated period, or refer such Bantu to an aid centre or to the district labour officer in that prescribed area or to the district labour officer of the area in which such Bantu is domiciled, shall complete the record card set out in the Thirty-fifth Schedule to these regulations in respect of such Bantu and shall advise the Bantu Reference Bureau accordingly.

12. If a Bantu is entitled in terms of paragraph (a), (b) or (c) of sub-section (1) of section *ten* of the Urban Areas to be in the prescribed area or is authorised thereto by paragraph (b) of sub-regulation (2) of regulation 10 of this Chapter, the municipal labour officer may permit such Bantu to seek employment in such area and shall in such event endorse the reference book of such Bantu as follows:

'Permitted to reside at .... and to seek work as (indicate class of work) .... within

the prescribed area of .... until
....................................,

(2) When a Bantu is referred to a prospective employer under sub-regulation (3) of regulation 10 of this Chapter, he shall be given a document substantially in the form set out in the Thirty-eighth Schedule to these regulations and he shall report back to the municipal labour officer within the period stated thereon or on his reference book, whichever is the later date.

13. When a Bantu fails to accept employment within the period stated in terms of regulation 12 of this Chapter or within any extension of such period or refuses to accept suitable employment offered to him, the municipal labour officer shall inquire into the reasons for his failing or refusing to accept employment and may:

(a) if suitable work is available in the prescribed area according to his records and if the Bantu refuses without reasonable cause to accept such work, cause such Bantu to be dealt with in terms of section *twenty-nine* of the Urban Areas Act;
(b) if suitable work is not available in the prescribed area according to his records, refer such Bantu to the district labour officer or to an aid centre;
(c) if the Bantu is unable to find or accept employment for some reasonable cause, deal with him in terms of instructions from the regional labour commissioner.

14. (1) No person shall by virtue of section *ten bis* of the Urban Areas Act take any Bantu into his employment in a prescribed area or have such Bantu in his employment unless permission to take up employment has been granted to such Bantu by the labour officer concerned in terms of these regulations.

(2) The permission referred to in sub-regulation (1) may be with-held or refused if the Bantu concerned has not been registered with the labour bureau as provided for in regulation 10 of this Chapter or if the employer of such Bantu has not been registered as an employer as provided for in sub-regulation

(1) of regulation 9 of this Chapter or if such employer failed to advise the labour bureau of the vacancy to which such Bantu is to be appointed as provided for in sub-regulation (3) of the said regulation 9.

(3) Every person to whom a workseeker has been referred under sub-regulation (2) of regulation 12 of this Chapter shall by an appropriate endorsement on the form prescribed in the Thirty-eighth Schedule to these regulations and handed to him by such workseeker, indicate whether or not he is prepared to accept such Bantu and such form shall be handed to the municipal labour officer by such Bantu within the currency thereof or within any extended period indicated thereon.

15. (1) Any person who takes a Bantu male or Bantu female into his employment in a prescribed area shall after taking such Bantu into his employment, if he is not otherwise prohibited under any law from taking such Bantu into his employment and if such Bantu is not prohibited under any law from being in or taking up employment in such area:

(a) within three days record in the appropriate column of the reference book or passport of that Bantu his name and address and the date on which such Bantu entered into his service;

(b) within three days complete a notification which shall be substantially in the form set out in the Thirty-sixth Schedule to these regulations, copies of which may be obtained free of charge from the local labour bureau, and deliver or post such notification to the municipal labour officer concerned;

(c) retain the acknowledgement by the municipal labour officer of the registration of such Bantu;

(d) with due regard to the provisions of regulation 6 of Chapter XI of these regulations keep a record of all Bantu in his employ at that address in the prescribed area.

(2) The provisions of sub-regulation (1) shall not apply in the case of a Bantu:

(a) who has undertaken to render service for a fixed period of less than three days;

(b) who has undertaken to render service as a casual labourer or as an independent contractor if such Bantu is authorised by the municipal labour officer concerned in terms of regulation 22 of this Chapter to take up employment as a casual labourer or as an independent contractor;
(c) who has been registered for the same employer in another area if such employment has not been cancelled, but subject to the provisions of regulation 8 of Chapter IX of these regulations.
(3) No person shall employ a Bantu in a prescribed area:
(a) who is not in possession of a reference book or passport or, in the case of a Bantu under the age of sixteen years, a document of identification;
(b) if it appears from such Bantu's reference book, passport or document of identification that such Bantu has entered into a labour tenant contract or a contract of employment with some other persons and such other person has not recorded in such reference book, passport or document of identification the fact that such contract has been terminated, unless a Bantu affairs commissioner has recorded in such book, passport or document the fact that such Bantu has been released from his obligations under the said labour tenant contract or that such contract of employment has been terminated or cancelled;
(c) who is under the age of sixteen years and is to work in a place other than on the land on which his parent or guardian resides or is employed unless such Bantu is in possession of a document of identification indicating that the father or guardian or the Bantu affairs commissioner has consented to such employment;
(d) born outside the Republic or the Territory of South West Africa unless such employer has obtained the permission prescribed in section *twelve* of the Urban Areas Act or is permitted by virtue of a lawful endorsement in the passport or identity document of such Bantu to take such Bantu into his employ in which event he shall complete the relevant columns of the passport or identity document of such Bantu.

16. (1) The municipal labour officer, on receiving the notification referred to in sub-regulation (1) of regulation 15 of this Chapter, shall:
 (a) if there is no other lawful reason why the employment of such Bantu should not be registered, register such employment by endorsing the record card of the Bantu concerned set out in the Thirty-fifth Schedule to these regulations accordingly or if no such card is available, register such employment on a record card completed for that purpose;
 (b) advise the employer of the fact that such employment has been registered by delivering or posting to the employer an advice of registration on a form substantially in the form set out in the Thirty-seventh Schedule to these regulations.

(2) The municipal labour officer on receiving the notification referred to in regulation 15 of this Chapter shall transcribe the information contained therein on to the record card set out in the Thirty-fifth Schedule to these regulations.

(3) The municipal labour officer shall, when he registers a contract of employment of a Bantu under this regulation, endorse the reference book or passport of such Bantu 'Permitted to remain in the prescribed area of .... while employed by .... as ....'

In the case of a Bantu who qualifies to be in that prescribed area by virtue of paragraph (a), (b) or (c) of sub-section (1) of section *ten* of the Urban Areas Act, he shall endorse the reference book of such Bantu:

'Permitted to be in the prescribed area of .... in terms of section *ten* (1)(a), (b) or (c) (as the case may be) of Act No. 25 of 1945, and to be employed by .... at .... as ....'

17. Any person referred to in sub-regulation (1) of regulation 15 of this Chapter shall, if the Bantu referred to in that sub-regulation, dies or deserts from his service or if the employment of such Bantu is terminated for any other cause, within three days of such death, desertion or termination having been brought to his notice, advise the municipal labour officer

concerned of such fact by delivering or posting to him a notification substantially in the form set out in the Thirty-sixth Schedule to these regulations and shall at the same time sign the reference book or passport of such Bantu, if available, in the column provided for such purpose.

18. When a municipal labour officer wishes because of mechanisation, audit considerations or any other local circumstances, to follow a procedure differing from that prescribed in these regulations or to use different forms or documents, he may, with the written approval of the regional labour commissioner, adopt such a variation or use such different forms of documents; Provided that no such approval shall have the effect of enabling the municipal labour officer to register a Bantu as a workseeker or to allow such Bantu to take up employment in or to be in the prescribed area when such Bantu could not under these regulations have been so registered, allowed to have taken up employment or to be in the prescribed area.

19. Every person who is authorised to employ a Bantu male in possession of a reference book, identity document or passport shall so long as such Bantu continues to be employed by him, within seven days of the commencement of each month, sign his name in and complete the appropriate columns of such reference book or passport to indicate that such Bantu is still employed by him.

20. For the purposes of these regulations, employment shall be classified as follows:
A. Private concerns and business establishments:
   1. Agriculture, forestry, fishing.
   2. Mining and quarrying.
   3. Manufacturing.
   4. Construction.
   5. Wholesale and retail trade.
   6. Financial institutions.
   7. Private transport.
   8. Accommodation and catering services.
   9. Other private business services.
B. Public Corporations.

C. South African Railways and Harbours.
D. Public authorities:
  1. Government Departments and Provincial Administrations.
  2. Local authorities.
E. Semi-government organisations.
F. Sundry services:
  1. Domestic servant.
  2. Other.

21. (1) No person shall introduce into a prescribed area a Bantu who is prohibited from remaining in that area save when he obtains the prior permission of the municipal labour officer and of the regional labour commissioner under this regulation and no person shall, with the intention of enabling such Bantu to be in such prescribed area contrary to the provisions of section *ten* of the Urban Areas Act, induce or assist such Bantu to enter or remain in such area.

(2) Any person who desires to introduce Bantu labour or a specific Bantu into an area from another area, may place a requisition substantially in the form set out in the Thirty-ninth or Fortieth Schedule to these regulations, as the case may be, with the municipal or district labour officer concerned and furnish to such labour officer such security as may be required by him for the return of such Bantu to his home on termination of his employment.

(3) No such introduction may be permitted without the prior approval of the regional labour commissioner concerned.

(4) A Bantu shall not be refused permission in terms of this regulation to re-enter a prescribed area after an absence therefrom of not more than twelve months, for the purpose of taking up employment, if a vacancy exists, with the employer by whom such Bantu was last employed in such area before leaving such area: Provided that if no such vacancy exists, such Bantu may, with the prior approval of the Bantu affairs commissioner in such prescribed area, be permitted to take up employment with some other employer in that area.

22. (1) No Bantu shall work in a prescribed area as a casual labourer or carry on any work on his own account in a

remunerative activity or as an independent contractor or perform work for a period of less than three days, without the permission of the municipal labour officer.

(2) The permission referred to in sub-regulation (1) shall not be granted to a Bantu:
(a) unless he qualifies under paragraph (a), (b) or (c) of sub-section (1) of section *ten* of the Urban Areas Act to be in the prescribed area or the regional labour commissioner has authorised the municipal labour officer concerned to grant such permission to a Bantu not so qualified;
(b) unless such Bantu occupies accommodation in a Bantu residential area which in the opinion of the municipal labour officer is suitable; or
(c) unless, in the case of the Western Cape, the regional labour commissioner has authorised the granting of such permission.

(3) When he grants the permission referred to in sub-regulation (1) the municipal labour officer shall:
(a) endorse the reference book of such Bantu 'Permitted to work in the prescribed area of.................... as a casual labourer/trader/independent contractor/......
.................until....................and to reside at..................', and
(b) endorse and sign the record card prescribed in the Thirty-fifth Schedule to these regulations accordingly.

(4) The permission granted to any Bantu to work as a casual labourer, trader or independent contractor in a prescribed area shall expire on the date shown on the endorsement referred to in sub-regulation (3) or any extension thereof.

(5) Any Bantu male permitted under this regulation to work in a prescribed area as a casual labourer or to carry on any work on his own account in any remunerative activity or as an independent contractor shall pay on or before the seventh day of each month, to the municipal labour officer who granted such permission a fee of twenty cents for every month or part thereof for which he has been granted such permission and shall

present his reference book not later than the seventh day of each month to the said officer for signature.

(6) Whenever the municipal labour officer is satisfied that a Bantu who has been permitted under this regulation to work as a casual labourer or to carry on work on his own account in any remunerative activity or as an independent contractor:
- (a) is no longer in his opinion a fit and proper person to hold such permission; or
- (b) is no longer pursuing the occupation in respect of which such permission was granted; or
- (c) has failed to pay the fee prescribed in this regulation;

he may terminate the permission granted to him.

* * *

28. (1) No permission need be obtained under these regulations for the employment of the following persons and no such person need register as a work-seeker and no fee need be paid under regulation 24 of this Chapter in respect of any such person, provided that such person is authorised under paragraph (d) of sub-section (1) of section *ten* of the Urban Areas Act to be in the prescribed area concerned, viz:
- (a) any advocate, attorney, notary public, conveyancer, medical practitioner, dentist, professor or lecturer at a university or university college;
- (b) ministers of religion who are marriage officers;
- (c) teachers whose salaries are paid or defrayed directly or indirectly in whole or in part by the Government or any provincial administration;
- (d) any policeman, warder, clerk or interpreter while in the service of the State (including the Railways Administration and any provincial administration and any Board constituted in terms of an Act of Parliament) or any body contemplated by paragraph (f) of sub-section (1) of section *eighty-four* of the Republic of South Africa Constitution Act, 1961 (Act No. 32 of 1961).

(2) Any Bantu who claims an exemption under sub-regulation (1), may at any time be called upon by an authorised

officer to produce proof of the fact that he falls within one of the classes set out therein and the labour officer concerned shall notify the Bantu Reference Bureau of every Bantu in his area who is thus exempted.

* * *

Influx Control

1. Only the following Bantu may under sub-section (1) of section *ten* of the Urban Areas Act be in a prescribed area for any period in excess of seventy-two hours, viz. a Bantu who produces proof that:
    (a) he or she has, since birth, resided continuously in such area; or
    (b) he or she has worked continuously in such area for one employer for a period of not less than ten years or has lawfully resided continuously in such area for a period of not less than fifteen years and has thereafter continued to reside in such area and is not employed outside such area and has not during either period or thereafter been sentenced to a fine exceeding one hundred rand or to imprisonment for a period exceeding six months; or
    (c) she is the wife or the unmarried daughter of or that he is the son under the age of eighteen years of a Bantu mentioned in paragraph (a) or (b) of this regulation and after lawful entry into such prescribed area, ordinarily resides with that Bantu in such area; or
    (d) in the case of any other Bantu, permission so to remain has been granted by an officer appointed to manage a labour bureau.

2. (1) If the municipal labour officer is satisfied that a Bantu qualifies under paragraph (a), (b) or (c) of regulation 1 of this Chapter to be in a prescribed area, he may endorse the reference book or document of identification of such Bantu as provided in sub-paragraph (c) to (g) of paragraph (i) of sub-regulation (1) of regulation 17 of Chapter II of these regulations.

(2) When a Bantu for any reason forfeits his qualification to be in the prescribed area or when the endorsement referred

to in sub-regulation (1) was made in error, the municipal labour officer or any Bantu affairs commissioner may cancel any endorsement made in terms of the said sub-regulation by writing across it 'Cancelled', signing such cancellation over his designation and dating it.

3. (1) Any Bantu permitted under Chapter VIII to be in or take up employment or to carry on work on his own account in a prescribed area, need not, so long as he lawfully remains in such employment or carries on such work, obtain any further permission under this Chapter to be in that area, provided that the reference book of such Bantu bears an endorsement as prescribed in sub-regulation (3) of regulation 16 of that Chapter.

(2) Any Bantu permitted under Chapter VIII to seek work in a prescribed area, need not, for the period during which he is authorised by such permission to be in the area, obtain any further permission under this Chapter to be in that area, provided that the reference book of such Bantu bears an endorsement as prescribed in sub-regulation (1) of regulation 12 of that Chapter.

4. (1) Any Bantu not qualified to be in the prescribed area who is desirous of being in that prescribed area for a period in excess of seventy-two hours for any purpose other than employment shall apply beforehand to the municipal labour officer for the requisite permission, furnish the information required by such officer and if such officer is satisfied that suitable accommodation in a Bantu residential area is available for such Bantu, he may permit such Bantu to be in such area for a period and purpose indicated by him. Any application for such permission shall, where that is practicable, be made through the office of the Bantu affairs commissioner of the area in which such Bantu resides.

(2) When the municipal labour officer grants any permission under sub-regulation (1), he shall endorse the reference book of such Bantu appropriately in the manner provided in regulation 17 of Chapter II of these regulations.

5. No permission need be obtained under this Chapter to be in the prescribed area in the case of a Bantu referred to in regulation 23 of Chapter VIII of these regulations.

APARTHEID IN PRACTICE—WORK AND VOTING

6. No permission need be obtained by a Bantu under this Chapter to be in the prescribed area in the case of a Bantu not born in the Republic or the Territory of South West Africa if such Bantu is in possession of a passport bearing a current valid endorsement made by a passport control officer or a Bantu affairs commissioner, authorising the presence of such Bantu in the area concerned for the period and the purpose indicated thereon.

7. (1) Any Bantu not authorised in terms of section *ten* of the Urban Areas Act or these regulations to be in a prescribed area, may if such Bantu is not arrested, be summarily ordered by the municipal labour officer to leave such area forthwith or be referred to an aid centre or to the district labour bureau.

(2) Where any order is made under sub-regulation (1) the reference book or passport of such Bantu shall be endorsed appropriately in the manner provided in regulation 17 of Chapter II of these regulations by the municipal labour officer.

8. If a Bantu has been registered at a local or district labour bureau for employment with a particular employer and if the reference book or passport of such Bantu has been duly endorsed by a labour bureau as prescribed in sub-regulation (3) of regulation 16 or sub-regulation (3) of regulation 23 of Chapter VIII of these regulations and duly signed by the employer as provided for in regulation 19 of the said Chapter, and such Bantu is required in the course of his employment to enter or be employed in another prescribed area, he shall not be refused permission to be in such other area, provided that:

(a) the employer has notified the municipal labour officer concerned beforehand of the fact that such Bantu is to be in that other prescribed area;

(b) the employer has satisfied such municipal labour officer as to the suitability of accommodation provided for such Bantu; and

(c) the reference book of such Bantu is endorsed as prescribed in these regulations authorising the presence of such Bantu in such other area.

NOTE—The effect of these regulations is *inter alia* to entrench the system of migratory labour with its extremely deleterious effect on

APARTHEID IN PRACTICE—WORK AND VOTING

health and family life. (See e.g. 'Let No Man Put Asunder', Special Issue of *Black Sash*, June/July 1964; and Brookes, E. H., and Hurwitz, N., *The Native Reserves of Natal*, Oxford University Press, 1957, Ch. VII.)

DOCUMENT 23. TRADE UNIONS. FROM *A Survey of Race Relations in South Africa*, 1965, COMPILED BY MURIEL HORRELL AND PUBLISHED BY THE SOUTH AFRICAN INSTITUTE OF RACE RELATIONS.

In its Special Report No. 277 the Bureau of Statistics gave detailed information about the membership of registered trade unions as at 31 December 1963 (including members not in good standing). No statistics relating to African unions were included, as these do not qualify for official registration.

The numbers of unions then were:

	White membership only	Coloured and/or Asian membership only	Mixed membership	Totals
Forestry and fishing	1	—	2	3
Mining	4	—	—	4
Manufacturing	25	18	27	70
Construction, electricity, etc.	10	2	2	14
Commerce, transport, etc.	31	9	5	45
Miscellaneous	18	7	11	36
TOTALS	89	36	47	172

The membership of these unions was as follows:

Whites	White membership only		Mixed membership		Totals
	M	F	M	F	
Mining and quarrying	33,598	950	—	—	34,548
Manufacture, construction	70,271	8,199	49,929	9,939	138,338
Commerce, transport	99,475	11,893	4,012	13,260	128,640
Other	30,178	4,463	3,792	4,792	43,226
TOTALS	233,522	25,505	57,734	27,991	344,752

	Coloured and/or Asian membership only		Mixed membership		Totals
Coloured	M	F	M	F	
Manufacture, construction	11,688	11,223	18,482	30,736	72,129
Commerce, transport	6,081	5	1,598	223	7,907
Other	7,674	812	1,256	365	10,107
TOTALS	25,443	12,040	21,336	31,324	90,143
Asians	M	F	M	F	
Manufacture, construction	3,762	131	14,348	3,681	21,922
Commerce, transport	1,225	5	6	—	1,236
Other	3,855	91	4,470	165	8,581
TOTALS	8,842	227	18,824	3,846	31,739

The combined membership was 466,634.

Membership of co-ordinating bodies

There are four co-ordinating trade union bodies in South Africa.

(a) The S.A. Confederation of Labour, with three constituent bodies, is on the right wing, and is composed of White workers. The Minister of Labour said in the Assembly on 23 February that there were 33 affiliated unions with 189,071 members, but the Confederation itself claims 26 unions with about 189,500 members. Among the affiliates are the Mine Workers' Union and seven Railway Staff Associations.

(b) The Trade Union Council of South Africa (Tucsa) is the central body, with 70 White, Coloured and/or Asian, mixed and African unions affiliated to it, having a total of 191,063 members (possibly about 22 per cent of them Non-White). Included in these totals are 8 unregistered African unions, with 2,012 members. Tucsa appears to maintain more careful membership records than do some of the other bodies.

(c) The Federation of Free African Trade Unions (Fofatusa) is an independent body which maintains liaison with Tucsa. Unlike Sactu, it has tried to steer clear of politics. It claims 13 affiliated African unions, and, according to Mr. A. Hepple, in 1964 the member-unions included some 14,000 individual workers. (The membership has decreased since then, *inter alia* because the 4,000-strong National Union of Clothing Workers has become affiliated to Tucsa, instead.)
(d) The left-wing S.A. Congress of Trade Unions (Sactu) has, in the past, allied itself with the A.N.C. and other members of the (political) Congress Group. Nearly all its original leaders are now under banning orders, or have been convicted of political offences, or have left the country, and its present membership (mainly African, with some Coloured) is unknown. The Security Police have continued to raid Sactu's offices from time to time, confiscating pamphlets and financial and other records.

The Confederation held a congress during January at which it decided that job reservation was essential to preserve industrial peace and equity, but that determinations should be flexible measures, subject to adjustment wherever the circumstances demanded this. The conference resolved that fragmentation of work should not be permitted unless agreed to by the trade unions concerned. Other resolutions dealt with training and employment opportunities for White workers.

As described below, during 1965 Tucsa has concerned itself increasingly with African workers. In January it sought an interview with the Minister of Labour to make a renewed plea for the official recognition of African unions; but the Secretary for Labour replied that such an interview would serve no useful purpose, as nothing had happened to change the Government's attitude. (In 1964 the Minister said that Africans had not yet reached the stage where they could exercise the functions and rights of trade unions without harmful results.)

In the Assembly on 23rd February, Mrs. Helen Suzman

APARTHEID IN PRACTICE—WORK AND VOTING

(P.P.) pointed out that the prohibition on African membership of registered unions not only deprived them of the benefits of collective bargaining, but also meant, in effect, that in 'White' areas, Africans were unable to become employed in any occupation in respect of which there was a closed shop agreement. Such occupations included baking, building, tailoring, clothing, the electrical industry, furniture, tobacco, the motor industry, and many more.

In preparation for decisions to be made at its annual congress, Tucsa sent a confidential questionnaire to some 4,500 African workers to ascertain their attitudes to trade unionism.

This congress, held in East London during March, was a 'mixed' one—nearly one-fifth of the delegates being Non-White. A four-year plan was adopted with the aim of approaching all unorganized workers, irrespective of race, and increasing Tucsa's membership very considerably. It was decided that seven more full-time organizers should be appointed. An economic research bureau and library would be established, at Tucsa's head office in Johannesburg, to provide the basic economic information needed by trade unions in preparing submissions for higher wages. A public relations service would be set up, and a training programme instituted for officials and leaders of the movement.

Among the resolutions passed were calls for the removal of the industrial colour bar, and for a vast expansion of educational facilities for all races. It was suggested that it be made a criminal offence for employers to replace a worker of one race by someone of another race *at a lower wage*. (Replacements, in themselves, were not objected to as long as the principle of 'the rate for the job' was maintained.)

Commenting on the proceedings in the *Rand Daily Mail* of 29th March, Mr. Pogrund said his firm impression was that the rank-and-file members of Tucsa were solidly and knowingly behind the non-racial policy. This was a new development. White trade unionists were increasingly appreciating that the key to strength lay in solidarity.

As mentioned on page 92, Tucsa sent observers to the annual International Labour Organization meeting in Geneva. It is preparing booklets and lecture-notes to assist African trade unionists. During October it suggested to the Minister of Labour that a mobile office of his department be sent to African townships, to make available to people who live and work long distances from existing labour offices, services provided for in labour legislation, and to enable African workers to discuss their problems. The Secretary for Labour replied that the plan was not feasible at that stage; but Tucsa intends pursuing the matter.

In 1963 the Government set up machinery outside the framework of trade unionism to make representations in regard to African wages and to intervene when labour disputes occur.

According to the July issue of *Bantu*, during 1964 officials of the Bantu Labour Board made appeals on behalf of 71,132 Africans for better wages and conditions of work. The wage increases that resulted totalled R4,293,440. During the previous year, 169,369 Africans had been thus assisted, the resulting wage increases amounting to R3,330,770.

The only African labour disputes to have been reported in the Press in 1965 were one between a bus company and its African employees in Cape Town (this was referred to the Wage Board for settlement), and a brief stoppage of work by African painters in Durban.

COLOURED DISFRANCHISEMENT

The following account of Coloured disfranchisement and the constitutional struggles connected with it is taken from the reasonably objective and admirably succinct account given by Professor H. M. Robertson of the University of Cape Town in his book *South Africa*, published by the Duke University Commonwealth-Studies Center (1957).

DOCUMENT 24. COLOURED DISFRANCHISEMENT. FROM *South Africa*, BY PROFESSOR H. M. ROBERTSON

In 1951, the Separate Representation of Voters Bill was introduced, and passed by the two houses sitting separately by a simple majority. It provided for the removal of the

Coloured voters of the Cape (then some 47,000 in a total electorate of 1.5 million) to a separate roll, through which they might elect four European members of the House of Assembly and two members of the Provincial Council, who might be either White or Coloured.

The validity of the act was challenged in the courts. In the Cape Provincial Division of the Supreme Court, a decision was given favourable to the Government. But the Court made it clear that this was only because, whether it agreed or not, it was bound to accept the Appeal Court's 1937 decision, that Parliament, being sovereign, could make laws in any way it thought fit. The case, which is reported as *Harris and others vs. the Minister of the Interior and another*, was then taken on appeal, and the appeal was allowed by a unanimous decision of a full bench of five judges, which had the result of rendering the act invalid.

The argument of the Counsel for the Government (Mr. A. B. Beyers, now Mr. Justice Beyers) had a major theme and two minor themes. The first minor theme was that the Cape Coloured voters were being deprived of no rights. They would still have the right to vote and, indeed, in a more effective manner than before. The second minor theme was that there must be certainty in the interpretation of the law, hence the Court was bound to accept the interpretation given in *Ndlwana vs. Hofmeyr* in 1937. The major theme was that, since the Imperial Conference in 1926 and the Statute of Westminster and the Status Act, the Union's Parliament was fully sovereign. The sovereignty of Parliament, as United Kingdom constitutional law and practice made plain, involved the right to come to decisions as it pleased. No previous decision of Parliament could bind Parliament for the future and no testing right existed by which the Court could pronounce on the validity of an act of Parliament.

On this he had to answer the question whether, in that case, the South Africa Act still had any validity as the basis of Union, or whether the Union of South Africa now had a purely unwritten constitution. His argument in this point was that the South Africa Act had become incorporated in South

Africa's common law constitution when sovereignty had been achieved.

The Government's counsel argued along these lines with considerable support from English authorities, steeped in the common law tradition. . . .

In the upshot, the Appeal Court rejected the argument that there was no deprivation of rights. It gave reasons for not being bound to follow the Court's decision in 1937 as representing a complete statement of the law. That case was decided on other grounds, and not only was the particular issue unnecessary to the decision of the case, but it was not seriously argued, nor was the judgment itself free of ambiguity. As regards the major issue, the court denied neither the sovereignty of Parliament nor the inability of the courts to pronounce upon the validity of acts of Parliament. But it did not accept the argument that the institutions of South African parliamentary government had, by implication, been assimilated to those of the United Kingdom Parliament, rendering the special provisions of the South Africa Act ineffective. Thus, without arrogating to itself the right to pronounce on the validity of acts of Parliament, the Court had the duty to pronounce that the removal of the Coloured voters of the Cape Province from the common roll was invalid, because it was not an act of Parliament, since the Separate Representation of Voters Bill had not been passed by Parliament so constituted as, according to the Constitution, was necessary for the particular purpose.

In my own view, there can be no doubt of the soundness of this decision, at any rate from the point of view of the substantial realities of political science, whatever doubts might exist in respect of the niceties of constitutional law. Indeed, from the start of the controversy I had held that a revision of the 1937 judgment was essential to *restore* the sovereignty of Parliament from encroachment by a judicial decision. The intention of the parliaments of both the Union of South Africa and the United Kingdom had been plain; and the various pieces of legislation enacted to give formal effect to the Union's complete sovereignty had been passed on the assumption that the constitutional safeguards of the South Africa Act

APARTHEID IN PRACTICE—WORK AND VOTING

remained in force. The South African Parliament had taken no decision to remove them, and if it has removed them, must have done so without intending to. The alleged method of removal was by way of an Appeal Court decision which implied that the two parliaments had removed them inadvertently. If, then, there has at any time been a change in the law brought about by judicial interpretation, this change was not introduced by the decision in 1952 in the case of *Harris vs. Minister of Interior*. It had surely been done via a judge's *obiter dicta* in the decision of 1937 in *Ndlwana vs. Hofmeyr*. The constitutional position which did not go beyond what Parliament itself had decided was restored only as a result of the careful revision of the Court's earlier judgment in 1952. However thwarted a Parliamentary majority which did not command the necessary two-thirds of the votes in both houses might feel, the fact remains that it was this decision, the effect of which was to prevent an insufficient majority taking advantage of what was essentially a piece of judicial law-making, in order to reinterpret the law differently from Parliament's own interpretation of it, that in reality reaffirmed Parliamentary sovereignty.

The present South African Government does not accept rebuffs with good grace. Its first reaction to the Appeal Court's decision was to introduce a High Court of Parliament Bill. This was duly passed in the ordinary manner (i.e., by a majority of less than two-thirds of each house, sitting separately) in the 1952 session of Parliament. It set up a new constitutional court, consisting of all members of the two houses, sitting together, which by a simple majority vote was empowered to confirm, vary, or set aside the Appeal Court's decision. The High Court of Parliament duly sat up in Pretoria (though all opposition members and senators boycotted its proceedings), and by unanimous vote it accepted a motion of the Minister of the Interior reversing the Appeal Court's decision. The legality of these proceedings was in turn contested in the Cape Provincial Division of the Supreme Court. They were declared invalid, and this decision was confirmed on appeal by the Government.

It is perhaps ironical that had the legality of the Separate Representation of Voters' Act gone on appeal from the South African Appeal Court to the British Privy Council, that body, more familiar with the conception of Parliamentary sovereignty inherent in the United Kingdom's unwritten constitution, might have given more weight to the contention that a Parliament, to be sovereign, must be bound by no rules save those it cared to adopt. But appeals to the Privy Council (virtually in disuse) had quite recently been abolished by Act 16 of 1950. . . .

The Government's next step was to attempt to secure a two-thirds majority for a revision of the South Africa Act, so as to do away with entrenchments. Although there was a break-away of four United Party members of Parliament, who wished to substitute compromise with the Government for unyielding opposition, this defection was not enough and the Government still failed to secure a two-thirds majority. Then the Appellate Division Bill was introduced, providing for a new Court of Appeal which should have exclusive jurisdiction in constitutional questions. This was dropped, however, in favour of a renewed effort to get sufficient support amongst opposition members to gain a two-thirds majority for the validation of the invalid Separate Representation of Voters Act. This was referred to a Joint Select Committee of House and Senate (with eleven Government and seven Opposition members) which reported back to the next session of Parliament (1954).

If it had been hoped, with compromises on both sides, to reach agreement in the Select Committee, there was no sign of this occurring. Immediately the last piece of oral evidence had been heard, instead of the usual motion of adjournment to consider the evidence, this was rejected by eleven votes of the Government supporters against seven Opposition votes, in favour of the immediate acceptance of the principle of separate representation. From then on, proceedings degenerated into what appears to have been a rather sordid manoeuvre to confine the proceedings to consideration of a brief report to which was annexed a ready-prepared draft bill for revalidating the invalid act, to prevent discussion of the evidence on its merits and, in particular, to make use of Parliamentary standing orders and procedures to prevent Mr. Harry Lawrence's getting on the record of the Committee's proceedings—even by moving it as an amendment—a minority report which he had prepared. So the Opposition members were manoeuvred into a position in which, after several unsuccessful appeals to the Speaker of the House of Assembly against the rulings of the Chairman of the Committee, they left no more positive record of their endeavours than a block of seven minority votes upon every division.

Some concessions were made in the majority report of the committee, for example rather more favourable terms were proposed for the constitution of an advisory Union Council for Coloured Affairs—though these have been modified again, less generously, in the latest legislation. One or two further concessions were also made in the later stages through which the bill was taken after the Select Committee had reported; but it emerged from the third reading with only 129 votes in favour, whereas 138 votes were necessary to secure a two-thirds majority of the two houses.

The next stage of the attempt to achieve the Government's aims was the appointment of five additional appeal court judges in March 1955, bringing the total number of such judges up to eleven. This was done administratively, and perfectly legally, for the law says only that the Court shall consist of the Chief Justice and as many other judges as are required. Then the Appellate Division Quorum Act was hurriedly rushed through. The relevant provisions of this are that where the validity of any act or purported act of Parliament is concerned, it will take all eleven judges of the enlarged Court to form a quorum, and a valid decision must be a decision of at least six judges.

The day after this act became law, the Senate Bill was introduced. The four senators elected by Africans were left unaffected (as, indeed, they had to be unless the new act was certain to be invalidated, in turn, upon the same grounds, since the right of the Natives to elect these four senators had been passed in 1936 by a two-thirds majority as an amendment of an entrenched clause, and was, therefore, itself entrenched). Quite recently, however, in June 1956, the Minister for Native Affairs revived a project which had been for some time in abeyance, when he declared that in due course the representation of Africans in Parliament must disappear, since other and more satisfactory ways of associating the Bantu with the Government of the country have been devised. He has, in effect, given notice that a further instalment of electoral *apartheid* will be introduced before long.

But the main feature of the Senate Bill was that it marked the abandonment of a direct attempt to deprive the Coloured voters of the Cape of access to the common voters' roll in favour of the creation of conditions in which a two-thirds majority in favour of their removal could be assured. Instead of each province's remaining on an equality in its representation in the Senate, with eight members apiece, the new bill destroyed this concession to provincial sentiment made at the time of Union. It provided for an increased number of elected senators, but they were to be apportioned between the different provinces in the same way as the distribution of seats in the House of Assembly is determined, according to the distribution amongst the provinces of the White voters. Thus, in the new Senate, there were twenty-seven elected members from the Transvaal and twenty-two elected members from the Cape, but only eight each from Natal and the Orange Free State.

Moreover, the system of proportional representation was abolished within the electoral colleges. Thus, the party with a majority in each provincial electoral college (which consists of the representatives of each constituency within that province both in the House of Assembly and in the Provincial Council) selects all the Senators for that province. The Senate no longer reflected the balance of voting strength in each Province. There were now no Senators for the Cape, the Orange Free State, or the Transvaal who were not Nationalists, while Natal's whole representation in the Senate belonged to the United Party.

The number of Senators nominated by Government was

doubled, from 8 to 16. The result was that, whereas in the old Senate there were 30 Government supporters (including 2 elected and 2 nominated Senators for South West Africa, who were first added in 1950) out of a Senate of 48 members, in the new Senate there were 77 Government supporters out of 89. This meant that the Government could count on at least a majority of 171 votes to 77 votes in a full attendance at a joint sitting of both Houses, and this was comfortably in excess of a two-thirds majority.

Once the Senate had been recast, the Government designed to make use of the enlarged and radically altered Senate to bring to a successful conclusion a measure which had been agitating the country for over five years by reintroducing its bill to validate the abortive Act of 1951 to remove the Cape Coloured voters from the common roll. The measure was now one in which considerations of prestige and refusal to be thwarted had become the major driving forces, since the fear of losing control of the machinery of government through the influence of the Coloured vote in some eight or nine Cape electoral divisions (a very real fear after the unexpected and narrow electoral victory in 1948) is no longer serious.

In due course, in February 1956, there was a joint sitting at which the removal of the Cape Coloured voters from the common roll was revalidated, and the removal of all entrenchments save those on equal language rights was passed by 174 votes against 68. The new Cape Coloured franchise was finally determined, in May 1956, by the two Houses sitting separately. It conceded the right to elect, through four separate constituencies, four members of the House of Assembly and also two Provincial Councillors; but it now confined these rights, in the Provincial Council as well as in Parliament, to the election of White representatives.

Immediately after the Joint Sitting two Coloured voters contested the Senate Act, claiming that it was a fraudulent attempt to defeat the entrenched clauses of the constitution by subterfuge, and basing their plea essentially upon the same grounds as had been successful in the second case of the series. But the new manoeuvre was more cunning than the old in so far as it was not linked directly with the invalidated Separate Representation of Voters Bill. Indeed the very fact that, incidentally to what was undoubtedly the main aim, it had involved such sweeping changes as the refashioning of the whole basis of provincial representation in the Senate, made it more difficult to substantiate the argument that it was so uniquely designed to overcome the lack of sufficient votes to bring about a legal change in an entrenched clause of the South Africa Act as to be itself *ipso facto* invalid. Suppose the new Senate had functioned for ten or twenty years without returning to the question of voting rights at the Cape, and had then participated in a joint sitting in which the Cape Coloured voters were removed from the common roll by a two-thirds majority. Could the validity of the changes then, after such an interval, have been successfully challenged? If not, how could they be challenged if it proceeded with such legislation straight away? The appellants were on more difficult ground than before.

The Cape Provincial Division of the Supreme Court shrank from admitting the far-reaching consequences that might seem to flow from admitting the applicants' arguments, which it rejected in a unanimous judgment delivered on 18 May 1956. If, in order to make the guarantees of the Cape franchise effective, the entrenchment of the Section 152 of the South Africa Act was meant to imply a limitation of Parliament's power to vary the composition of the Senate under Section 25, the Court held that such an intention would have been expressly stated in the act.

The case then went on appeal. Although the validity of the newly enlarged Senate went for final decision to a newly enlarged Appeal Court, that did not mean that the judgment was a foregone conclusion. Even where political motives for appointment to the Bench have been apparent, the independence of the South African judiciary is well established. The appeal was, however, dismissed by a majority judgment of ten against one. The same Chief Justice who had delivered judgment against the Government in the High Court of Parliament case delivered judgment in favour of the Government in the Senate case.

His judgment, while favourable to the Government on the legal issues, cannot be regarded as complimentary upon the moral ones. The Government, he suggested, had hardly attempted to deny that the sole reason for reconstructing the Senate was to render nugatory the safeguards of the entrenched clauses. But if Parliament sitting bicamerally had plenary power to reconstitute the Senate, its real purpose was irrelevant. Because the enlargement of the Senate in no way purported to affect the appellants' rights it could not be said to render them nugatory. Even had the Senate been reconstituted by limiting it to supporters of the Government whose names were set forth in the act itself, this would not in itself be *ultra vires*. It still required a further legislative step to destroy the appellants' rights, namely the passage of an act in conformity with the proviso in Section 151 of the South Africa Act. This had been done in joint session with the aid of the newly created two-thirds majority, and the distinction between entrenched rights and unentrenched rights goes no further than that requirement.

If this meant that the legal safeguards of the South Africa Act had proved inadequate, he suggested that the framers of the Constitution might have foreseen the possibility though doubting the probability of circumvention. But they might have felt that 'the supreme legislative power in relation to any subject matter is always capable of abuse, but it is not to be presumed that it will be improperly used. If it is, the only remedy is an appeal to those by whom the legislature is elected.'

Mr. Justice Schreiner gave an equally closely argued dissenting judgment. He insisted that where pieces of legislation in apparently separate fields form successive steps in a legislative plan, with the ultimate effect of merging to accomplish an unlawful result, then in substance the separate fields become one. The complementary pieces of legislation must therefore be invalid because the combined purpose is invalid. 'In general,' he argued, 'the parts of a whole take their character from the whole. A scheme to defraud is an obvious example; another is a scheme to get round a legislative obstacle.'

APARTHEID IN PRACTICE—WORK AND VOTING

Mr. Schreiner received no support for his judgment. Thus at great cost, the Government had its way with the Coloured vote—and, incidentally, rendered it more difficult for an opposition party successful at the polls to obtain control of the Senate as well. It must be recognised that what has occurred in South Africa is virtually a revolution, which the Government itself, for reasons of policy, has conducted against the South Africa Act, which was the basis of Union. In the end, after a series of mishaps, this revolution has been carried through without apparent illegality, yet, despite that, it amounts essentially to a revolution.

ABOLITION OF AFRICAN REPRESENTATION
IN PARLIAMENT

Act No. 46 of 1959, from which the following quotations are taken, provides for an elaborate system of African local government through tribal, regional and territorial authorities, and almost incidentally abolishes African representation in Parliament.

DOCUMENT 25. FROM THE PROMOTION OF BANTU SELF-GOVERNMENT ACT, NO. 46 of 1959.

WHEREAS the Bantu peoples of the Union of South Africa do not constitute a homogeneous people, but form separate national units on the basis of language and culture:

AND WHEREAS it is desirable for the welfare and progress of the said peoples to afford recognition to the various national units and to provide for their gradual development within their own areas to self-governing units on the basis of Bantu systems of government:

AND WHEREAS it is therefore expedient to develop and extend the Bantu system of government for which provision has been made in the Bantu Authorities Act, 1951, with due regard to prevailing requirements, and to assign further powers, functions and duties to regional and territorial authorities:

AND WHEREAS the development of self-government is stimulated by the grant to territorial authorities of control over the land in their areas, and it is therefore expedient to provide for the ultimate assignment to territorial authorities of certain rights and powers conferred on or assigned to the Governor-General or the Minister or the Trustee referred to in the Native Trust and Land Act, 1936, in terms of any law:

AND WHEREAS it is expedient to provide for direct consultation between the various Bantu national units and the Government of the Union:

AND WHEREAS it is expedient to repeal the Representation of Natives Act, 1936:

AND WHEREAS it is expedient to provide for other incidental matters:

BE IT THEREFORE ENACTED by the Queen's Most Excellent Majesty, the Senate and the House of Assembly of the Union of South Africa, as follows:

* * *

15. (1) The Representation of Natives Act, 1936, is hereby repealed, but the repeal shall have no effect in relation to any person duly elected as a senator or member of the House of Assembly or a Provincial Council in terms of that Act and holding office at the commencement of this Act.

(2) Notwithstanding the repeal of the Representation of Natives Act, 1936, no person shall be entitled to have his name included in any list of persons qualified to vote at elections of members of the House of Assembly or of a Provincial Council, in which he would, but for the repeal of the said Act, not have been entitled to have his name included.

(3) Any person whose name is at the commencement of this Act included in the Cape native voters' roll framed under section *seven* of the Representation of Natives Act, 1936, shall retain all the rights and privileges to which he would, but for the repeal of that Act, in terms of any other law have been entitled as a registered parliamentary voter in the province of the Cape of Good Hope.

16. This Act shall be called the Promotion of Bantu Self-government Act, 1959.

APARTHEID IN PRACTICE—WORK AND VOTING

ABOLITION OF INDIAN REPRESENTATION

The Asiatic Land Tenure and Indian Representation Act (No. 28 of 1946) placed restrictions on the purchase of land by Indians, but also gave them a limited community franchise for Parliament and the Natal Provincial Council. By Act No. 47 of 1948, printed below, this franchise, which had never come into actual operation owing to the opposition of the Indians themselves, was repealed—be it noted, at the earliest possible opportunity—by the newly elected Parliament.

DOCUMENT 26. FROM THE ASIATIC LAWS AMENDMENT ACT, NO. 47 OF 1948.

ACT to amend the Asiatic Land Tenure and Indian Representation Act, 1946.
BE it enacted by the King's Most Excellent Majesty, the Senate and the House of Assembly of the Union of South Africa, as follows:

1. Section *thirty-one* of the Asiatic Land Tenure and Indian Representation Act, 1946 (Act No. 28 of 1946), hereinafter called the principal Act, is hereby amended by the deletion of paragraph (a) of sub-section (1) and the substitution therefor of the following new paragraph:

'(a) by the substitution for the definition of "Asiatic" of the following definition:

" 'Asiatic' means any member of a race or tribe whose national home is in Asia, other than a Turk, or a member of the Jewish or the Syrian race or a person belonging to the race or class known as the Cape Malays, and includes any woman, to whichever race, tribe or class she may belong, between whom and a person who is an Asiatic in terms of the foregoing provisions of this definition, there exists a marriage or a union recognized as a marriage (whether or not of a monogamous nature) under the tenets of any Asiatic religion;".'

2. Sections *forty* to *fifty-seven* inclusive of the principal Act are hereby repealed.

3. The preamble to the principal Act is hereby amended by the deletion of the words; 'and to extend to Indians in the said provinces a special franchise to the end that they may be represented in Parliament and in the Provincial Council of Natal:

AND WHEREAS it is desirable that these matters should be dealt with together in one enactment:'

4. The short title of the principal Act is hereby amended by the deletion of the words 'and Indian Representation'.

5. The long title of the principal Act is hereby amended by the deletion of the words: 'to make special provision for the representation in Parliament of Indians in the Provinces of Natal and Transvaal, and for the representation in the Provincial Council of Natal, of Indians in that province'.

6. This Act shall be called the Asiatic Laws Amendment Act, 1948.

PART VIII

The Group Areas Act

Perhaps no measure of *apartheid* has been more far-reaching than the Group Areas Act. Some of the relevant clauses of the original Act No. 41 of 1950 are quoted below. The Act has been amended and re-amended many times, but the essentials as given below still remain. Extracts 28 and 29 give further information about the Group Areas system.

DOCUMENT 27. FROM THE GROUP AREAS ACT, NO. 41 OF 1950.

2. (1) For the purposes of this Act, there shall be the following groups:
 (a) a white group, in which shall be included any person who in appearance, obviously is, or who is generally accepted as a white person, other than a person who although in appearance obviously a white person, is generally accepted as a coloured person, or who is in terms of sub-paragraph (ii) of paragraphs (b) and (c) or of the said sub-paragsaphs read with paragraph (d) of this sub-section and paragraph (a) of sub-section (2), a member of any other group;
 (b) a native group, in which shall be included:
  (i) any person who in fact is, or is generally accepted as a member of an aboriginal race or tribe of Africa, other than a person who is, in terms of sub-paragraph (ii) of paragraph (c), a member of the coloured group; and
  (ii) any woman to whichever race, tribe or class she may belong, between whom and a person who is, in

terms of sub-paragraph (i), a member of a native group, there exists a marriage or who cohabits with such a person;

(c) a coloured group, in which shall be included:
   (i) any person who is not a member of the white group or of the native group; and
   (ii) any woman, to whichever race, tribe or class she may belong, between whom and a person who is, in terms of sub-paragraph (i), a member of the coloured group, there exists a marriage, or who cohabits with such a person; and

(d) any group of persons which is under sub-section (2) declared to be a group.

(2) The Governor-General may by proclamation in the *Gazette*:

(a) define any ethnical, linguistic, cultural or other group of persons who are members either of the native group or of the coloured group; and

(b) declare the group so defined to be a group for the purposes of this Act or of such provisions thereof as may be specified in the proclamation, and either generally or in respect of one or more group areas, or in respect of the controlled area or of any portion thereof so specified, or both in respect of one or more group areas and of the controlled area or any such portion thereof.

(3) A proclamation under paragraph (a) of sub-section (2) may provide that only persons who have in accordance with regulation been registered on application, or who have been registered under any other law, as members of the group referred to in the proclamation, shall be members thereof.

(4) A member of the native group or of the coloured group who is or becomes a member of any group defined under paragraph (a) of sub-section (2) shall, to the extent required to give effect to any proclamation under paragraph (b) of the said sub-section, be deemed not to be a member of the native group or of the coloured group, as the case may be.

3. (1) The Governor-General may, whenever it is deemed expedient, by proclamation in the *Gazette*:
(a) declare that as from a date specified in the proclamation, which shall be a date not less than one year after the date of the publication thereof, the area defined in the proclamation shall be an area for occupation by members of the group specified therein; or
(b) declare that, as from a date specified in the proclamation, the area defined in the proclamation shall be an area for ownership by members of the group specified therein.

(2) Proclamations under paragraphs (a) and (b) of sub-section (1) may be issued also in respect of the same area.

(3) No proclamation shall be issued under this section:
(a) except with the prior approval in each case by resolution of both Houses of Parliament: Provided that any such proclamation may be issued without such approval:
  (i) if it is issued before the expiration of a period of five years from the date of promulgation of this Act, in respect of a group area for a group other than the native group or a group defined under sub-section (2) of section *two* consisting of members of the native group, in the province of the Cape of Good Hope or of Natal; or
  (ii) if it is issued in respect of an area in the province of the Transvaal for the coloured group or a group defined under sub-section (2) of section *two*, consisting of members of the coloured group, the whole or the greater part of which consists of an area assigned or set apart, as at the commencement of this Act, under paragraph (d) of section *two* of Law No. 3 of 1885 of the Transvaal or section *ten* of the Municipal Amending Ordinance, 1905 (Ordinance No. 17 of 1905) of the Transvaal, or of land described in sub-section (10) of section *one hundred and thirty-one A* of the Precious and Base Metals Act, 1908 (Act No. 35 of 1908) of the Transvaal;
(b) unless in each case the Minister has considered a report

by the board and has consulted the Administrator of the province concerned, and in the case of an area situated wholly or partly on land which, in terms of any law relating to mining, is proclaimed land or deemed to be proclaimed land or upon which prospecting, digging or mining operations are being carried on, also the Minister of Mines, and in the case of an area situated wholly or partly within a controlled area as defined in section *one* of the Natural Resources Development Act, 1947 (Act No. 51 of 1947), also the Natural Resources Development Council established by section *two* of the said Act;
(c) by which there would be included in any group area the whole or any part of :
  (i) any land situated in an area which is a scheduled native area or a released area in terms of the Native Trust and Land Act, 1936 (Act No. 18 of 1936);
  (ii) any location, native village or native hostel referred to in section *two* of the Natives (Urban Areas) Consolidated Act, 1945 (Act No. 25 of 1945), or any area approved for the residence of natives under paragraph (h) of sub-section (2) of section *nine* of the said Act;
  (iii) a coloured persons settlement as defined in section *one* of the Coloured Persons Settlement Act, 1946 (Act No. 7 of 1946);
  (iv) any mission station or communal reserve to which the provisions of the Mission Stations and Communial Reserves Act, 1909 (Act No. 29 of 1909) of the Cape of Good Hope, or of the said Act read with section *sixteen* of the Coloured Mission Stations and Reserves Act, 1949 (Act No. 12 of 1949), apply; or
  (v) any area which is a national park in terms of the National Parks Act, 1926 (Act No. 56 of 1926), or any land which forms part of such a park.
4. (1) As from the date specified in the relevant proclamation under paragraph (a) of sub-section (1) of section *three*, and

notwithstanding anything contained in any special or other statutory provision relating to the occupation of land or premises, no disqualified person shall occupy and no person shall allow any disqualified person to occupy any land or premises in any group area to which the proclamation relates, except under the authority of a permit.

(2) The provisions of sub-section (1) shall not render it unlawful for any disqualified person to occupy land or premises in any group area:

(a) as a *bona fide* servant or employee of the State, or a statutory body or as a domestic servant of any person lawfully occupying the land or premises;

(b) as a *bona fide* visitor for a total of not more than ninety days in any calendar year of any person lawfully residing on the land or premises or as a *bona fide* guest in an hotel;

(c) as a *bona fide* patient in a hospital, asylum or similar institution controlled by the State or a statutory body or in any such institution in existence at the commencement of the Act, which is aided by the State, or as an inmate of a prison, work colony, inebriate home or similar institution so controlled; or

(d) as the *bona fide* employee (other than a domestic servant) of any person or as the husband, wife, minor child or dependant of any person (including a domestic servant or employee) who is lawfully occupying such land or premises: Provided that the provisions of this paragraph shall apply in respect of any group area or any part of any group area only if the Governor-General has by proclamation in the *Gazette*, declared them to apply in respect of that group area, or that part thereof, and only to the extent and subject to the conditions (if any) which may be specified in the proclamation.

(3) Any provision in the title deed of any immovable property situate in any group area referred to in sub-section (1) prohibiting or restricting the occupation or use of such property by persons who are members of the group for which that area has been established shall lapse as from the date referred to in the

said sub-section, and no such provision shall thereafter be inserted in the title deed of any immovable property in such group area.

* * *

19. No person shall acquire or hold on behalf or in the interest of any other person any immovable property which such other person may not lawfully acquire or hold in terms of this Act.

20. (1) If any immovable property:
(a) is acquired or held in contravention of any provision of this Act or is dealt with or used contrary to any condition of a permit under the authority of which it has been acquired or is held; or
(b) has at the commencement of this Act been acquired or is at the said commencement held in contravention of any provision of any law repealed by this Act or in pursuance of any agreement which is null and void in terms of any such provision, or is registered in favour of any person who is in terms of any such provision debarred from holding it, or is dealt with or used contrary to any condition of a permit or any term of a certificate issued under any such provision, under the authority of which it was acquired or held,

the Minister may, after not less than three months' notice in writing to the person concerned and to the holder of any registered mortgage bond over the property, cause the property to be sold either out of hand upon the terms and conditions agreed to by the person concerned and approved by the Minister after consultation with the mortgagee or if the property has not been so sold, within such period, not being less than one month, as the Minister may allow, then by public auction upon such terms and conditions as the Minister may determine.

THE CASE FOR THE ACT

The extract which follows, taken from the Hansard of the South African Senate for 14 June 1950, is the presentation of

THE GROUP AREAS ACT

the Act by the Minister in charge of it on its first introduction into the South African Senate. The Act has since been repeatedly amended, but the main principles have remained the same, and this speech is relevant to them. Senator Jackson, former M.P. for Ermelo, was a United Party Whip in the Senate, the late Senator Conroy had been Minister of Lands in the United Party Government, and the late Senator Heaton Nicholls had been at different times Administrator of Natal, High Commissioner for South Africa in London and Leader of the United Party in the Senate.

DOCUMENT 28. FROM A SPEECH BY THE MINISTER OF THE INTERIOR, INTRODUCING THE GROUP AREAS ACT, 14 JUNE 1950.

The Minister of the Interior: Mr. President, the underlying principle of this Bill is to make provision for the establishment of Group Areas, that is, separate areas for the different racial groups, by compulsion if necessary. Legislative sanction must be given, in other words, to the idea of establishing these groups. That, I submit, is a plain and straightforward issue of principle which can allow of no misunderstanding or misapprehension. The setting aside of areas for non-Europeans is not novel in our legislative history. The Precious and Base Metals Act of 1908, the Mission Stations and Communal Reserves Act of 1909, the Bethalsdorp Settlement Act of 1921 and various other Acts—legislative measures which are referred to in the White Paper—are examples of areas which by law are reserved for certain specific racial groups. This Bill is an extension of the principle to all the racial groups in any part of South Africa. So far there has been, by legislation, no area which is set aside for Europeans exclusively. In terms of this Bill this is now also done. The Bill, I must remind Hon. Senators, merely provides the machinery for demarcating these various group areas. It does not presume to make the demarcation itself. Hon. Senators will have observed that the establishment of group areas will therefore not be a thing which takes place instantly on the passing of this Bill. The provisions of the Bill provide for the gradual demarcation into group areas over a period of years. With that as a background we were naturally faced with the immediate problem of the interim period—what is to happen before the group areas can be declared? And the first problem we had to face here was to prevent any further deterioration in the existing position. We had to see to it that the mixed areas which have grown, which have continued in the past years, will not be allowed to continue further; that there shall not be any deterioration as far as that aspect of the question is concerned and, therefore, the Bill provides for the idea of a controlled area which comes into operation as soon as the Bill is applied to any particular part of South Africa. It further provides for proclamations cutting out part of the controlled area and making it, on the one hand, either what is called a specified area, or, on the other hand, what is called an open area—all within the controlled area. The idea, as I say, is that all these various types of areas are merely preliminary to the proclamation of the group area and it is to see that the existing position does not become worse. That is why provision is made for your controlled area and your specified area. Now the change-over from the existing system to the new system envisaged by the Bill naturally is not an easy matter. If we had simply provided for expropriation, for demarcation and expropriation after demarcation, we may have solved the problem in a shorter period of time, but I am afraid we would have made the transfer from one system to the other not so smooth as it is attempted in the present Bill. We have avoided the method of expropriation, and although that is a recognised method for obtaining results of a national or of a wider importance in our existing legislation, we have not resorted to that method in this Bill. Now, it is this attempt to make the change-over from the old system to the new as smooth as possible that introduces all the complications and the difficulties in this Bill. The principle, the ideal, is simple and clear. The scheme is also simple, but to make the passage from the one system to the other system work with the least amount of irritation—that is what makes the Bill complicated. We have

THE GROUP AREAS ACT

attempted, as far as possible, to remove all the sources of irritation which we could possibly remove without sacrificing the ideal and principle of this Bill. As I have said, the scheme of the Bill is also quite simple. In the first place you have the immediate institution of control wherever the Act is proclaimed, except land under Clause *three*, sub-clause (3)(c). That is excluded. But as soon as the Act is proclaimed to apply to any particular part of South Africa, control is automatically instituted there. That is the first part of the scheme. The second part is the gradual proclamation of group areas within that controlled area. That means group areas for occupation or for ownership or for both occupation and ownership by members of a particular group. Then, as I have said, in between the controlled area and the group area, you may have a specified area, or on the other hand an open area as provided in Clause *ten*, sub-clause (3). The three main groups follow the pattern of the Population Registration Act. They are the European, Coloured and the Native groups. The last two groups are also susceptible of division into subgroups, depending on the desire of the persons concerned to be separated from other people and dependent, too, on general considerations of policy. I think I should now say a few words as to what the position is in a controlled area and in a specified area and then in a group area. First of all in a controlled area there can be no change of ownership to a member of another group than that of the existing group, without a permit. In the second place there can be . . .

Senator Conroy: That controlled area is practically the Union, with certain exceptions?

The Minister of the Interior: Wherever the Act is declared to apply, it immediately becomes a controlled area.

Senator Heaton Nicholls: How much of the Union do you anticipate the Act shall not apply to?

The Minister of the Interior: What we have said the Act will not apply to is those parts specified in Clause *three*, sub-clause (3)(c). Now as far as occupation in a controlled area is concerned, there can be no change of occupation to a member of another group than that of the owner, without a permit. In other words, as far as occupation is concerned, the colour of the particular premises is determined by the colour of the owner, not of the occupier.

Senator Jackson: So, if an Indian lives on a white man's property . . .

The Minister of the Interior: I will explain all that. I want to explain the whole scheme and I want to do it fully. I would not like Hon. Senators to anticipate what I am going to say. Now as far as a controlled area is concerned, that is the position in regard to ownership and in regard to occupation. The issue of permits is under Clause *fourteen*. That can only be done after a report by the Land Tenure Board which is envisaged in Clauses *twenty-six* and *twenty-seven*. Such a report by the board is only made after due notice and opportunity for representations. In other words, before the board, with certain minor exceptions, proceeds to make recommendation in regard to a permit, it publishes that such and such an application has been made, and that any interested party can make written representations. In fact the board, which is really modelled on the lines of the board instituted under the Asiatic Land Tenure Act of 1946, has allowed all interested parties to appear before it and to state their case; to hear their arguments before making recommendation. That, I take it, will continue to be the position. In other words, there will be full opportunity for representations by interested parties. Judging from what I have said, it must be obvious to Hon. Senators that the large majority of land transactions involving ownership or occupation will continue undisturbed as at present. Any question of a transfer of ownership within the same group carries no impediment as far as that is concerned—as far as occupation is concerned in a controlled area—and with the proviso that the colour of the occupant is deemed to be the colour of the owner on that date, there can also be free transfer within the same group. It is only when you go outside the group that a permit is needed. Now, in regard to a specified area, the position is slightly different. I think I may perhaps illustrate it by giving a practical example to Hon. Senators of how the various degrees of control affect a change in ownership or occupation. Now take the controlled

THE GROUP AREAS ACT

area. I have already explained that if you have an Asiatic owner on the date on which the proclamation applies the Act to a certain part of the country, but a European occupier, then the Asiatic owner can eject—if he can do it under his contract—or he can get rid of the European occupier after his contract is over. He can then put an Asiatic occupier in his place; or he can go and live there himself, because he is the owner on the specified date and the occupant is deemed to be of the colour of the owner. In a specified area the position is otherwise. There, if on a specified date when the area is declared, you have an Asiatic owner and a European occupier, then the European occupier can only be superseded by another European occupier. We had hoped that we would have been able to make the whole controlled area really the specified area, but we were faced with the practical difficulty of deciding what the occupation was on a specified date. It is easy to say what the ownership was on a specified date. You merely have to go to the Deeds Registry, but in order to find out what the colour of the occupant was on a specified date is a matter which becomes more difficult with the passage of time. The Asiatic Land Tenure Act, which was passed in 1946, applies this principle. Although only four years have elapsed, there are already difficulties of proof encountered in deciding who was the occupier on the specified date. (I think it was in January, 1946.) For that reason we have not made that the general pattern, but any area—if it is desired that it be declared a specified area—may on application to the board be declared a specified area. The board will then have to consider the matter. I just want to say that there is another side of the question too, because if you have a European owner and an Asiatic occupier, then under the specified area the European owner cannot put in a European occupier if there was an Asiatic occupier on the specified date. Under the controlled area the European owner can supersede the Asiatic occupier by a European occupier. It cuts both ways and, therefore, it is a matter which in a particular locality they can apply for by proclamation.

Senator Conroy: Can that position go on permanently?

The Minister of the Interior: No. This is all in order to peg the position preliminary to a group area being declared. Even where no group area is concerned, you can always by proclamation make a controlled area into a specified area, or *vice versa*, you can deproclaim a specified area and make it a controlled area.

Senator Clarkson: Nobody will ever know what the position is going to be.

The Minister of the Interior: It is quite simple. As soon as there is a group area then all your uncertainties are removed and that is, after all, the primary purpose of this Bill which is to provide for the group area. The other is the interim measures and to a large extent we want to leave it open for the interested parties to come and say what form they prefer, and their representations will then be considered and if they are found to show good cause those representations will be acceded to. Now let me just recapitulate. As far as ownership is concerned you have the controlled area, the specified area and the open area. In a controlled area there can be no transfer of ownership to a member of another group without a permit. As far as a specified area is concerned, it is the same. As far as an open area is concerned, it is the same. So, as far as ownership is concerned, there is no difference between a specified area and a controlled area or an open area. The provision in all three cases is that you cannot sell to a person of another group without a permit; that is as far as ownership is concerned. The difference between these three types of control is classified when you come to the question of occupation. In a controlled area you can have no occupation by a member of another group than that of the owner without a permit. In the case of a specified area you can have no occupation by a member of another group than that of the occupier at the date of the proclamation without a permit. In the case of an open area occupation is uncontrolled. Hon. Senators will see that as far as the transfer of ownership is concerned there is no difference. It is only when it is a question of occupation that there is a difference between these three types. Now I want to say a few words about the procedure which leads up to the proclamation of a group area. The first point that I want to make clear is that a group area can only be declared after a report by the board. The board must investigate. It must hear the interested parties. It must make a recommendation. The board can only report after due notice and an opportunity for representations from interested parties. Then when you have a recommendation from the board that is brought to the Minister, and the Minister can only approve of it after consultation with the Administrator of the province concerned, and in certain cases with the Minister of Mines or the Natural Resources Development Council, if they are interested. Then you have this final provision that no proclamation proclaiming a group area can be done except with the prior approval of both Houses. That is the general principle to which there are two exceptions. The two exceptions are the following. The first is that within five years of the date of promulgation of the Act—that is in Clause *three* (3)(a), in the Cape and Natal—such a proclamation can be issued without the prior approval of both Houses of Parliament, and, secondly, in the Transvaal it can also be done without the approval of Parliament in certain specified cases, cases namely where Parliament has already in the past given its approval to the setting aside of that particular area for a particular non-European group. In such a case it is not necessary to come before Parliament again. That is the procedure which leads up to the proclamation . . .

Senator Conroy: You have not given us a reason for that five-year period during which you need not come to Parliament. What is the reason for that?

The Minister of the Interior: The reason for that is the following. In the first place, in Natal, in terms of the existing Asiatic Land Tenure Act of 1946, you have a similar provision in regard to the international areas, the released areas, that is the areas in which there is free for all purchase. The Minister may extend those areas without coming to Parliament in the first five years. That is the principle that has been adopted here.

Senator Dr. Brookes: Those five years end in 1951, so that is no answer.

The Minister of the Interior: Yes, those five years will end in 1951, but the principle which was accepted in 1946 was five

THE GROUP AREAS ACT

years, and it is the same principle that is accepted here. The only difference is that this Bill is four years after the other Bill.

Senator Byron: What is the reason?

The Minister of the Interior: What is the reason? I should imagine Hon. Senators on the opposite side would be better acquainted with the reason for imposing such a condition in 1946. I am adopting that reason. But I do it also for this reason, that there are a large number of areas which can be and should be declared group areas immediately. There are areas which are predominantly of the one or the other group, and we want to have them declared as soon as possible. We do not want to have any delay as far as they are concerned, because the declaration of a group area for a European group will mean immediate security for the people who are living in that group.

Senator Clarkson: They have that today under the Land Tenure Act.

The Minister of the Interior: Not in the Cape. No, they have not got it in the . . .

Senator Clarkson: No, it is all right. I am thinking of Natal.

The Minister of the Interior: No, they have not got it under the Land Tenure Act in Natal either.

Senator Clarkson: Oh yes, they have.

The Minister of the Interior: No, it is subject to a permit. It is like the specified area, not the group area. The position under the Asiatic Land Tenure Act is very much the same as the position under the specified area would be. But there is today no area in the whole of Natal where you can say that ultimately that area will be exclusively European or exclusively Indian. That was admitted by the Rt. Hon. Leader of the Opposition in Another Place when he introduced that Bill. There is no provision for that.

Senator Dr. Brookes: Why does the Hon. Minister single out the Cape for five years?

The Minister of the Interior: Because in the Cape we have not even got what we have in Natal and the Transvaal today, a specified area to protect them in the meantime.

Senator Dr. Brookes: Why single out the Cape?

THE GROUP AREAS ACT

The Minister of the Interior: The Cape is not singled out. The Cape is now brought into line with the others. And as I say, in the Cape particularly—judging by the representations and petitions which have been brought in—there are a large number of areas in the Cape—in the Cape Peninsula, in Port Elizabeth and East London—which could immediately be declared as group areas, to give security for the inhabitants that their property will not be depreciated by the purchase—which is today free in the Cape Province—by a non-European next door to their property. That is why we say that this must be done with the least possible delay and impediment. Now the result of the proclamation of a group area is the next point to which I want to devote some attention. The position as far as a group area is concerned is that it may be a group area for ownership only, or it may be a group area for occupation only, or it may be a group area for both occupation and ownership. Now, I deal first with the question where a group area is for ownership only. There, where a group area has been declared for ownership only, there can be no acquisition of property in that area by a disqualified member without a permit, but a disqualified member holding property in such an area may continue to hold it until he dies. In other words, he is given an opportunity of getting rid of it if he is disqualified. There is no expropriation of his property. He can continue to own it until his death, but he will not be able to leave it to a disqualified person. If he leaves it to a disqualified person it will be sold and the proceeds will go to the disqualified person, but the ownership of the property cannot pass to a disqualified person after the existing disqualified person has died. In the case of companies who own land, the position is different. A company legally has no end. It is a *persona* which does not die. So in the case of a company we say that a disqualified company which owns property—it cannot acquire property—at the time the group area is declared, is permitted to continue owning that property for a period of ten years. Within ten years it will have to get rid of that property. But for ten years it may continue to own that property. Now if you have a group area for occupation only, then the ownership provisions as for a controlled or specified area will apply there. In other words, there cannot be a transfer from one group to another group without a permit. This is in a group area for occupation only. The ownership provisions are still controlled in this sense that you require a permit if you want to sell to somebody of a different group.

Senator P. W. Le Roux Van Niekerk: Why does the Hon. Minister bring in a permit?

The Minister of the Interior: Because we do not want the ownership to change, unless there is some control over it, just as in the controlled area. We are not proclaiming it a group area for ownership; it is only for occupation. Later on I will explain why we have this type of group area for occupation only. Firstly, as far as ownership is concerned, the ordinary provisions for a controlled or specified area will apply. But as far as occupation is concerned where you have declared a group area for occupation only, then anybody who is disqualified to live in that area must relinquish his occupation within a period fixed in the Proclamation, declaring it a group area, and that period, which must be fixed in the Proclamation, shall not be less than twelve months. In other words, the Board will have to recommend within what period the occupiers will have to relinquish their occupation, but they may not specify a period which is less than twelve months after the Proclamation is issued declaring that a group area for occupation only. Now where the period has elapsed, provision is made for the issue of permits for continued occupation in clear cases of hardship, or where it is clearly in the interests of that particular group that this disqualified person should continue to occupy there. There are two cases in which permits will be issued. The first is where the period has expired for a disqualified person to relinquish his occupation, but there is a clear case of hardship if he were required immediately to leave and in such a case he may be given a permit extending the period within which he must get out of that area.

Senator Conroy: Supposing he does not get a permit and he has to get out, where does he go? Is there another group where he can go?

The Minister of the Interior: That is why you have the permit system. If there is any case of hardship this is to carry him for a longer period.

Senator Conroy: If you refuse to carry him any longer? It is possible. Where is this man to go?

The Minister of the Interior: Yes. I can only say that if a permit is refused then it must be because he has not been able to make out a clear case of hardship. That seems to me to be the meaning of this provision. The other provision is where a man will be given a permit even if the period has expired, if his continued occupation in that area is in the interest of that particular group; for instance, where you have a non-European group, a European chemist or a doctor or a teacher may, in the interest of the non-European group, be allowed in that area. In such cases they can continue to remain there under a permit.

Senator Heaton Nicholls: Europeans can remain in those areas?

The Minister of the Interior: If it is in the interests of the non-Europeans. And the converse too. This does not apply to the one or the other only. If it is in the interests of the Europeans that a particular non-European should continue to occupy premises there, then he will be allowed to do so under a permit.

Senator Conradie: Where does 'apartheid' come in?

The Minister of the Interior: The Hon. Senator asks me where 'apartheid' is . . .

Senator Conroy: I do not want to interrupt the Hon. Minister, but I would like him to make this quite clear. Supposing a person is not qualified and a permit is not given to him because, as you say, a distinct case of hardship is not proved and he has to move; and supposing there is no group for that disqualified person where he can go. What happens to him?

The Minister of the Interior: He can then go to a controlled area. He can go and occupy the place which a person of the same group occupied in a controlled area, or he can get a permit if there has to be a change of group in the controlled area. Naturally one would like the group area to be cleaned up as soon as possible, whichever group area it is. That is the first thing we would like to have. It is only in distinct cases of hardship where we will give a permit in a group area for continuance of occupation, or where it is clearly in the interests of the group itself that the person remains there. Now, the reason why we make provision for a group area for occupation only is because the non-Europeans are not in a position to own all the property in a non-European group area. We must provide for it that there will still be European owners in non-European areas, because the non-European has not sufficient capital to provide for his own housing. Naturally, in that area, as I say, the provisions of a controlled area will apply. In other words if a European owns property in a group area which has been declared a group area for occupation by non-Europeans only, and he wants to sell to a non-European, then the permit allowing him to sell will naturally be granted. The only point is that we do not insist that the non-Europeans must own all the property in a non-European area, else we are going to have the trouble that there will not be sufficient housing for them.

Senator Clarkson: What about a transfer from a European to a European in that area?

The Minister of the Interior: In an area for occupation only?

Senator Clarkson: Yes.

The Minister of the Interior: That can pass freely.

Senator Clarkson: By permit?

The Minister of the Interior: No, no permit. If a non-European in that area wants to sell to a non-European, that can be done without a permit. Other areas, of course, can be declared as for both ownership and occupation. That, I take it, will be the form which will be employed where the financial resources of the group permit of their ownership of all the land in that particular group area. Provision in regard to trading is the next point to which I want to refer. That is, that no licence to trade may be issued in respect of premises where the proposed holder of the licence, as well as the persons who will be in actual control of the business, have not the right of occupation. We are making the right to trade dependent on the right to occupy. You will not be allowed to trade in premises which you have not the right to occupy.

Senator Jackson: What does the Hon. Minister mean by the issuing of a licence?

The Minister of the Interior: Anybody who has a licence for trade, that is, a licence which is a yearly one. It is not a licence in perpetuity.

Senator Jackson: You do not apply for the renewal. You just go and pay and get a receipt.

The Minister of the Interior: Yes, but it is only given for a year. All these trading licences are only given for a year.

Senator Hosking: What about existing rights?

The Minister of the Interior: As far as the occupier is concerned, if he has not the right to occupy there, then he cannot trade there. Hon. Senators will have an ample opportunity of raising the question of vested rights and I shall deal with that. Now I come to the Land Tenure Advisory Board which is really, as far as the machinery is concerned, the crux of this Bill. That board is set up for carrying the objects of this Bill into effect. They will be the persons who will investigate all particular cases and who will have to recommend. They hear evidence and they recommend. The board is modelled on the lines of the Asiatic Land Tenure Act under the 1946 Act, with an increased personnel to cope with the extended duties which they will have under this Act. The existing board in Natal have, I think, carried out their duties with conspicuous success. They maintain a very high degree of impartiality and efficiency and fairness. In paying a tribute to the work of that board I can merely express the wish and, I think, the certainty that the new board will carry on along the lines which were so well laid by the old board.

Senator Byron: Will you allow non-Europeans on the board?

The Minister of the Interior: The idea is that there will be seven and they will be able to sit in panels. I think that the existing board has four members.

Senator Dr. Brookes: There is no provision against it?

The Minister of the Interior: As far as the Bill is concerned, there is no provision against it, but I see no reason for allowing non-Europeans on the board. There is no provision against it.

THE GROUP AREAS ACT

Senator Dr. Brookes: So a better Government might put them on?

The Minister of the Interior: Another Government may; to that extent I may agree with the Hon. Senator. This board, in the existing set-up, will be assisted by inspectors and other officials who will be armed with the necessary powers to ensure the proper carrying out of their duties. This is very much modelled on the lines of the existing Act again. The powers which the officials will have are very much on the lines of the existing Act. Now another very important point in this Bill is contained in Clauses *six* and *seven* which provide for a measure of training in local government by non-European groups. It is provided in those two clauses that in certain group areas, you may allow a measure of self-government by the inhabitants of that particular group. The measure of that self-government will depend upon the stage of development of the group concerned and their capacity for shouldering the responsibilities attaching to those duties. No hard and fast rule can be laid down, because, naturally, the position will differ from one group to another. Even within the same group you may have varying degrees of capability and for that reason no hard and fast rule is laid down, but provision is made for some form of local government, and provision is made that that local government may be either wholly or partly elected by the inhabitants of that group. Again, we cannot lay down any hard and fast rule at this stage. It will have to be an experiment which we are undertaking—an experiment in training in self-government and democratic procedure for these non-European groups. They will be under the supervision of the local authority, and it is provided that no such form of self-government shall be instituted unless the local authority has been consulted, and unless the Administrator and the Minister have, in consultation, agreed to it. This is a matter in which the local people are in the best position to see whether an area of this nature should be established or not. There is a safeguard, as I say, for their proper administration by the supervision of the local authority. On the other hand we want to ensure that the local authority does not neglect them, and therefore in Clause *seven* provision is made that if the

THE GROUP AREAS ACT

Minister has reason to believe that any such group area is not being fairly dealt with by the local authority, he may ask the administrator to institute an inquiry, and if the inquiry reports that certain services or amenities must be provided, then the local authority can be instructed to provide those services or amenities. If they fail to do so, the administrator may do so and charge it to the local authority concerned. I hope it will never be necessary to make use of this clause, but it is there as a safeguard to ensure that persons in those areas are not neglected by an unsympathetic local authority.

Senator Heaton Nicholls: May I ask the Hon. Minister whether this rules out the Health Commission in Natal which has power under the Natal Ordinance to take over any municipality which fails in its health duties.

The Minister of the Interior: This is merely a provision under this Bill. They may develop into any other form of local authority. There is no period put to their development. They may develop in the Cape—I do not know what the various forms of local government in Natal are—but in the Cape they may for instance, develop afterwards into a local board or a village management board, but that is under the provincial ordinances; we have nothing to do with it. This is merely the initial training to make them ripe for development. Now, inevitably, in a Bill of this nature there have to be provisions to avoid the circumvention of the law by the formation of companies, and particularly of private companies. To a large extent our experience has been very unhappy in this respect in past legislation. Hon. Senators will recall that there has been a continuous process of stopping up loopholes—and ingenious persons discovering new loopholes and our having to stop those loopholes again, and you have that continuous spiral. Well, what we have here represents, if I may say so, the accumulated wisdom and experience in regard to this matter extant at the moment of drafting this Bill. It is mainly taken over from existing legislation and also, as I have said, where we have foreseen other loopholes we have tried to provide against them too. That is inevitable in a Bill of this nature because no sooner has it been placed on the Statute Book than attempts are made to evade its provisions. And the necessary sanctions must be provided, because you must have penalties of such a nature as to discourage the evasion of the law. Now that, I think, gives Hon. Senators the broad outline of the Bill as such, but before sitting down I want to refer to certain features of the Bill as a whole, apart from any particular provisions. The first point I want to make—and I think that is the outstanding feature—is that this Bill is a major measure towards the realisation of one of the main objects of the policy of apartheid, that is to eliminate friction between the races in the Union by providing separate areas for the different races. There is a four-point control. Hon. Senators from Natal will realise what that means. There is control in respect of both ownership and occupation, and for both residence and trading. That is the four-point control which we have embodied in this Bill. Now this, as I say, is designed to eliminate friction between the races in the Union because we believe, and believe strongly, that points of contact—all unnecessary points of contact—between the races must be avoided. If you reduce the number of points of contact to the minimum, you reduce the possibility of friction. Contact brings about friction, and friction brings about heat, and may cause a conflagration. Therefore, in this Bill, we see one of the means of relieving the stresses and strains in our racial relations as they exist today.

Hon. Senators: Hear, hear!

The Minister of the Interior: We want to remove one of the root causes of it, and we believe that this is the way to do it. If you are continually having contact between your brakes and your tyres, you cause friction; the friction engenders heat, and it can lead to very grave trouble with your motor-car. Now, we want to avoid those root causes of that trouble, as shown in the past.

Senator Clarkson: Build plenty of houses for the Indians and the Natives and 75 per cent of that trouble will disappear.

The Minister of the Interior: Yes, that can still continue. Now it will be planned. All the local authorities can do so now, but they can do it on a much better planned scale. We know the danger of having a mixture of races in an area. In the past, only too frequently, it has been the cause of trouble. And it is

THE GROUP AREAS ACT

not only between Europeans and non-Europeans. It is also between non-Europeans *inter se*. We know this—and I think it is a very important thing—that the Durban riots of last year took place in a mixed area. They took place where you had Indians and Natives, and we want to avoid a repetition of that kind of thing, and that is why we say we must have separate areas for them, to remove the friction which caused that conflagration in Durban last year.

Senator Heaton Nicholls: We question that statement. The Durban riots occurred in the middle of Durban.

The Minister of the Interior: The other main feature of this Bill is that this object . . .

Senator Clarkson: The Durban riots occurred in Grey Street.

The Minister of the Interior: Oh no.

Senator Heaton Nicholls: Oh yes.

The Minister of the Interior: The main scene was Cato Manor.

Senator Clarkson: It developed into Cato Manor.

The Minister of the Interior: If Hon. Senators say that the boy who was hit by the Indian was hit in a street in Durban, I will not deny it, but the real trouble was Cato Manor. That was the trouble.

Senator Jackson: Where were the Newclare riots?

The Minister of the Interior: If Hon. Senators want to make the general proposition they are free to make it. I deny it. I say that the cause was the putting of people of different races together. The result of putting people of different races together is to cause racial trouble.

Hon. Senators: Hear, Hear!

The Minister of the Interior: That is the point. If they want to deny it, let them get up and deny it.

Senator Jackson: I asked the Minister a simple question. I am not trying to make contact with him to cause friction.

The Minister of the Interior: I am not acquainted with what happened at this particular place that the Hon. Senator mentioned. It does not mean that you will not have racial conflict otherwise too, but I want to avoid any additional causes and irritations which will bring about racial conflict. The second feature of this Bill is that this object is achieved without recourse to discrimination between the various races, because restrictions imposed upon one group are also applicable to the other groups. In other words, each group surrenders certain of its rights for the common good of all groups. Each group is required to do that. If the right to purchase for the non-European is restricted in the Cape Province today, the right of the European in the Cape Province will also be restricted and therefore, I say I think it is a feature of this Bill that we attain the object of eliminating friction by providing separate areas without having recourse to discrimination between the races. The third feature, I have already explained, is the provision for a training in democratic procedure and in self-government by persons in group areas for non-Europeans. That is a form of positive apartheid and I think it is a feature of this Bill which ought to be welcomed on all sides. The fourth feature is that the change-over which is provided for in this Bill is calculated to take place gradually with the least disruptive effect. The Bill seeks to combine the guarantee of future certainty with the minimum of present inconvenience. That is what the Bill seeks to do and I think to a large measure it succeeds in that. The harsh method of expropriation has been avoided. Large areas can be proclaimed immediately without any inconvenience. Other areas require the liquidation only of isolated pockets. In some areas the intermixture is great and the problem difficult, but the Bill is so elastic in its nature that it provides the means of coping with all these various types of cases and allows each one to be dealt with according to its degree of difficulty and the extent of admixture that has taken place. Those are the main features of this Bill, and I think if one comes back to what I started with, the underlying purpose is to provide separate areas for the different races as we believe that that is the only alternative to intermixture—racial trouble leading to an intermingling of the races in the future of South Africa. We believe that this Bill will be one of the cornerstones for preserving a White South Africa, while doing justice to the non-European elements and allowing them to develop each within his own area to the fullest extent of their capabilities. I move.

THE GROUP AREAS ACT

THE CASE AGAINST

The following extracts are from the speech on the main Group Areas Act in the Senate by Senator Edgar H. Brookes and the speech some years later in the House of Assembly on one of the many amending Group Areas Acts, by Mrs. Helen Suzman, the one representative of the Progressive Party in the South African Parliament. They speak for themselves.

DOCUMENT 29A. FROM A SPEECH ON THE GROUP AREAS ACT IN THE SENATE BY DR. EDGAR H. BROOKES, 14 JUNE 1950.

Senator Dr. Brookes: Mr. President, the Hon. Senator who has just taken his seat has given me the starting point of my speech by referring to this extraordinary document—the Joynt Report. I call it an extraordinary document because it has about it all those elements of sharp practice and disingenuousness which are associated with this Bill from beginning to end, in its conception, its introduction and its presentation to this House.
The Minister of the Interior: Is that fair to people who cannot defend themselves?
Senator Dr. Brookes: I charge those qualities to the Minister. He can defend himself if he likes but every commission has got to stand criticism in this House.
The Minister of the Interior: I think it is a scandalous statement.
Senator Dr. Brookes: I will repeat the statement. Mr. President. This report is an extraordinarily misleading document. It is a document which is produced under extraordinary auspices and put before Parliament in an extraordinary way. It is the first parliamentary Blue Book which has been edited by a Minister before its publication.
Hon. Senators: Hear, hear.
Senator Dr. Brookes: It was put in in the other Place, so near to the time of the Bill that there was not time to study it properly by the members there. This report is full of inaccuracies. It is a completely one-sided document. When I compare it with the

two Broome reports, Mr. President, the difference is as the difference between light and darkness. Now, I do not make a grave statement of that without chapter and verse. I am going to prove my statement which the Hon. Minister has taken so badly. The Hon. Minister has said in his introductory note to this report that the report is a lengthy one, and chapters one and two respectively deal with the position historically, before and after Union up to 1946. So there is no history recorded in this, but in Chapter IV, Paragraph 288, it says: 'A perusal of the evidence summarized in Chapters I to III hereof says that the Indian came to South Africa as an indentured labourer against the wishes of the European inhabitants of Natal.' Now, Mr. President, the European inhabitants of Natal may or may not have made a serious political error. That is a different question. But here is a statement made in a report which the Minister wants to defend. The statement is alleged to be fact that as a matter of history the Indian came to Natal against the wishes of the European inhabitants. The historical chapters which are supposed to support that are suppressed. I do not know what they contain. I would like to give some of the facts with regard to this. On the 18 June 1855, a public meeting of the citizens of Durban, called by the Town Council, by a very large majority, got the following paragraph inserted in an address to Sir George Grey: 'Independently of measures for developing the labour of our own Natives, we believe your Excellency will find occasion to sanction the introduction of a limited number of coolies or other labourers from the East in aid of the new enterprises on the coast lands, to the success of which sufficient and reliable labour is absolutely essential.' Three times the Government of India was asked to send that labour: three times they refused, but pressure came continually from the people of Natal for this labour. In 1859 the Legislative Council of Natal passed an ordinance in favour of this immigration. Twelve of the sixteen members of that Council were elected. In 1864 the Legislative Council made a further request for immigration of Indian labour. The Chamber of Commerce of Natal, after the Indians had been $3\frac{1}{2}$ years in Natal approved this report. It was signed by R. Acutt, C. Behrens, W. Snowden and R. Hawse. This is the report: 'Your Committee considers that the slow process of introducing coolies at present obtaining, is totally inadequate to the wants of the sugar, coffee and cotton planters. Your committee strongly advocates that the Government borrow money in England for the purpose of keeping up a regular and constant stream of immigration adequate to the demand.' The *Natal Mercury*, in one article said: 'Coolie labour is the vitalising principle.' In another article in 1865, five years after the first batch of Indians arrived in Natal, the *Natal Mercury* advocated that the Indians should be encouraged to take up land. It said: 'We can see that private planters and land owners might find it remunerative to encourage small coolie growers to cultivate for themselves, by offering patches of leased or bought land and to crush their cane at their landlord's mill.' The first batch of Indians to arrive in Durban were greeted with a torchlight procession by the European citizens. Now these are mere facts of history, Mr. President, they can be proved. I have my references for all these things and he presents us with a report like this which he—I was going to say which he has the audacity to defend— defends and which tells us that a perusal of the evidence shows that the Indian came to South Africa as indentured labour against the wishes of the European inhabitants here. Let me give another illustration of the value of this report. Page 8, Paragraph 321: 'The commission regarding Cape Coloureds found that Coloureds should have their own township which should be separate from those of the Natives, and two leading members of the commission held that European, Native and Coloured townships should be separate from each other.' Could any possible meaning be attached to that, Mr. President, by the ordinary reader than that the commission, or at any rate, a minority of the commission recommended legislation of the kind that we have before us now? That is the context in which it is put. I have turned up Paragraph 236 of this report and it is just a minor inaccuracy that it is the wrong paragraph altogether. Paragraph 236 says: 'The Act provided for the appointment of an inspector of white labour; the inspector was required to keep a register, etc.' but I went to the trouble to look through the report until I found the relative paragraph. It is Paragraph 732(a), not Paragraph 236. 'The commission recommended that wherever ground is set aside for the establishment of a location or township for non-Europeans, that in such location or township set aside the Coloured people should be segregated from the Natives. In the footnote, in this connection Drs. Wilcox and de Villiers hold that when townships are established by local authorities the demarcation between European, Coloured and Native areas should be distinct.' Who would differ from that? That is simply in new cases and in cases where townships are established. What is the good of a commission of this kind? It disgusts me, Mr. President; I cannot say otherwise when I am given information of this kind. In this commission no evidence is taken from the Cape at all. There is no evidence from either side. Let me say that of the bodies which were invited to give evidence by this commission, these committees with the exception of the Institute of Race Relations, all of them represented the Europeans only. It was a packed set of witnesses to produce a packed report and in the whole Cape Province no evidence is produced, and on the basis of no evidence at all from the Cape Province they want to take away rights which the Cape Coloured people have had during our history, the Cape Coloured people who are now to be subjected to compulsory segregation. My, how they must hate the Minister! The curses are not loud but deep in the minds of the Coloured people as far as he is concerned and also his party. There has been no instance in our history such as the betrayal of the Cape Coloured people by the Nationalist Party. There is more to it than this, Mr. President. I know the Minister is going to be annoyed. I hope to make him feel thoroughly annoyed.

The Minister of the Interior: I think you flatter yourself.

Senator Dr. Brookes: But I do say that the Minister has double-crossed the Indian delegation about this Bill. He has told them that he is introducing a Bill which will treat everybody alike. He knows very well that the effect of this Bill is intended to increase the restrictions on Indians. One story is told in New Delhi, another story is told in Durban.

Even the little bit of window-dressing which puts the Indians with the Coloureds into one group so that you can say there is no differentiation against Indians, is offset by the creation of ethnic groups. When the Hon. Senator Viljoen talked about it he told us that the intention was quite clearly four groups, Europeans, Asiatics, Natives and Coloureds. He made no bones about it and he said that the object of the Bill was to hound these people out of the Cape Province. That is how he gets votes from Port Elizabeth. He told us so quite unashamedly. I ask you, Mr. President, what hope is there for South Africa in the international world with discreditable manoeuvres of this kind; how far have we fallen in the scale of the international world? It is no use bringing these cheap little arguments and cheap little victories before the standard of world opinion. There are grave moral questions involved, grave political questions involved. If the Hon. Minister is in any doubt as to the opinions of people on these benches, I hope I shall remove it. We object to this Bill in principle because we object to compulsory segregation in principle. We accept fully and frankly the fact that in general terms the people of South Africa are living and will continue to live their lives apart residentially. We believe this has been attained quite as much as it needs to be attained at the present time, and we are going to move a direct negative to this Bill. The Hon. Minister has asked us to believe a statement which is a complete fallacy, namely, that by separating people you promote friendly relationships. May I ask the Hon. Minister what his views on marriage are?

The Minister of the Interior: Certainly on mixed marriages, I am.

Senator Dr. Brookes: May I ask the Hon. Minister to look at the map of Europe. I am not talking about mixed marriages. I am talking about marriages. I ask the Hon. Minister if he thinks that a man's relations with his wife will improve by permanent separation. I ask the Hon. Minister to look at the map of Europe, at Switzerland where French and German-speaking people have lived together in amity with one short civil war in 600 years, and in France and Germany where the principle of apartheid has been consistently and thoroughly applied they have had three wars in the last 80 years, major wars into which they have dragged the whole world including ourselves. He is basing his views on a fallacy. It does not necessarily mean that because people are separated they are going to live more happily. There are certain objections which we have to this Bill which I want to point out—working, unfortunately, against time as all of us are. It is very difficult to get in all I want to say in the time I have been allotted to make these points. Our first objection to this Bill is that it aims ultimately at a state of rigidity. I note that it is not rigid in its present form, far from it, but it is aiming at rigidity. It is aiming at a state of affairs ultimately, as soon as the Minister can bring it about, where everything is fixed, where there are no exceptions. You cannot have life with no exceptions in a country like South Africa. We on these benches will never accept that position. There are exceptional cases and exceptional cases must be dealt with fairly, but we are concerned much more with the unfairness of this Bill. This is a racial Bill and it is a Bill in which one race is prosecutor and judge. The Minister has said that he does not intend to have any non-Europeans on his board. He need not have told us. We know that. This is a Bill in which the white man is to divide up the land between himself and the others and he is going to decide which part each shall have. I need not read more than a few lines to remind the House of one of the most famous stories about President Kruger. I read from Manfred Nathan's life. 'Two brothers had a dispute regarding a piece of land which had been left to them in undivided shares and they could not settle which portion each was to receive. They appealed to the President. He said to the elder brother: "You divide the land into two portions and let the younger brother have the first pick." ' Will the Minister do that? No, of course, he will not. He wants to divide it and to have the first pick too. We know what we are talking about on these benches. The people we represent have been subjected to compulsory segregation and we know what every honest member of this House will admit—hon. members who have been on the

Native Affairs Commission in this House will admit—that what you get for a Native location in an urban area is a bit of land which nobody else wants. Just what is left. They know that. They know that that is so all over the country. Do you suppose, Mr. President, that if there is any allocation of land between Europeans and Coloured in the Cape Peninsula, that the Coloured people would get Newlands or Kenilworth? The Hon. Minister knows they will not. He knows what happened in Durban when we tried to get land for Indians even for things like a technical college or a sports ground. I went to a lot of trouble to get a site for a school for Indians employed by the Municipality of Durban, and do you know what they offered me? Land, later on, when it was built up, which they were building up from the rubbish dumps of Durban. That is what they offered me to build a school on. This is the nature of this Bill: compulsory segregation administered by one race. And I do not trust the Hon. Minister to hold the scales equally between the races; I do not trust him in the least, to do so. All his administration of Indian affairs in the last two years has shown that in that respect he is partisan. He should not be the person who hounds on public opinion and benefits by it; he should be the person who holds the balance evenly between the represented and unrepresented people, and tries to handle the situation fairly, as Ministers of the Interior—including his own Prime Minister—did before him. Incidentally, referring to his own Prime Minister, will it be believed that this report only refers to the Cape Town Agreement as 'negotiations for repatriation having broken down'? Not a word about the Cape Town Agreement. This is the report to which the Hon. Minister asks me to accord respect because of the people who signed it. We object to this Bill because there has been no consultation of the people concerned. There has been absolutely no consultation with the Cape Coloured people. Their rights are being taken away over-night without consultation; without even investigation. I should be ashamed if I were the Hon. Minister, to be defending a Bill of this kind. I remember the days when the Hon. Minister stood for a liberal policy, when he said that nationalism and liberalism came to the same thing. I remember the Hon. Minister saying good things about the inclusion of the Coloured people, generally speaking, in the European community.

The Minister of the Interior: This is the same as in the 1946 Act.

Senator Dr. Brookes: We object to this Bill, Mr. President. We object to it because of the part which political considerations have played in it. Of course it is easy to get an excited public meeting worked up against Indians or Coloured people —a public meeting of Europeans. Anybody can do that; it is like shooting a sitting bird. But that is not statesmanship. That is politics of the worst and lowest kind. We want statesmanship in a country like South Africa. The Hon. Senator Viljoen can well boast of getting votes in Port Elizabeth as the Hon. Minister hopes to get votes in Durban. I do not want to be self-righteous, but thank heaven I am not that sort of politician; I should prefer to have another kind of profession. We object to this Bill because of the power which it gives to the Hon. Minister and to the Government generally, not only to the exclusion of Parliament in important respects, but to the complete exclusion of the law-courts of the country, so that the very Bar Council of the Bar of which the Hon. Minister is a member, even if it has not protested against this Bill, has protested against exactly the same principles in another Bill. The Bar of the country is upset. If the judges will allow—well, I had better not talk about the judges; the Hon. Minister, at any rate, does not seem to have much confidence in them— but the judges are cut out of practically every situation which this Bill provokes. And they have always been the protection of unrepresented groups in the past. But it is not only this, it is the lack of publicity. The Hon. Minister must report to Parliament the proceedings and the results of the recommendations of his Land Tenure Board to be appointed under the Bill, but there is no undertaking that the hearings of that board shall be public; that has gone. That is one of the main differences from the 1946 Act. There is no provision in this Bill for public hearings on the part of the commission.

The Minister of the Interior: This is exactly as in the 1946 Act.

THE GROUP AREAS ACT

Senator Dr. Brookes: Will the Hon. Minister deny that there have been public hearings in the past?

The Minister of the Interior: There was public hearing, and I said today that that would be the position today.

Senator Dr. Brookes: Does the Hon. Minister say that there will be public hearings in the future?

The Minister of the Interior: I have said that.

Senator Dr. Brookes: I thank the Hon. Minister, and I accept his word for that.

The Minister of the Interior: I have said that; just as in the past they will carry on in the same way, because the provision in law is the same.

Senator Dr. Brookes: I accept the Hon. Minister's word for that, but it would be as well to have it put explicitly into the Bill, because it is always the same with assurances of that kind that future Ministers are not bound by a previous Minister's assurances.

The Minister of the Interior: The Hon. Senator did not ask for an assurance on the 1946 Act.

Senator Dr. Brookes: I voted against the 1946 Act, Mr. President. I do not know what the Hon. Minister thinks he is gaining by taunting me about the 1946 Act, because I voted against it.

The Minister of the Interior: The Hon. Senator did not ask for this.

Senator Dr. Brookes: Yes. My time is limited, and I must pass on. I can hardly attack the Hon. Minister and plead with him at the same time—one has to pay one's price for attacks—but nevertheless I hope that he will consider the position of the Native population in this Bill. I have an amendment coming forward which will preserve for the Native population all protection given under the Land Act of 1946 and its amendments, and no further protection. It is a very reasonable thing to ask and I hope the Hon. Minister will accept that amendment. You can hardly segregate the Native people more than they are now. With regard to the Cape Coloured people, I have said what I have to say. There can hardly be a more disillusioned group of people in the world than the Cape Coloured

THE GROUP AREAS ACT

people at the present time. If this Bill is carried—as it probably will be, by one vote, again—all that we can do is to protest on every occasion against legislation of this kind. I would like to feel clean; I would like to feel that I am not associated with manoeuvres of this kind. I would like to feel that I was human —according to the old Cape and the old South African traditions—and above all I would like to feel that I was fair. And let me, in conclusion, Mr. President—I am not surprised that my hon. friend is glad I am going to conclude, I did not appeal for Indian votes as their dear fellow-comrade when they had the vote, and then turn against them when they had lost it. I am being consistent...

Hon. Senators: Hear, hear!

Senator Dr. Brookes: I want to conclude what I have to say by reading a letter from someone whose name, I think, will be revered on both sides of this House. I want to read a letter from Jan Hendrik Hofmeyr.

Hon. Senators: (Inaudible.)

Senator Dr. Brookes: So Hon. Senators are worried about Jan Hendrik Hofmeyr.[1] It is from 'Onze Jan' that I am going to read—Jan Hendrik Hofmeyr, Senior—though I would be very proud to read something from Jan Hendrik Hofmeyr, Junior. This is from 'Onze Jan' dated the 22 March 1909. Mr. Hofmeyr received a letter from the Coloured People's Vigilance Committee of Cape Town, expressing the undying gratitude of the whole of the Coloured people for his championship of the Coloured and Native franchise, and this is what he wrote:

> Avondrust, 22nd March, 1909, Gentlemen,—Allow me to thank you cordially for the kind letter you sent me on the 14th under the instructions of the Executive of the Coloured People's Vigilance Committee, and for the flattering terms in which you

[1] Jan Hendrik Hofmeyr Senior ('Onze Jan') was the founder of the Afrikaner Bond in the Cape Colony, a body which sought to further the interests of the Afrikaans-speaking people within the wider loyalty to the British Empire. The younger Jan Hendrik Hofmeyr was the very able lieutenant of General Smuts, more than once Acting Prime Minister of South Africa, and very sympathetic to the aspirations of the non-white groups in South Africa.

THE GROUP AREAS ACT

referred to the slight service which I tried to render to my Coloured fellow-countrymen. I, however, hardly deserve their particular thanks, for in saying a kindly word on their behalf I did not think of their interest exclusively, but quite as much of those of my white fellow-South Africans.

This is the true voice of South Africa, Mr. President. This is the true voice of the man who began South African politics as South African politics. This is the true voice of the people of South Africa as untainted by the continental importations and thoughts of the last twenty years. And he goes on to say this:

With a European population of only a million at the southern extremity of a continent occupied by some two hundred million, mostly barbarians and semi-barbarians, I cannot help feeling, whatever my own prejudices of race and colour may be, that the political and social security of South Africa would be none the worse for retaining the goodwill of the five million of Coloured and aboriginal inhabitants with whom we live interspersed, and for reconciling them with our political institutions. When the political union of all South Africa shall have been fully established, it would be a bad day for our new Commonwealth if, in addition to protecting our northern frontiers against the teeming millions of Darkest Africa, we had to be continually on our guard against a malcontent Coloured and Native population in our midst, outnumbering us by five or six to one.

That is what Jan Hendrik Hofmeyr said in 1909. That we stand by today. I stand, on these benches—I always have done and I still do—not simply as representing one section of the community, my own electorate—but as standing for the interests of South Africa as a whole, and I am convinced that to force legislation of this kind on the unrepresented racial minorities of South Africa, to ram it down their throats against their will and against the better judgment of half this Parliament, is going to bring about great dangers for the future—dangers which it is our duty to try to avert. I move: To delete the word 'now' and to add at the end of the Question the words 'this day six months'.

THE GROUP AREAS ACT

DOCUMENT 29B. FROM A SPEECH ON AN AMENDMENT TO THE GROUP AREAS ACT IN THE HOUSE OF ASSEMBLY BY MRS. HELEN SUZMAN, 23 FEBRUARY 1961.

Mrs. Suzman: Mr. Speaker, before commencing with my criticism of the Bill presently before the House, I want to tell the hon. member for Innesdal (Mr. J. A. Marais) that no amount of legislation introduced in this House will help people preserve their identity. That is something that individuals must look after for themselves. No Immorality Act, no Mixed Marriages Act and no Group Areas Act will preserve for people their own identity if they do not wish to preserve it for themselves. And that is the attitude of this party, that we do not wish to force integration on anybody, neither do we wish to force segregation. We wish to leave it to the normal traditional courses of this country. We will force neither segregation on the population of South Africa, nor will we force integration.

Before I get on to my main theme I want to say to the hon. member for Parow (Mr. Kotzé) that he last night made a passionate speech about the remarkable achievements in housing and in slum clearance on the part of this Government.

Mr. Van Der Walt: Ask the City of Johannesburg.

Mrs. Suzman: That had nothing whatever to do with Group Areas, and that is the point I am trying to make. You do not need a Group Areas Act to clear slums; there is a Slum Clearance Act under which one can quite readily clear slums; and one does not need a Group Areas Act to put up great housing schemes. That, also, has nothing whatever to do with the operation of the Group Areas Act. That is all I wish to say to that hon. member.

When the original Group Areas Act was passed in 1950, the then Prime Minister, Dr. Malan, declared that the enactment of the Group Areas law would mean a fresh start for South Africa because, he said, it heralded a new period. He made it clear at the time that the Government regarded—and it is quite clear that it still regards, the Group Areas as one of the most important of all apartheid measures. He stated:

> What we have in this Bill is apartheid. It is the essence of apartheid policy which is embodied in this Bill.

THE GROUP AREAS ACT

Now if this Bill for Group Areas and its trail of amending Acts is the essence of apartheid, one can only say that it has failed. I do not want to labour the point which has been made by other hon. members in this House, that this is the eleventh amending Bill that we have had to consider in Parliament since 1950 when the original measure was passed. None of these amending Bills has made the original Act any more practicable, and no amending Bill which the hon. the Deputy Minister will have to introduce in the future—and certainly he will have to introduce more amending Bills—will make it more practicable.

The hon. the Deputy Minister stated in his introductory speech that this Bill contained some important concessions. He also made it quite clear that no deviation from basic policy is intended by this Bill. It interested me to notice, when I read the Deputy Minister's speech in the Other Place—which, naturally, is practically identical to his speech here since he is introducing the same Bill—when I read that speech I noticed that he had omitted to issue this warning to the hon. Senators. Why, I wonder, did he find it necessary to warn this House that no deviation of policy was intended, but he did not find it necessary to warn the Upper House?

The Deputy Minister of the Interior: Did the hon. member read my reply to that debate?

Mrs. Suzman: Yes, I did, but I am talking of the hon. the Minister's introductory speech, and I am coming to the point the Minister is making now. It is possible that he found it necessary to issue this warning when he replied to the debate in the Other Place and when he introduced the Bill here because he was rather startled at the laudatory notices which his initial introductory speech had received in the so-called Opposition Press. One leading newspaper, the *Star*, actually went so far in an article on the 9th, after the hon. the Deputy Minister introduced the Bill in the Upper House, the *Star* went so far as to say that the amendments to the Group Areas Act were 'a message to the Indians of South Africa that the Nationalist Government accept them and are prepared to accommodate them'. They said 'It is a new phase, almost a

THE GROUP AREAS ACT

reversal of Nationalist policy'. Now it is clear to me that having read that laudatory remark the hon. the Minister was at pains to tell everybody, perhaps his own supporters more particularly, that no new policy was intended and that this was no reversal of Nationalist policy. I want to tell the Deputy Minister that to those of us who have made a study of the Bill, he need not have been at such pains because it is obvious that there is indeed no basic change in policy in this Bill.

The Deputy Minister of the Interior: I am in full agreement with you.

Mrs. Suzman: I want to follow on the careful analysis of this Bill which was made by the hon. member for East London (North) (Mr. van Ryneveld) last night, and I want to start with the most important clause, Clause 12, which the Minister said contained an important concession—I use his own words—and will make it possible for trading areas to be proclaimed for racial groups without attaching thereto the implication coupled with the proclamation of group areas. It will also, he said, have the advantage of terminating occupation for residential purposes without depriving the person concerned of his means of earning a livelihood. Now on the face of it this seems an important concession, but I am afraid that on closer examination of the clause it is robbed of its rosy hue. Firstly, I cannot see how this clause resolves the difficulty in areas already proclaimed as group area, unless the Minister is prepared to de-proclaim these areas. Will the Deputy Minister tell us in his reply whether it is his intention to de-proclaim any areas?

The Deputy Minister of the Interior: No.

Mrs. Suzman: Well, he mentioned in his speech yesterday that this would solve the problem in metropolitan areas like Johannesburg. Well, it appears that in those parts of Johannesburg, Klerksdorp, Pretoria, Durban and Pietermaritzburg, where group areas have already been proclaimed, there will indeed be no concessions made whatever, so this already considerably waters down this important concession.

An Hon. Member: Now that is feminine logic.

Mrs. Suzman: Feminine logic is very accurate sometimes, if

THE GROUP AREAS ACT

only the Minister would listen to it occasionally. As far as the rest of the clause is concerned, I have some other bits of feminine logic to offer to the Minister and perhaps he can tell me whether it is correct or not. That is that this clause extends only to defined areas, which are very limited in scope, and indeed may even on certain other interpretations further limit the existing rights of Indians in those areas. In other words, previously Indians who occupied property in so-called defined areas could do so for any purpose whatsoever providing they have occupied those premises prior to 31 March 1951. Now, under the new Section 16*bis*, if the Governor-General proclaims that the premises previously occupied by Indians for residential purposes should now be suitable only for industrial purposes, they will have to leave both their homes and their businesses, even though the area has not yet been declared a group area. Is that a correct interpretation? So, it could really mean further restrictions.

Thirdly, there is another difficulty I have in construing this clause as making any important concession at all, and that is how it affects Indians in rural areas. Indians who trade in rural areas which are not controlled by any local authority. It seems to make the tenure of such Indians even more precarious. Because whereas previously they could continue in occupation even if they did not have written leases, it now seems to me that a further amendment has been introduced which does away with the validity of verbal leases and makes it necessary for these Indians now to have written leases if they are to continue to enjoy these privileges. That is the amendment to Section 17.

Then Clause 14 is another important one. The Minister told us that this clause was introduced to assist disqualified mortgagees who have difficulty in taking over properties in areas for which they were not qualified. Well, he has helped them in one regard, but he has imposed certain other restrictions, because it now appears that the property has to be alienated within a certain period of time. Now the Minister could always give a permit anyway, even before Clause 14 was introduced. Now he makes it possible for himself to give a permit with restrictions, which previously he could not do, and naturally the precious principle of apartheid and of the Group Areas Act would be violated if a disqualified mortgagee was allowed to take over a property for an indefinite period of time. So this, too, is an additional restriction. In any case, as far as the issue of permits is concerned, I want to say that to us this business of governing by permit is a very bad principle indeed. You make overriding restrictions and then release people by issuing permits. You apply job reservation, but with exemptions. The whole position becomes impracticable. We are completely against the idea of government by permit because it is a bad principle. In any case, what the Minister is permitted to do is one thing, and what he is prepared to do is another thing. What the Group Areas Board is permitted to do is one thing, and what it is prepared to do is another thing. The entire history of the administration of the Group Areas Act has shown that these officials are not prepared to make the necessary concessions which will bring any real relief to the hardships suffered. I was horrified to read only a year or so ago that the Chairman of the Group Areas Board actually considered that one of the duties of the Board was to seek to curtail the number of Indian traders on the ground that Indians at present have too large a share of trade. So permits do not help if the basic policy goes against the wishes of the people who are being governed by permits.

The other astonishing condition the Minister laid down in Clause 14(b) is that a person who acquires a permit shall carry out any alterations or erect such structures on the property as the Minister may deem to be necessary. That to me is an astonishing inroad into the normal rights of a property owner. Finally, this business that the mortgagee must dispose of the property within a limited time is not of much help if the person is thereby forced to dispose of his property in a falling market.

Clause 16 is the other really important clause, and it amends Section 20. This enables the Minister to do piecemeal what he formerly had to do *in toto*. It assists him now in doing slowly what he formerly had to do in one job. He stated: 'I am convinced that the changes proposed in Clause 20 will be

THE GROUP AREAS ACT

welcomed by all right-minded people.' I do not know who the Minister considers to be right-minded people, but these changes are certainly not welcomed by us. He said that this procedure was in accordance with the assurances given by the Minister and by himself that no person who cannot be provided with alternative accommodation will be uprooted. That is a good principle, but then I do not want to uproot any people at all. That is the difference between the Minister and us. The Minister said this was in accordance with his assurances, but I wonder whether it is also not in accordance with the Supreme Court decision in the Natal Supreme Court in the case of Lockat v. the Minister of the Interior, where the Minister found he was not able to enforce the Group Areas Act over a large area simply because it was shown that the persons who were about to be displaced could not be provided with alternative accommodation. Perhaps that is one of the main reasons why this piecemeal clause has been introduced.

Now, I have two big objections to this amendment. The first is that it lays itself open to the grossest abuse. I do not believe that it is the correct principle of procedure to allow officials to single out individuals who may stay in a certain place and others who may have to move. Secondly, there is another limiting factor, namely that the notice period for the removal of people has now been cut down to three months. Under the existing Act it could be a seven-year period, and now it is one year, but after the first year it is three months, so that people live with an ever-constant Sword of Damocles hanging over their heads, not knowing when the sword will fall and they will be given three months' notice after the first year in which to move to other areas, and this is grossly inequitable.

Clause 23 provides for the repeal of the old Section 31 and replaces it with a new one. This does two things. The first is an amendment which is introduced simply because it was found that the existing provision was redundant, i.e. the application for trading licences, because the Board could not refuse to give a certificate to the person who was entitled to occupy the premises, and if he was not entitled to occupy the premises he could be ejected even if he had the trading licence. So clearly this was a redundant provision and the Minister has done away with it. The fact that it has been removed will make very little difference, except that some unnecessary inconvenience in applying for trading licences no longer has to be gone through. Unfortunately in removing this one restriction the Minister has filled the gap by another restriction, which was perhaps also brought on by another Supreme Court case. This Government constantly has to come back to the House to plug loopholes in the original Act which people have found in normal life, and the courts have ruled against the Government. This case was heard in the Cape Supreme Court. . . .

The Deputy Minister of the Interior: Is this the first Government that ever did so?

Mrs. Suzman: No, but this Government really gets the Oscar. Of course this is not the first Government which ever did it, but it is the first to do it so often. The Government holds the Oscar for plugging loopholes in Acts, and if they will take a little advice from this side of the House, these Acts would not be passed in the first place, and that would save a great deal of time and money in litigation. The latest loophole that is being plugged now is the one where an Indian could put in an agent and use premises in an area which has been proclaimed for another group. Now this loophole is plugged so that an Indian cannot even have a warehouse in a proclaimed area, and that is carrying things too far.

That completes my detailed criticism of the Bill. I simply want to say that our policy is quite clear. We will continue to press for the repeal of the Group Areas Act. We are completely against the compulsory removal of people and while we are quite agreed that provision might be made for people to live among their own people, we are equally agreed that provision could and should be made to allow people to live in mixed groups if they prefer to do that. We do not want to force integration or segregation on the people of South Africa. Finally, I want to say that the Minister of the Interior, when one of these amending Bills was introduced, said that the object envisaged could not be attained 'without difficulty, inconvenience and sacrifice'. Well, there has indeed been difficulty, inconvenience and sacrifice, but unfortunately the gross disproportion of it fell on one side of the colour line. A grossly disproportionate burden of sacrifice has been placed on the non-Whites. What this Act means is the mass uprooting of settled communities. It has also entailed the disruption of commercial life. Even temporary postponement which was permitted under the permit system does not help, because material damages are nevertheless suffered in the interim by virtue of the very uncertainty of the lives of the people under the permit system. You have restriction of credit, curtailment of overdraft facilities, the calling up of bonds, a reduction in the volume of trade and deterioration in the value of property. These are all material discomforts, most of which are suffered by the non-Whites. Worst of all are the strains and tensions that are engendered by the uncertainty. The most crushing anxieties are introduced into the lives of law-abiding citizens who know that at any time in future the permits under which they carry on business may be withdrawn. No amount of amending legislation can make the Group Areas Act an equitable measure because its very nature is discriminatory and it therefore cannot be administered with equity. It is a rankly discriminatory measure. The Deputy Minister called this Bill another example of the desire to administer the Group Areas Act with equity and reason, but I say it is just another example of what Dr. Johnson called 'the triumph of hope over experience'.

* * *

We may add the following article, *Group Areas Anniversary*, by Brian Barrow, printed in the *Cape Times*, Cape Town, on 26 November 1966:

> Four years ago this week an elderly Coloured couple were ordered under the Group Areas Act to leave their 150-year-old family home in Newlands. The offer of a 'nice new home' did much to lessen the shock of removal. But what actually happened to them? Here is an investigation into the lives they led before their removal and what life has meant to them since.
>
> Group Areas is not really apartheid: it is merely separate development. And separate development is not really so bad; it

is the best possible thing for everyone concerned. 'They', that is, the people who are mostly affected by it, are not considered inferior, but only different. Removal does not bring hardship or suffering; rather the opposite; it gives 'them' a new chance in life. So in the long run, you see, everything will be for the best. Mark my words, soon the day will come when no-one will even think about it.

This is the kind of facesaving rationalisation of *apartheid* that seems to be gaining currency these days, the sort of thinking that many people in high and powerful places are trading as the truth; and if the truth is what you *want* to see or think then in all fairness it must be conceded that, to them, it *is* the truth.

But what of Mr. and Mrs. Janey? To them the truth happens to be something rather different. It certainly is not what they *want* to see or think; nor is it something that can be hidden behind euphemism. To them the truth is something real and inescapable—a now arid and empty life moving to its rather soulless end after a shattering blow struck in the name of the Group Areas Act.

These people in high and powerful places might even think of asking: But who on earth are Mr. and Mrs. Janey? They are not in the telephone directory! In any case, it is no longer Group Areas; it is the Department of Community Development.

In fact, Janey is not their real name, which is being withheld at their own request. But their first names are Christine and Seyster; and these are real. Today they would be living out their lives in contented obscurity if it wasn't for two things: first, an act of God—the colour of their skins; second, an Act of Parliament—Group Areas.

Mrs. Janey's family lived in a small cottage in Newlands for more than 150 years. Her mother was born in it and so was she. She continued to live in it after her marriage to Seyster 47 years ago. She was one of eight children, all of them brought up within the bosom of the church and a strict but happy home.

Her elder brother who is still alive—in Kimberley—was the manservant of Cecil Rhodes. He was at Rhodes' death-bed, cooling the empire-builder's last hours with a large ostrich feather fan. As a young woman she and her friends used to collect wood on the slopes of Newlands Ravine and it was there that she met Smuts on several occasions. 'He got to know us and often stopped to talk with us, always advising us to work hard.'

And this the whole family did. The sons soon went to work and got married. Most of the daughters got married too. Christine stayed at home to take care of her ageing parents in the same little cottage where eventually both parents died. She and her husband then took it over to make it a home for their children and for themselves when they grew old.

It was still their home exactly four years ago this week. She was then 70, he 69. He worked as a liftman in Cape Town earning R12 a week. They knew many people. They felt safe and happy in the security of a large circle of relatives and friends. The prospect of old age held no fears for them.

'You see, gentlemen, we were lucky, we had everything we could wish for,' Mrs. Janey says. 'It was not a large home but after those many years and events it had become a very intimate part of our lives. Yes, we loved it; it was our world, you might say. Everything was close by—shops, trains and buses not far away, our own telephone and only 10 minutes' walk to St. Paul's church. And we had friends all round us. Most of our neighbours were white and we lived in the greatest harmony among them. Another near neighbour was the State President but, of course, we did not know him. Yes, we were not far from Westbrook. We had a lovely garden, gentlemen, full of shrubs and flowers in the front and the back; japonicas, hydrangeas, vine, loquats, guavas, peaches, roses and pomegranates, all planted by ourselves.

'Friends used to come and go at all times and we never had any trouble with our European neighbours. We never borrowed or interfered or did anything like that. We were always taught rather to go without than to borrow. But we had many friends and wonderful parties at night with coloured lights and lanterns hanging in the fruit trees. Somehow there was no feeling of time. The days and the weeks just flew by but we never seemed to grow any older.'

Christine Janey could reminisce for hours about the days in the Newlands cottage, a place that was so meaningful to her that it became almost an extension of her own being. They did not own it, but spent all their savings maintaining it. Seyster did all the patching, plastering and painting. He installed electricity and made other improvements which cost him in all R200. She did the gardening and kept house. There was not much furniture, but what they had was simple except for a huge four-poster double bed, made of wrought iron and with big brass knobs on. The rent was R6 a month.

'The joy of it was that we were free. Day or night we came and went as we pleased. No one would have dreamed of interfering with us. We knew every face and almost every flower in the neighbourhood.'

Then suddenly, four years ago this week, that life of theirs in Newlands ended; not by death, war or disaster, but by a knock at the front door. It was a man from the Group Areas office. He had certain information for them. He told them what it was, and they stared at him in anguished disbelief, overwhelmed and speechless.

The Group Areas man came again and they prayed and begged and pleaded. But it was no use. 'I am only the man they send to tell you,' was his reply. 'I can do nothing.' Nor could anyone else do anything because there was nothing anyone could do. This was the law.

And today Mr. and Mrs. Janey are in Bonteheuwel. I found their small, dust-blown house after some difficulty. The first thing I saw were two frightened old faces at the window and their hesitancy to open the front door was the first hint that fear and isolation had become the essence of their lives, fear of practically everything; their neighbours, the people who pass by in the street, fear of venturing out of the two small rooms that now confine them, fear of their loneliness, fear of losing their last hold on respectability, fear of looking too far into the future or even back into the past, even fear of nothing.

And the next strongest emotion is, ironically, gratitude; gratitude for having a roof over their heads and simply being able to live.

This is what two old people have been reduced to in four years. How did it happen? Mrs. Janey told their story.

The Group Areas people promised them a 'nice new home', but the house they moved into at Bonteheuwel was surrounded by sand. It came up to the front doorstep and started again when they opened the kitchen door onto the back yard. The floors were of cement and walls were whitewashed brick. There was a sitting-room, a bedroom, a kitchen and a bathroom without a bath. There were no interleading doors. There was no room for all the furniture, or for the piano they had had at Newlands. The bathroom had no ceiling. Wind and dust blew in from under the eaves. Worst of all there was no communication. There was no telephone and suddenly there were no friends or familiar faces. The shops were far away and there was no church. There were no trees or flowers, but only great expanses of emptiness between rows of uniformly built hutments. There was in fact nothing left of the life that they had been accustomed to.

There was not even a doctor and Seyster's health had been broken completely by the shock of their removal. He had to give up his job and their income was reduced to the R2 a month they received as a dual pension. The friendly and peaceful atmosphere in which they had once thrived was gone. Most of the people who lived in the neighbourhood were roisterous. Scores of skollies walked the streets which were dangerous by day and places of terror by night.

'We have lost all touch with the world we knew,' said Mrs. Janey. 'Our only pleasure is the wireless and visiting the grave of our daughter in Maitland where we sing hymns and pray together. Many a night and day we just sit and look at each other. I have not been out of here for two years, not even to Cape Town. I dare not. We're afraid of having to come home in the dark. We have had one burglary already, gentlemen. We have nothing to do with our neighbours, we dare not. If we did we'd lose the last little independence we have and that we must hang on to at all costs.

'Somehow everything seems to have been shattered. We have lost touch with all our old friends. Some of them have moved away; others have promised to come and see us, but they can't find us in this place. It all looks the same. They don't know where we are. They don't know how to get here, and they're also afraid of the skollies. I'm afraid to go out. My grandchildren come and see us sometimes and that we always look forward to. They want me to go and see 'The Sound of Music' in Athlone. But for three weeks I've not been able to make up my mind to go. That's when the skollies wait for you, gentlemen, they wait for you to come out of the bio.

'If you knew what we had had before you would realise what we go through now, gentlemen. I long for trees and green grass. But look out there. It is all sand and wind and dead bush. Nothing will grow here. We brought as many plants as we could from our home, but everything died. Only a rose tree survived and it got its first flower the other day, the very first; and you know, one of these ruffians walking past just tore it out. I saw him do it. But what could I say. If I'd opened my mouth we would have been for it.'

In the four years they have been there three murders have been committed in broad daylight within a stone's throw of their house. Every day they wait alone. Every night they are terrified. Their only companions are a cat, a dog and a rooster whose unearthly crowing seems to spell out the desolation of their lives.

'The cat and dog sleep with us in the house, we feel safer when they do,' Mrs. Janey said. 'But we are still grateful. Things could be very much worse. At least we have a roof over our heads and ... well, we are old and we cannot have everything. Time goes on and as you wait to die the world changes.'

Yes, time does go on and the world does change. When we left the Janeys we went to see what had happened to the cottage they once lived in in Newlands. It wasn't there. It had been bulldozed out of existence. One of the loquat trees was all that remained on a stretch of steam-rolled rubble. Cement mixers were at work and the air was full of the blasphemous clatter of pneumatic hammers. Obviously the area must have been zoned for flats. The new block will probably be ready in about six months time. It promises to be a rich, spacious, gleaming structure of glass, facebrick and steel, a splendid example of community development; another euphemism, this time in concrete.

The small Newlands cottage has been pounded to dust beneath it. Operation Group Areas is nearly complete. The wound is being sewn up and will now begin to heal. Before long there will be no trace of it. No one will even remember it. No one will even think about it any more.

And those people in high and powerful places will be able to say with their own kind of logic: 'But what are you talking about. Such things never happened in South Africa. Just go along to Newlands and see for yourself.'

PART IX
Apartheid in Practice—Social Consequences

MARRIAGE AND IMMORALITY LAWS

The following extracts are taken from Gwendolen M. Carter's book, *The Politics of Inequality* (Thames and Hudson, 1958). To save quoting a multiplicity of Statutes we have turned to Gwendolen Carter's book, which, though critical of the doctrines of apartheid, is extremely reliable in its facts.

DOCUMENT 30. FROM *The Politics of Inequality*, BY GWENDOLEN M. CARTER, 1958.

The Prohibition of Mixed Marriages Act, 1949

One of the earliest of the Nationalist measures struck at the marriages still taking place infrequently between Europeans and non-Europeans, that is, chiefly, the Coloured. These marriages could still be solemnized in the Cape and Natal, though no machinery for so doing existed in the Transvaal. Between 1943 and 1946, less than 100 mixed marriages a year were consummated in the Union, the figures running 92, 99, 92 and 77 for the respective years. European marriages in 1945 and 1946, in contrast, amounted to 24,071 and 28,308, so the problem was a small if irritating one.

Miscegenation, out of which the Cape Coloured arose originally, has long been socially unacceptable in South Africa. As far back as 1685, Europeans were forbidden by law to marry freed slaves of full colour, though marriages with half-breeds were allowed. In 1927, the Hertzog Nationalist-Labour coalition passed an Immorality Act penalizing extra-marital relations between Europeans and Africans. The Prohibition of Mixed Marriages Act, 1949, and an amended

Immorality Act passed the following year, extended these provisions to the relations between Europeans and Coloured.

The difficulty here was not just of colour, or even of shade. Because the Coloured are a very mixed people, no satisfactory definition has been reached by which to differentiate them. In the Liquor Act of 1927, for example, a Coloured was defined as one who is neither a European, an Asiatic nor a Native. Habitual association with an acceptance as Coloured was subsequently used as a distinguishing feature for the Population Register. The possibility, and indeed the prevalence, of light-skinned Coloured 'passing' as white, coupled with the fact that some of the oldest and most distinguished Afrikaner families in the Cape have some admixture of coloured blood, made the issue both sensitive and, to the Nationalists, of pressing importance.

As the parliamentary debate made clear, the Nationalists were not concerned so much with race purity in the biological sense as with strengthening the barriers against increasing infiltration by the Coloured. The special urgency of the problem, they emphasized, arose from the process of industrialization and consequent urbanization which inevitably brought Europeans and non-Europeans into closer contact both in their places of employment and their dwelling areas. The characteristic theme of self-preservation of the European race appears throughout the Nationalist speeches on the bill.

By introducing this particular measure before either the Immorality Amendment Bill or the Population Registration Bill, and also by presenting it in rather loose and careless wording, the Nationalists provided the United Party with an opportunity of which the latter took full advantage. United Party members pounced on the problems of defining a Coloured; the criteria to be used by marriage officers, whom the law made responsible for refusing to solemnize such marriages; the procedure for voiding a marriage; the consequences for the children; and the distasteful use of informants. So penetrating were they that Dr. T. E. Dönges was forced to accept a wide range of clarifications and improvements in the statute. For these the United Party smugly claimed so much credit that

APARTHEID IN PRACTICE—SOCIAL CONSEQUENCES

C. R. Swart finally countered with the remark that it was 'no disgrace' if the Opposition showed 'some intelligence' and assisted the Government in placing 'something better' in the bill.

The atmosphere in this debate was much friendlier than in most discussions of apartheid measures, and no divisions were called in either the committee or report stages. But these facts hardly conceal the underlying dilemma which the United Party faced over the measure. Smuts had immediately expressed the United Party's opposition to mixed marriages, but strongly stated that this type of 'prohibiting legislation' did not provide 'a practical solution'. On the contrary, the elimination of mixed marriages was a matter for public opinion and race pride, he declared, voicing the typically empirical approach of the United Party to race relations. Others reinforced the point that this was no matter for law as in the comment that:

> This was a contest between the Minister of the Interior and the Creator. He is trying to lay down a definite line where no definite line can be drawn.

A more basic approach to the problem, which several United Party members voiced, would be to eliminate the advantages of 'passing' by improving the status of the Coloured and to strengthen the white strain by immigration (to which a Nationalist backbencher, J. H. Abraham, objected characteristically that the hearts of these immigrants would be corrupted on arrival by the liberals).

Sharp divergencies thus existed, in fact, between Nationalists and the United Party over whether the measure should be passed at all. In the background lay the contrasting approaches of their respective churches. Dönges declared the three Dutch Reformed Churches had asked for the measure. Mrs. Ballinger, senior among the Natives' representatives, pointed out, on the other side, that neither the Anglican nor the Roman Catholic Church would recognize the State's right to interfere with the sacrament of marriage. Subsequently the South African Anglican Synod protested the measure for this reason.

Yet the United Party was not willing to push its dislike of the character of the legislation to the point where it opposed the measure as such. A United Party member accused the Government of deliberately attempting to embarrass his party with the legislation; a Nationalist backbencher, A. Steyn, underlined the point in saying:

> The party over there dare not go to the country and say that because here and there a person is not purely white or coloured, he may stand in the way of the whole people. You cannot do it. It is your duty to side with this party. The people will call you to account.

Moreover, Dönges could point constantly to the example of the United States to justify incorporating such provisions in legislation (e.g. 30 American states with similar laws; 15 with a marriage officer to administer them).

Also, the press gave the United Party little incentive to fight. The *Natal Witness* said the bill was 'realistic', asserting that public opinion was not 'a sufficient safeguard'. The *Natal Daily News* called the measure 'horrible' but did not elaborate. The Convention of Coloured Organizations opposed it as useless. On the whole there was not much interest in the measure.

The limited application of the law did not escape comment. One of the Nationalist experts on colour questions, W. A. Maree, was joined by Labour's N. G. Eaton in asking why the provisions of the bill were not extended more widely to ban marriages between the three non-European groups: Africans, Coloured and Asiatics. Dönges declared this was under consideration, though no action has ensued. In fact, the Mixed Marriages Act falls into the category of European protective legislation. Perhaps even more truly, however, its purpose was expressed by one of the Nationalists, Dr. J. H. Steyn, who felt the measure was neither practical nor necessary, but saw its worth as 'a documentation' of the South African way of life. Practical or not, it was an assertion of the special position of the white race.

Few prosecutions have taken place under the Mixed Marriages Act. No one obviously Coloured would attempt, henceforth, to marry someone obviously European. Most of the cases have come before the courts through informers and commonly the partners have been genuinely unaware that they fell within the purview of the Act.

One of the most talked of mixed marriages in recent times, that of Seretse Khama (titular chief of the Bamangwato tribe of Bechuanaland) to an Englishwoman, took place about the same time as the Mixed Marriages Bill was proceeding through Parliament. The tribe's decision to accept Seretse as chief despite his marriage touched the Protectorate's nearest neighbours, South Africa and Rhodesia, on a sensitive spot. The *Star* commented, on 27 June 1949, that if the British Government approved the tribe's decision, it would scandalize many whites in South Africa, whereas rejection might 'irretrievably' offend the Bantu; its own view, expressed next day, was to leave the situation to itself. *Die Burger* and *Die Transvaler* strongly disapproved the marriage, and the Dutch Reformed Church passed a resolution that Seretse should not be recognized as chief. *Die Vaderland* called on the British Government 'to honour the principle of apartheid'.

The British Government's decision, early in 1950, to withhold recognition from Seretse Khama for five years met enthusiastic Nationalist press reactions. *Die Transvaler* declared, on 10th March, that Britain had given in to the demands of apartheid and two days earlier had commented with satisfaction that 'the time for expediency in colonial politics had passed'. *Die Vaderland* wondered why the ban was only for five years. *Die Burger* was more basic in its approach, noting that while 99 out of 100 whites in Africa would approve, an equal percentage in Britain would disapprove, indicating the serious gulf over racial problems between the British at home and white settlers in Africa.

Yet the English language press was far from sure that the British decision was wise or justified. The *Cape Argus*, it is true, felt it to be the wisest thing to do in unusual and difficult circumstances. The *Star*'s impression of the decision, however, was that it was 'unmitigatedly bad', while the *Cape Times* and *Daily Despatch* could not see any justification for it. The *Friend* declared it might be 'a pyrrhic victory for Dr. Malan', but felt the British would not depart from paths of justice and fair dealing. The *Forum*, a liberal monthly, thought the decision would do much harm to White-Black relations. If South African opinion was a factor in the British decision, it was not that of the Opposition press.

As for the non-Europeans, the one formal protest was that of the South African Indian Congress made directly to Prime Minister Attlee. For the others, the *Bantu World* wrote sadly that the Seretse issue had been 'confused by politics and emotion'.

Amendment to the Immorality Act of 1927, 1950

The companion legislation to the Mixed Marriages Act was the amendment to extend to the Coloured the provisions of the Immorality Act of 1927 (Act No. 5, 1927) or, as its full title read, the Act to prohibit illicit carnal intercourse between Europeans and Natives and other acts in relation thereto. The purpose of the 1950 legislation, in fact, was not to check immorality as such but, as Dr. Dönges expressed it, 'to try to preserve some sort of apartheid in what one may call prostitution'; in other words, to prevent further admixture of European and Coloured blood.

The United Party was somewhat handicapped in opposing the amendment to the Immorality Act by the fact that it had agreed to the early measure and that Smuts had said in the debate on the Mixed Marriages Bill that illicit relations between Europeans and Coloured were the real evil. None the less, they reiterated justifiably many of the same arguments they had used in debating the Mixed Marriages Bill, notably the difficulty of differentiating Europeans from Coloured in certain cases. In an amendment which condemned miscegenation but opposed the measure, Colin Steyn, leader of the United Party in the Orange Free State, argued, on 1 March, 1950, that white civilization had maintained itself for 300 years without this prohibition, that the evil was on a small scale and the measure unworkable. He declared that the bill cast a slur on the Coloured and would create ill feeling between them and the Europeans.

APARTHEID IN PRACTICE—SOCIAL CONSEQUENCES

The United Party was on particularly firm ground when it pointed out that if the bill was to be introduced at all, it should include prohibitions against illicit intercourse between all racial groups. P. A. Botha, Nationalist Secretary in the Cape, agreed that miscegenation between Coloured and Native should also be penalized so that the Coloured might gradually develop a 'sense of nationhood'. Mrs. Ballinger went to the root of that particular problem, however, when she pointed out that prostitution was an inevitable result of African migratory labour, with its disastrous effect on the African family unit. Other points in the legislation which the United Party criticized were placing the onus of proving innocence on the accused, the power the measure gave to the police to enter and search private premises, and punishment by imprisonment rather than fines.

United Party opposition to the measure, in which it was joined tacitly but not actively by the Labour Party, proved unavailing, however, as the second reading passed by 66 to 55. Thereafter the measure secured virtual unanimity. The committee stage was remarkable for its harmony, the Minister of the Interior accepting, on 28th March, a United Party amendment that it would be sufficient defence if the accused had 'reasonable cause' to believe he was a person of the same race. The report stage passed unopposed, and the third reading without a vote.

Part of the reason for the rapid petering out of the United Party attack was that the Nationalists were not slow to point out inconsistencies in the United Party position as well as to engage in their customary frontal attacks. If the number of instances was small, they asked, how could the enforcement problem be large? If the measure was not necessary, why lighten the penalty? If, as the United Party felt, foreign sailors were to blame in most instances, how could public opinion help to prevent this? S. M. Loubser, a Nationalist backbencher, added in his customary vehement way that others than sailors responsible for miscegenation were the Communist Party, which accepted no line of demarcation between European and non-European, and liberals 'attending

APARTHEID IN PRACTICE—SOCIAL CONSEQUENCES

dances' and associating 'as equals' with the Coloured. Europeans in South Africa would have to work out their own salvation, he asserted, for world opinion believed in equality.

The Nationalists were not hesitant to accuse the United Party of favouring the Coloured to gain their votes. Another argument was that under the influence of its liberals the United Party was no longer the champion of 'pure blood' and was prepared to let things slide until the white race perished. F. W. Waring, in reply, charged that the measure was a cheap political stunt so the Nationalists could go to the *platteland* and say the United Party favoured miscegenation. In fact, as on so many other occasions, the United Party was outmanoeuvred, partly because it had no answer to the problem of miscegenation except educating public opinion, partly because the Nationalists exploited so well their advantage in having a more clear-cut, simpler but not necessarily more valid approach to the problem.

A few prosecutions have taken place under the amendment to the Immorality Act, notably in instances where European and Coloured, though not married, have been living together over a period of time. In these instances, the family was broken up, and the customary penalty of three months in jail imposed. Whether the result justified the personal hardships involved depends upon the point of view. It has, moreover, been noted in Parliament and the press that, under the present act, Coloured or African females have been found guilty and sentenced, while their European male partners have, in a separate trial, been acquitted.

PETTY APARTHEID

The following account of an exchange between Mrs. Helen Suzman and the Minister of Community Development is taken from the Hansard of 2 June 1965. It illustrates as well as any document can do the kind of problems which arise in South Africa under this particular head.

The summary of 'Petty apartheid' in 1965 which follows is taken from the *Cape Times* of 15 October 1965.

APARTHEID IN PRACTICE—SOCIAL CONSEQUENCES

DOCUMENT 31A. DEBATE BETWEEN MRS. HELEN SUZMAN AND THE MINISTER OF COMMUNITY DEVELOPMENT, 2 JUNE 1965.

Mrs. Suzman: The tradition in Cape Town was to have mixed entertainments. What I want to ask the hon. Minister is whether he has decided on what the criteria are, because it will be of great assistance to the entire country if one knew what the criteria are. It started off by not allowing mixed audiences; then one could have mixed audiences as long as there were separate amenities within the hall itself: then one could only have mixed audiences if facilities were not available in the areas set aside for the different races themselves; then one could only have these mixed entertainments if the particular event could not be repeated; then one could only have them providing it was only a non-White orchestra with a non-White choir, not a White audience and mixed group of performers on the stage. So we would like to know what the criteria are. You have this absurd nonsense, that the 'Messiah' for instance in Johannesburg recently was interfered with. Let me tell the hon. member for Vereeniging that it has been traditional that the 'Messiah' should be performed in Johannesburg with an African choir, with a White orchestra and a White conductor. Indeed so traditional has it been that the Government's own political organ *Bantu* came out with a triumphant article 'Messiah choir has great success'. It devoted two pages to pictures of the Black choir, and parts of the White orchestra are shown. That was the traditional thing and we are proudly told that this is one of the highest standards of musical entertainment ever presented in Johannesburg. But now this cannot be allowed. Now this is forbidden, because now it is no longer tradition, because the hon. the Minister and the member for Vereeniging have discovered that it is not traditional to allow a Black choir to sing in front of a White audience with a White orchestra and a White conductor. So they have to have a Black conductor and they were allowed a White organist instead of an orchestra. The nonsense of all this goes beyond words, it surpasses belief. Nobody knows where we are getting to in this country with this complete nonsense. (Interjections.) Mr. Chairman, may I have your protection against the interruptions by the hon. member for Vereeniging? I did not say one word when he was uttering his nonsense. Why can he not keep quiet for a few minutes?

The hon. Minister does not bother to give us statistics any more. I have asked him on two occasions to tell us about the number of permits that have been applied for, how many were refused and how many granted? The hon. Minister says it is too much work for his Department to assemble these statistical details. I might say that his colleagues, other Ministers in charge of this nonsense, the Minister of Planning and the Minister of Bantu Administration were able to give us statistics. This hon. Minister is not able to. I put it to him that the reason is that he is being swamped by applications for permits, so that he does not know whether he is coming or going. His Department does not even bother to tell people when they apply for permits that they do not need to apply for permits in certain cases. For instance, as I understand it, the legal position is that only public entertainments *per se* in fact are affected by Proclamation R.26.[1] But people are so nervous of breaking the law that they come along to the Minister and apply for permits for private functions, such as weddings, which do not fall under 'public entertainment' at all. But the Minister's Department does not even bother to tell people that they need not apply. They keep them hanging around and waiting, and in some cases they were actually refused permits. I would like a direct answer from the hon. the Minister to this question: Is it correct, legally, that permits are in fact not required for private functions? In other words, for a wedding, which is not a public entertainment, which is by invitation only? Are permits required or not required in terms of Proclamation R.26? Because there is a considerable amount of confusion over this particular point. I think the hon. the Minister will save his Department a lot of trouble if he would

[1] The Proclamation, dated 12 February 1965, defining 'occupation' under the Group Areas Act in such a way as to affect attendance at entertainments.

at least publicize the fact that permits are indeed not required for private functions. I say that this proclamation R.26 had made us ridiculous in the eyes of the outside world, absolutely ridiculous. Incidentally, I do not consider it an issue of petty apartheid. I disagree with people who think that this is petty apartheid. I think it is a grievous insult to human dignity, and I believe that it is in that light that this matter is viewed by the non-White people to whom this applies. I also think that it is a severe injustice, because where people were spending peaceful leisure hours watching soccer matches and other matches, they are now prevented from so doing. For instance, at the Rand Stadium and the Wanderers Stadium, those people are now turned back on their own resources and have no way in which to enjoy their leisure hours peacefully. What are we trying to do? Are we intent on turning more people into delinquents with no facilities for decent recreation? The hon. Minister said that millions of Rand were spent by his Department and the Department of Indian Affairs and Bantu Administration to provide facilities for these people in their own areas. It just is not so.

* * *

The Minister of Community Development: There is one further question to which I must reply. We have been asked on what basis we act and what the norm is we follow in making provision for separate facilities. In the first place we say that where there are separate facilities of the same kind in the case of functions which can obviously be repeated, such as cinema shows and so forth, separate facilities must be provided, such as separate cinemas, separate halls and so forth.

In the second place we say that where a stage or film show is not of a repetitive nature, in other words, where, if one brought about absolute separation, one would be depriving some of those people of the privilege of attending such a show, we allow the Coloureds to attend under permit. The only condition we make is that separate seating and entrance facilities must be provided. I want to tell hon. members that a very fine thing has happened since this arrangement was introduced and that

APARTHEID IN PRACTICE—SOCIAL CONSEQUENCES

is that separate facilities have since been provided at numbers of places where the separate facilities available were of a very unsatisfactory nature, in other words, where the non-Whites were placed in an inferior position if they wanted to attend those functions, and it is actually to the advantage of the Coloureds that this decision was taken. I can mention numbers of examples of cases in which we have said: 'We realize that in this case we must allow Coloureds to attend but only under certain conditions.' The improvements which have been brought about in the facilities for Coloureds as a result of this have obviously been to the advantage of the Coloureds. In the third place, when we consider whether a permit must be granted or not, we consider whether or not hardship will be caused if the permit is not granted. In the fourth place, we consider how the community will be affected and what is to its advantage. These things are not done arbitrarily or out of hatred. We believe that by means of this system we can create conditions in South Africa under which both Whites and Coloureds can live their own lives.

An attack was made here today upon the Department's application of the policy of the resettlement of people from White residential areas. It was said that we are arbitrarily uprooting people from areas where they have lived for hundreds of years and placing them in new areas. Can hon. members give me an example of a peaceful area which is a mixed residential area? Give me one example in the world. Take England and America; mention one urban area to me where there is peace and quiet in a mixed residential area.

I want to conclude by saying that we do resettle people. That is true. But every person who is resettled is adequately compensated for his property after a proper and independent valuation has been made of that property. People who have no property and who are resettled in this way usually find themselves living under far better conditions than those which they experienced under slum conditions and admixing in the residential sphere. I think that I have now replied to all the questions put to me.

Mrs. Suzman: Will the hon. the Minister please reply to the

APARTHEID IN PRACTICE—SOCIAL CONSEQUENCES

question of whether permits have to be obtained for the holding of private multi-racial functions in halls? I am thinking, for example, of wedding receptions.

The Minister of Community Development: Our interpretation of this matter is that they must be public places of entertainment. We do not interfere in private matters. The merits of the case are first considered before a permit is granted. I suggest that the hon. member advise her friends to make certain before they hold such a function. They must first make sure from the regional office before they hold such a function.

DOCUMENT 31B. FROM THE *Cape Times*, 15 OCTOBER 1965.

Cape Times records, and readers' reactions in the Afrikaans- as well as the English-language Press, indicate that there have been more cases of so-called 'pinprick' or '*klein*' (small) *apartheid* in 1965 than in any other year. In no other year since the present Government came into power in 1948 have so many *apartheid* notices been put up, or has so much money been spent on separate entrances, toilets, seating arrangements and other trappings of *apartheid*.

Following are some of the many 'pinpricks' that have been reported, and which have evoked considerable comment this year:

The granting of Government permission for Coloured people to watch rugby at Newlands B field on condition that a 6-foot wire fence is built between them and the White spectators.

The turning away of 200 Coloured people from the Eve Boswell show at the Luxurama Theatre, Wynberg. Many of them had to wait in their cars in the car park till the show was over and White patrons had moved their cars.

The removal of three Coloured children from the Luxurama at a performance at which Whites were present. The formerly multi-racial theatre was later declared to be for Coloured people only. The UCT Ballet Company was not allowed to dance *Romeo and Juliet* there.

The refusal of Government permission for the prize-winning Afrikaans writer and artist, Breyten Breytenbach, now living in Paris, to bring his Vietnamese wife to South Africa to meet his parents.

The refusal of permission for a Johannesburg Indian couple to bring their baby, born prematurely during a visit to India by its mother, into South Africa. After several appeals, this decision was reversed.

The cancellation of a proposed visit to Cape Town of the United States aircraft-carrier *Independence*, after the South African Government had insisted that its pilots who landed here must be White.

The whole future of South African Chinese basketball eopardised by the news that Chinese players will not be allowed to take part in the national basketball tournament in Cape Town.

The refusal of permission for White children to take part with non-White children in a Red Cross pageant at Maynardville, Wynberg, and insistence that the audience be racially separated.

The barring of MPs and MPCs from addressing meetings of their constituents in Coloured rural areas.

The refusal of a loan application for a new St. Joseph's Home for crippled children at Philippi—a multi-racial institution.

The intrusion of four detectives at a symphony concert in the Cape Town City Hall to take the names of a handful of Coloured music-lovers in the audience.

The subsequent application, by Government order, of *apartheid* at the City Hall, with separate entrances, partitions, screens, ticket office, seats and toilets.

The appearance of a Government notice in a Knysna newspaper that an investigation is to be held into *apartheid* on the rocks among anglers.

The Government's directive that there must be no 'mixed' celebrations on South Africa's national days.

The refusal of permission for White judges to officiate at a Coloured beauty contest in Paarl.

The provision of separate reading tables in the central municipal library in Cape Town, though Whites and non-Whites use the same books.

APARTHEID IN PRACTICE—SOCIAL CONSEQUENCES

The considerable inconvenience caused to a blind White girl accompanied by a Coloured maid after she had been told by a White taximan in Cape Town that he could not carry White and Coloured passengers in the same car.

The turning away of large numbers of African sports enthusiasts from boxing and soccer matches in Cape Town, Pretoria, Johannesburg and Durban, and the prohibition on Whites from watching a non-White golf tournament at the 'White' Glendower golf course, Johannesburg, in which the Durban Indian champion 'Papwa' Sewgolum was taking part.

The removal of 14 Coloured people from the gallery of a Durban theatre during the interval, though there were no Whites in the gallery.

And many other 'pinpricks' throughout the Republic flowing from the 'mixed audiences' proclamation.

Other *apartheid* pinpricks in recent years have been:

1964—The refusal of Cabinet Ministers to attend diplomatic and other receptions at which non-White guests are present.

The directive to scientific bodies—including the South African Bird-watchers—to exclude non-Whites from their membership.

The removal of Sammy Davis, Junr., the American Negro film star, from cinema posters in Durban soon after Louis Armstrong, the veteran Negro jazz singer and trumpeter, was refused a visa to visit South Africa.

1963—'Papwa' Sewgolum receives his Natal Open golf trophy outside in the rain because he is not, as a non-White, allowed in the clubhouse.

1962—The Pretoria City Council's refusal to allow a visiting team of crack Japanese swimmers to use its Hillcrest swimming bath.

1958—The Government's directive that no more Coloured people may be employed as traffic constables, firemen or ambulance drivers in Cape Town.

Perhaps the most lasting pinprick applied in Cape Town is the form in which bus *apartheid* has been applied here since 1956, in a compromise arrangement between the National Transport Commission and the City Tramways Company.

APARTHEID IN PRACTICE—SOCIAL CONSEQUENCES

This system is so complex, *apartheid* being operative only on certain sections of the Sea Point/Wynberg route in certain parts of the buses at certain times of the day, that an attempted explanation of how it worked took up a whole column in the *Cape Times* when it was first introduced.

THE REDUCTIO AD ABSURDUM:
IMPROPER INTERFERENCE

What seems to be the furthest point to which apartheid can go is contained in the Prohibition of Improper Interference Bill of 1966 detailed below. The Bill provoked so much opposition that it was referred to a Select Committee and will probably not be enacted in the form given below. Readers should note carefully that this is *not*, at the time of writing, part of the Statute Law of South Africa, but the fact that it could be introduced was significant.

DOCUMENT 32. FROM THE PROHIBITION OF IMPROPER INTERFERENCE BILL, 1966.

Bill

To prohibit interference in the political sphere in the affairs of any population group by persons not belonging to that population group, to make certain incidental amendments to the Electoral Consolidation Act, 1946, and the Separate Representation of Voters Act, 1951, and to provide for other incidental matters.

WHEREAS the traditional way of life of the Republic of South Africa requires that every population group shall develop independently within its own group, but with mutual co-operation and assistance;

AND WHEREAS every population group has an inalienable right to live and to strive according to its own traditional way of life, as being the only foundation for ensuring lasting peace and good order;

AND WHEREAS the whites as the guardians of the other population groups accept their mission to lead the non-white population groups to self-realisation and to safeguard them against political exploitation by others as the sole guarantee for the continued existence of both their own and the other population groups:

BE IT THEREFORE ENACTED by the State President, the Senate and the House of Assembly of the Republic of South Africa, as follows:

1. In this Act, unless the context otherwise indicates— (i) 'Minister' means the Minister of the Interior; (ii) 'population group' means any of the following groups, namely:
   (a) the Bantu population group which includes all persons who have been classified as Bantu in terms of the Population Registration Act, 1950 (Act No. 30 of 1950);
   (b) the white population group which includes all persons who have been classified as white persons in terms of that Act;
   (c) the Indian group which includes all persons who have been classified as members of the Indian group in terms of that Act; and
   (d) the Coloured population group which includes all persons who have been classified as members of the Cape Coloured group, the Malay group, the Griqua group or the other Coloured Group in terms of that Act.

2. (1) No person shall directly or indirectly:
   (a) give assistance to any member of a population group to which such person does not belong, with regard to any act relating to such member's registration under any law as a voter at an election of any body of whatever nature; or
   (b) take part in or give assistance with regard to the establishment or organisation of any political party, or any group or other form of organisation the objects or any of the objects of which are to propagate, discuss, study or encourage political views, to which members of such a population group belong; or
   (c) be a member of or take part in any activities of any political party or group or other form of organisation

referred to in paragraph (b) to which members of such a population group belong; or
(d) (i) give financial assistance; or
(ii) make, prepare or disseminate propaganda; or
(iii) give any other assistance,
in support of or in opposition to any political party or group or other form of organisation referred to in paragraph (b) to which members of such a population group belong or of any candidate at an election in terms of any law of persons to any body which consists of members of such a population group or an election in terms of any law at which only members of such a population group may vote; or
(e) at any poll in connection with an election in terms of any law convey members of such a population group to any polling station for the purpose of enabling them to vote thereat, or give any assistance in connection with such conveyance; or
(f) in the case of any person who has been nominated as a candidate at an election at which only members of such a population group are entitled to vote, or who represents persons who are such members on any body, intimate to such members that he is or was a member or supporter of any political party, or any group or other form of organisation the objects or any of the objects of which consist of the propagation, discussion, study or encouragement of political views, to which persons other than members of such population group belong, or enlighten such members in regard to principles described by him to such members as the principles of such a political party or group or form of organisation; or
(g) do anything which in the opinion of the Minister may have the effect of defeating the objects of this Act and which he has prohibited by notice in the *Gazette*.
(2) For the purposes of subsection (1)(f) all persons who are entitled to vote at an election under the Separate Representation of Voters Act, 1951 (Act No. 46 of 1951), shall be deemed to belong to the Coloured population group.

(3) A prohibition under subsection (1)(g) may apply to all persons or to any class or group of persons or to all persons not belonging to any particular class or group.

(4) The provisions of subsection (1):
(a) shall not apply in relation to the exercise of his powers or the performance of his functions or duties by any person in terms of any law or in relation to the performance by any person in a professional capacity of any act which has not been prohibited by the Minister under subsection (1)(g);
(b) shall not be deemed to prohibit:
   (i) any person who has been nominated as a candidate for any election from taking part in meetings of persons who may vote at that election, for the purpose of securing the support of such persons in connection with his election; or
   (ii) any person who represents such persons on any body from taking part in meetings of such persons for the purpose of giving an account of the proceedings of such body or discussing matters relating to his actions as the representative of such persons; or
   (iii) any such candidate or any person who so represents such persons from informing those persons of his views in connection with any political party, or any group or other form of organisation, the objects or any of the objects of which are to propagate, discuss, study or encourage political views, to which such persons belong.

(5) The provisions of subsection (1)(d) shall not be deemed to prohibit any person from giving financial or other assistance or making, preparing or disseminating propaganda in support of or in opposition to any candidate who has been nominated for election under the Separate Representation of Voters Act, 1951, and for whom such person is entitled to vote at such election.

(6) The provisions of this section shall not apply with reference to the performance of its functions by any newspaper registered under the Newspaper and Imprint Act, 1934 (Act No. 14 of 1934).

(7) The provisions of this section shall, in so far as they can be applied, also apply in relation to any corporate body, and for that purpose such a body shall be deemed to belong to a particular population group only if all persons having controlling interests, as defined in the Group Areas Act, 1966, in such body are members of that population group: Provided that the Minister may by notice in the *Gazette* declare that any body specified in the notice shall not be deemed to belong to a population group so specified, even though all persons having such controlling interests therein are members of that population group, if in the opinion of the Minister the activities of such body are calculated to defeat the objects of this Act.

(8) The Minister may from time to time by notice in the *Gazette* amend or withdraw any notice issued under subsection (1)(g) or (7).

3. (1) The Minister may by notice in the *Gazette* exempt any person or class or group of persons from any or all of the provisions of this Act for a definite or an indefinite period and either conditionally or unconditionally.

(2) The Minister may exclude any person belonging to any class or group of persons from any exemption granted under subsection (1) in respect of that class or group of persons.

(3) The Minister may by notice in the *Gazette* withdraw any exemption granted under subsection (1).

4. The Minister shall lay on the Table in the Senate and in the House of Assembly copies of any notice issued by him under section 2(1)(g) or (7) or section 3 within fourteen days after publication thereof if Parliament is then in ordinary session, or, if Parliament is not then in ordinary session, within fourteen days after the commencement of its next ensuing ordinary session.

5. (1) Any person who contravenes any provision of section 2 shall be guilty of an offence and liable on conviction:
(a) in the case of a first conviction to a fine of not less than three hundred rand or more than six hundred rand or imprisonment for a period of not less than six or more than twelve months or to both such fine and such imprisonment; and

(b) in the case of a second or subsequent conviction to a fine of not less than one thousand rand or more than two thousand rand or imprisonment for a period of not less than one year or more than two years or to both such fine and such imprisonment.

(2) If any person who has at any time been convicted of an offence under subsection (1) is subsequently again convicted of an offence under that subsection, he shall for a period of five years from the date of the subsequent conviction be disqualified from being or remaining registered or voting under the provisions of the Electoral Consolidation Act, 1946 (Act No. 46 of 1946), or the Separate Representation of Voters Act, 1951 (Act No. 46 of 1951), or the Coloured Persons Representative Council Act, 1964 (Act No. 49 of 1964), or any other law.

(3) If in any prosecution under this section it is proved that financial assistance has been given to or for the benefit of any candidate referred to in section 2(1)(d), it shall be presumed, unless the contrary is proved, that such assistance was given in support of the election of that candidate.

(4) No prosecution in respect of an offence under this section shall be instituted except on the express direction of the Attorney-General concerned.

6. Section 8 of the Separate Representation of Voters Act, 1951 (hereinafter referred to as the principal Act), is hereby amended by the addition of the following subsections:

'(4) Notwithstanding anything to the contrary contained in any law, no person shall be capable of being nominated or of sitting as a senator in terms of this Act:

(a) if at any time during the period of three years immediately preceding the date on which the nomination takes place, or, in the case of the first nomination after the commencement of the Prohibition of Improper Interference Act, 1966, of a person who at such commencement is such a senator, at any time as from the date immediately preceding the day on which the nomination takes place, he has been a member of or has in any manner taken part in any activities of any political party, or any group or other form of organisation the objects or any of the objects of which are to propagate, discuss, study or encourage political views, to which members of the white population group mentioned in section 1 of that Act belong, or associate himself in any manner with the organisation of any such party or group or form of organisation or received assistance of any nature from any such party or group or form of organisation;

(b) unless before his nomination there has been submitted to the Minister a statement in which such person:
 (i) declares that he is not by virtue of the provisions of paragraph (a) incapable of being nominated or of sitting as a senator; and
 (ii) undertakes that if nominated he will not during his term of office become a member of any political party, group or form of organisation referred to in paragraph (a) or take part in any activities or associate himself with the organisation thereof or receive assistance from any such party, group or form of organisation;

(c) if he has at any time during the period of five years immediately preceding the day on which the nomination takes place, been convicted of an offence under section 5 of the Prohibition of Improper Interference Act, 1966, or under subsection (5) of this section.

(5) Any person who:

(a) in any statement made by him for the purposes of subsection (4)(b)(i) makes a false statement; or

(b) acts contrary to any undertaking referred to in subsection (4)(b)(ii),

shall be guilty of an offence and liable on conviction, in the case of a conviction under paragraph (a), to any penalty which may be imposed in respect of the crime of perjury, and, in the case of a conviction under paragraph (b), to a fine not exceeding two hundred rand or imprisonment for a period not exceeding one year or to both such fine and such imprisonment.

(6) Any senator who has been convicted of an offence under subsection (5) of this section or under section 5 of the Prohibition of Improper Interference Act, 1966, shall forthwith vacate his seat.'

7. Section 10 of the principal Act is hereby amended by the addition of the following subsection:

'(4) The provisions of paragraph (a) of section 8(4) relating to a senator referred to therein shall *mutatis mutandis* apply with reference to any member of the House of Assembly referred to in this section, and for that purpose any reference in that paragraph to the date on which the nomination of such a senator takes place shall be construed as a reference to the date on which the sitting of the nomination court in respect of the election of such a member of the House of Assembly takes place.'

8. Section 12 of the principal Act is hereby amended by the addition of the following subsection:

'(4) The provisions of paragraph (a) of section 8(4) relating to a senator referred to therein shall *mutatis mutandis* apply with reference to a member of the provincial council of the province of the Cape of Good Hope referred to in this section, and for that purpose any reference in that paragraph to the date on which the nomination of such a senator takes place shall be construed as a reference to the date on which the sitting of the nomination court in respect of the election of such a member of the said provincial council takes place.'

9. Section 20 of the principal Act is hereby amended:

(a) by the substitution for subsection (3) of the following subsection:

'(3) At elections of members of the House of Assembly or provincial councillors under this Act no member of the Senate or the House of Assembly or a provincial council shall act as a presiding officer for absent votes, and no person other than a non-European shall be nominated or appointed as such a presiding officer or as an election agent or a subagent, polling agent or messenger.'; and

(b) by the addition of the following subsection:
'(6) For the purposes of subsection (1), section 36 of the principal Act shall be construed as if the following subsections were added thereto:
'(10) No candidate shall be deemed to have been duly nominated:
(a) unless before the close of the sitting of the nomination court concerned there is lodged with the returning officer an affidavit or a solemn declaration made before a magistrate by the candidate in which the candidate:
  (i) in the case of a candidate for election as a member of the House of Assembly, declares that he is not in terms of section 10(4) of the Separate Representation of Voters Act, 1951 (Act No. 46 of 1951), incapable of being elected or of sitting as a member of the House of Assembly, or, in the case of a candidate for election as a member of the provincial council of the province of the Cape of Good Hope, declares that he is not in terms of section 12(4) of the said Act incapable of being elected or of sitting as a member of that provincial council; and
  (ii) undertakes that if elected he will not during his term of office become a member of any political party, group or form of organisation referred to in section 8(4)(a) of the Separate Representation of Voters Act, 1951, or take part in any activities or associate himself with the organisation thereof or receive assistance from any such party, group or form of organisation;
(b) if he has at any time during the period of five years ending on the day immediately preceding the day on which the sitting of the nomination court concerned takes place, been convicted of an offence under subsection (11) of this section or section 5 of the Prohibition of Improper Interference Act, 1966.
(11) Any person who:

APARTHEID IN PRACTICE—SOCIAL CONSEQUENCES

(a) in any affidavit or declaration made by him for the purposes of subsection (10)(a)(i) makes a false statement; or
(b) acts contrary to his undertaking referred to in subsection (10)(a)(ii),

shall be guilty of an offence and liable on conviction, in the case of a conviction under paragraph (a), to any penalty which may be imposed in respect of the crime of perjury, and, in the case of an offence under paragraph (b), to a fine not exceeding two hundred rand or imprisonment for a period not exceeding one year or to both such fine and such imprisonment.

(12) Whenever a member of the House of Assembly or of the provincial council of the province of the Cape of Good Hope is convicted of an offence under subsection (11), the provisions of section 178 shall *mutatis mutandis* apply as if such member had been convicted of an offence referred to in paragraph (a) of that section and as if a penalty referred to in that paragraph had been imposed in respect of such offence.'

10. Whenever the Minister has reason to believe that any person who has been nominated as a candidate at an election of a member for the House of Assembly or a provincial council is not qualified to be elected or to take his seat as such a member, the Minister may apply to the competent division of the Supreme Court for an order declaring the nomination to be void, and any court of the said division may on such application set aside or confirm the nomination and issue such other orders as it may deem fit.

11. This Act shall be called the Prohibition of Improper Interference Act, 1966.

SUMMARY

This statement by the editor of these Documents attempts to sum up, as far as possible in non-technical language, the measures which the Government of South Africa has taken to silence criticism and destroy effective opposition. It is by no

APARTHEID IN PRACTICE—SOCIAL CONSEQUENCES

means an exhaustive statement. There are many other forms of control not listed here. Nor are the full particulars given under any head. It can, however, be said that the paragraphs which follow are accurate, balanced, objective, and free from distortions. It seems necessary to include this statement in order to show how the Government is able to enforce the legislation referred to in previous sections of this book and to silence opposition.

DOCUMENT 33. BANNING, BANISHMENT AND OTHER RESTRICTIVE MEASURES.

1. Banning of organisations

The Communist Party of South Africa was banned by special legislation in 1950.

Under the Unlawful Organisations Act (No. 34 of 1960) the following organisations, *inter alia*, have been banned:
  The African National Congress
  The Pan-African Congress
  The Congress of Democrats
  The South African Indian Congress and its Provincial Branches.

2. Banning of Individuals

Under the Suppression of Communism Act of 1950, as amended in 1954, the Minister of Justice was empowered to ban individuals deemed by the Minister to be promoting any one of the aims of Communism. There is no trial and no appeal to the Courts. There is not even an administrative appeal by which the victim is notified of the details of his offence and permitted to plead his own case before the appropriate administrative officer.

As belief in racial equality is one of the aims of Communism it has been possible to ban persons who favoured racial equality but were not Communists—indeed who were in some cases pronounced anti-Communists.

A very large number of persons—running into the hundreds —have been so 'banned'.

Banning orders vary from person to person, but in general their provisions are as listed below:

(i) Most bans are for a period of five years. There is no guarantee that the ban will be lifted at the end of this period and in not a few cases the ban has been renewed.

(ii) The banned person is usually restricted to the magisterial district in which he lives. (In a few cases a neighbouring magisterial district has been included.)

(iii) In most, though not all, cases, the banned person has to report personally at regular intervals, usually once a week, to the police.

(iv) Banned persons may not communicate with one another.

(v) A banned person may not speak at public meetings, write to the newspapers, or publish articles or books. To quote a banned person is a punishable offence.

(vi) A banned person may not enter any educational institution. (Some exceptions have been made in the case of banned teachers or students.)

(vii) A banned white person may be excluded from non-white areas and from factories.

(viii) A banned person is almost without exception precluded from belonging to any political organisation.

These rules are administered strictly, and within the knowledge of the writer a young man of twenty-two and an old man of eighty have been charged in Court for inadvertent failure to report to the police on the prescribed day of the week.

Some bans have been withdrawn or modified, but most of them stand and are a potent force of intimidation.

In some cases the ban is accompanied by house-arrest. In a fair proportion of these cases this is a 24-hour provision, leaving a man a prisoner in his own home.

3. Banishment

An Act of 1956 permitted the Government to banish Africans from their homes. It would appear that from 100 to 150 persons have been so banished from time to time. No appeal to the Courts is allowed, but a banished person, if he applies *after* obeying the banishment order, will be furnished by the

Minister with the reasons for the issue of the banishment order, and so much of the information on which the Government's decision was based as can, in the Minister's opinion, be disclosed without detriment to the public interest.

Banishment is almost inevitably to a remote area where the banished man finds himself among an ethnic group different from his own and speaking a different language.

Huts are supplied, but not necessarily furniture or housekeeping equipment. Some freedom of movement within a prescribed area is allowed.

A man's family may accompany him, the fares being paid by the Government. If they prefer to stay and maintain their rights on the cultivable plot which they occupy at home they may pay the banished man visits. In exceptional cases of hardship a rail warrant will be provided for such visits.

A nominal amount is paid to the detainee and if there is suitable employment available he may be offered it—usually at rates of from R8 to R12 (£4 to £6) a month.

The majority, but by no means all, of the banished persons have subsequently been allowed to return to their homes under stringent conditions.

4. Deportation or voluntary expatriation

In some cases persons who were not South African nationals have been deported.

Restricted persons have sometimes managed to escape from the Republic. Others have on request been given an 'exit permit' by the Government. None of these can return without special permission, which is not normally likely to be granted.

Many South Africans have left their country voluntarily, seeing no hope of improving conditions by remaining. Other opponents of apartheid have seen their duty differently and have remained to take the risks of opposition. A large proportion of those who have left have been professional or academic persons and this 'brain drain', the exact figures of which have never been published, but which is considerable, constitutes a real problem in South Africa's academic life.

APARTHEID IN PRACTICE—SOCIAL CONSEQUENCES

5. Detention without trial

By the General Law Amendment Act (No. 37 of 1963) police officers may without warrant arrest and detain up to ninety days on any particular occasion persons suspected of committing, intending to commit, or having information about, specified types of political offences. Apart from a weekly visit from a magistrate, these detainees may be held absolutely *incommunicado*.

There is nothing to prevent the ninety day period being extended for a further ninety days immediately on its expiration, or even for a third ninety-day period, and such cases are known. There is no appeal to the Courts.

At the time of writing these notes, the 'ninety-day clause' has been suspended, but it may be re-introduced at any moment in the Minister's unfettered discretion. There is no need for further Parliamentary enactment. There is no appeal to the Courts.

A large proportion of the ninety-day detainees were subjected to solitary confinement, with, in some cases, marked psychological results.

The importance of the 'ninety-day clause' has lessened considerably since the enactment of the Criminal Procedure Amendment Act (No. 96 of 1965) by which whenever in the opinion of the Attorney-General there is any danger of tampering with or intimidation of any person likely to give material evidence for the State in any criminal proceedings, or there is fear that any such person may abscond, or whenever the Attorney-General deems it to be in the interests of such person or of the administration of justice, the person concerned may be arrested and detained until the conclusion of the criminal proceedings concerned, or for a hundred and eighty days, whichever may be the shorter period. The detainee will be visited by a magistrate once a week, but otherwise may be kept *incommunicado*.

There are certain further provisions which aggravate this law, but the essence of it is as shown above.

Opponents of the Government contend that this clause may be used and has been used to intimidate unwilling witnesses.

6. Advocating civil disobedience

The question may be raised by persons unfamiliar with the situation in South Africa whether methods of civil disobedience may not or should not be used by opponents of the Government to press their case. The answer to this question is to be found in the Criminal Law Amendment Act (No. 8 of 1953). This measure renders it an offence to advise, encourage or incite anyone to commit an offence by way of protest against a law or in support of a campaign against any law. Maximum penalties for such incitement are a fine of R1000 or five years' imprisonment, or ten lashes, or a combination of any two of these. The penalty imposed for a second or subsequent conviction must include either whipping or imprisonment.

Further the Act renders it an offence to solicit or accept any financial or other assistance for organised protest or resistance against the laws of the country. The penalties for such offences are as stated in the preceding paragraph, and the money or other articles received may be confiscated. Convicted persons who are not South African citizens may be deported.

7. Meetings

A series of enactments virtually leaves the control of African public meetings within the complete discretion of the Government. In addition to legal difficulties the holding of racially 'mixed' public meetings is much hampered by the unwillingness of public bodies to lend halls for this purpose. Even all-white public meetings may be subjected to control in certain circumstances.

8. The Security Police

The existence of a large and increasing force of Security Police makes the work of legal and institutional opposition to the Government's policies difficult. The very presence of the police at meetings acts as an intimidation to many. There are many forms of intimidation from many sources, so that it requires considerable moral courage to come out as an opponent of the apartheid policy.

POSTSCRIPTA

A.

Intimidation

In the original draft of this work a Document on Intimidation was included. It has since been represented to the editor that its publication might lead to further measures against his informants, and with reluctance he has decided not to publish this full and detailed statement. It would, however, be an incomplete picture of *apartheid* if no reference at all were made to the effects of intimidation in reducing to a minimum public protests and opposition to the Apartheid policy.

The presence of members of the Security Police at a lawful meeting, taking notes, assisted by tape-recorders, collecting names and sometimes photographing individuals, is in itself terrifying to many law-abiding people. In this and in other more serious ways such as those detailed in Document 33, it has become apparent that persistent and public opposition to Government policies is attended with grave personal risk. When comment is made as to the silence of friends of civil liberty within South Africa, these facts should be borne in mind.

B.

U.D.I. and Rhodesia—The South African Reaction

'U.D.I.' in Southern Rhodesia, and the measures taken by the British Government in response have, to a large extent, polarised opinion in the Republic of South Africa, swinging to the side of Apartheid many who had previously been neutral or even mildly in support of liberal policies. The battle for more liberal policies in the Republic has also been made more difficult by the constant press reports of happenings in the new independent African States, particularly, but not exclusively, in the Congo. While it may be argued with some force that all atrocities or acts of tyranny are 'news' and settled policies of progress are not, the best friends of emergent Africa must admit that not all the actions of the new States are helpful to those fighting Apartheid in South Africa. In South Africa there are pan-Africanists and also Liberals. The policies of pan-Africanism are not acceptable to Liberals, who stand for genuine non-racial democracy and parliamentary government, and not for a one-party state. More need not be said too illustrate the great difficulties which happenings to the north, in Rhodesia and elsewhere, add to the almost tragic situation of South African opponents of Apartheid.

Select Bibliography

No attempt is made here to give a full bibliography of Apartheid. Such a bibliography would be very extensive and of very unequal value. There are so many books available that it has been difficult for me to make a choice, but I have been guided by the principle of trying to give books which show both sides of the question.

CARTER, Gwendolen (ed.), *Five African States*, London: Pall Mall Press, 1966. A study of modern government in the Congo, Cameroun Federal Republic, South Africa, Rhodesia and Nyasaland, and Dahomey.

COPE, John, *South Africa*, London: Benn, 1965. A study by a liberal-minded and very reliable author.

HANCOCK, Sir Keith, *Survey of British Commonwealth Affairs*, Vol. II, Part II, London: Oxford University Press, 1937. A study which, though dated, is still valuable, by one of the greatest of Commonwealth historians.

HILL, C. R., *Bantustans*, Cape Town: Oxford University Press, 1964. A careful study of Bantustans by the Assistant Director of the Institute of Race Relations.

HOUGHTON, D. Hobart, *The South African Economy*, Cape Town: Oxford University Press, 1965. A reliable and informative study by an outstanding South African economist.

KUPER, L., *An African Bourgeoisie*, New Haven: Yale University Press, 1965. A study of the emerging African middle-class by a former Professor of Sociology at the University of Natal, South Africa.

MARQUARD, L., *The People and Policies of South Africa*, London: Oxford University Press, Revised Edition, 1966. A most reliable and impartial study by a liberal but dispassionate South African who has spent most of his life studying race relations.

MARAIS, Ben, *Colour, the Crisis of the West*, Cape Town: Howard Timmins for Geo. Allen & Unwin, 1953. A study, *inter alia*, of race relations in South Africa, the United States and Brazil by a theological professor of the Dutch Reformed Church.

SELECT BIBLIOGRAPHY

MARAIS, Ben, *The Two Faces of Africa*, Pietermaritzburg: Shuter & Shooter, 1964. A further stimulating study of race relations by the writer of the previous book.

PIENAAR, S. and SAMPSON, A., *Two Views of Separate Development*, London: Oxford University Press, 1961. An attempt to give, in the same volume, the arguments for and against apartheid, both expressed with reasonable moderation.

READER, D. H., *The Black Man's Portion*, Cape Town: Oxford University Press, 1961. A study of both practical and academic value by a well-known social anthropologist.

ROBERTSON, H. M., *South Africa: Political and Economic Aspects*, Durham: Duke University Press, 1957. A record of lectures given at Duke University by the Professor of Economics at the University of Cape Town. Outspoken but reasonable.

RHOODIE, N. J. and VENTER, H. J., *Apartheid*, Pretoria: H.A.U.M., 1960. A presentation of the case for apartheid.

SMITH, Prudence (ed.), *Africa in Transition*, London: Max Reinhardt, 1958. A most valuable and representative series of essays, contributions coming from every one of the racial groups into which South Africa is divided.

TATZ, C., *Shadow and Substance in South Africa*, Pietermaritzburg: University of Natal Press, 1962. A study of the inter-relations of land and franchise policy in South Africa by a South African who is now an authority on Australian Aboriginal Administration.

TINGSTEN, H., *The Problem of South Africa*, London: Gollancz, 1955. A record of impressions gained on the subject by the Editor-in-Chief of the Swedish paper *Dagens Nybeter*.

THOMPSON, L. M., *Politics in the Republic of South Africa*, Boston: Little Brown, 1966. An up-to-date study by a most distinguished South African historian now in the United States.

VAN DEN BERGHE, Pierre, *Caneville*, Middleton: Wesleyan University Press, 1964. A sociological study of race relations in a South African sugar town based on personal observation.

VAN DEN BERGHE, Pierre, *South Africa, a Study in Conflict*, Middleton: Wesleyan University Press, 1965. A study based on research on the spot of how the white man in South Africa is, in the words of the author, 'digging his own grave'.

Novels such as Alan Paton's *Cry the Beloved Country* (London: Cape, 1948, issued as a Penguin Book, 1953) and *Too Late the*

SELECT BIBLIOGRAPHY

Phalerope (Cape Town: Frederick L. Cannon for Jonathan Cape Ltd., London, 1953), Harry Bloom's *Episode* (London: Collins, 1956), Gerald Gordon's *Let the Day Perish* (London: Methuen, 1952) could be very helpful, also such books as Arthur Keppel-Jones' *When Smuts Goes* (Pietermaritzburg: Shuter & Shooter, 1955) and Alan Paton's *Hofmeyr* (London: Oxford University Press, 1964).

Subject Index

Agriculture, aspects of
  Gardening, 60
  Overcropping, 13
  Soil Conservation, 60
  Soil Rehabilitation, 13, 31
  Tree Planting, 60
  Water Conservation, 31
American Board of Missions, 52
Anti-Semitism, xxviii
Asiatic Religions, 128
Assembly, House of, see House of Assembly
Associated Scientific and Technical Societies, 91

Bantu (See also Natives)
  Administration, Dept. of, 42, 188, 189
  Affairs Commissioner, 103, 106, 110, 111
  Affairs, Division of, 42, 47
  Authorities Act (1951), 126
  Congregational Church, 55
  Development Authority, 42
  Education, 41–60
  Education Account, 61, 66
  Education Act (1953), 47, 48, 52, 54
  Education, Dept. of, 42, 43
  Labour Board, 116
  Languages, 44–46
  Local Authorities, 42, 45
  Peoples, xviii, 12, 13, 29, 30, 32, 33, 42, 45, 46, 48, 50, 63, 98–111, 122, 126, 127, 183, 195
  Reference Book (or Passport), 99–111
  Reference Bureaux, 98, 100, 109
  Technical Services, Dept. of, 42
  University Colleges, 61
'Bantustans', xxxii, 60
Beyers, Mr. Justice, 117, 118
Bible, The, xviii
'Bill of Rights' (Liberal Party), 39
'Black Peril', 3, 4
Boards, Bureaux, Councils and Local Authorities
  Appeal Board, 24, 25
  Bantu Affairs Commissioner, 103, 106, 110, 111
  Bantu Labour Board, 116
  Bantu Local Authorities, 42, 45
  Bantu Reference Bureaux, 98, 100, 109
  Communal Councils, 32, 33
  District Labour Officers, 101, 106
  Group Areas Board, 24, 170
  Labour Bureaux, 97, 98, 101, 102, 109, 111
  Land Tenure Advisory Board, 140, 149, 150, 162

SUBJECT INDEX

Boards, Bureaux, Councils and Local Authorities—*cont.*
  Legal Aid Bureaux, 23
  Local Authorities, 73, 74, 150, 169
  Municipal Labour Officers, 98–102, 104–111
  National Council for Child Welfare, 24
  National Resources Development Council, 134, 143
  Native Affairs Commission, xxiii, 48, 49, 161
  Natives Representative Council, xxvi, 16, 33
  Provincial Councillors, 123
  Provincial Electoral Colleges, 122
  Regional Labour Commissioners, 105–107
  Transvaal Provincial Administration, 23
  Union Council for Coloured Affairs, 121
Books, referred to or quoted
  Civil Liberty in South Africa, 75n
  Dawie 1946–64, 1, 2
  Native Reserves of Natal, 112
  South Africa, 116–126
  Survey of Race Relations, 23–25, 112
  The Churches and Race Relations in South Africa, 76–85
  The Politics of Inequality, 179–186
  Where We Stand, Archbishop Clayton's Charges 1948–57, 74–76
British Influences
  Administration, xviii–xxiv,
    xxxiii, 117, 118, 183, 184
  Administrators and Others:
    Attlee, Lord, 184
    Campbell-Bannerman, Sir Henry, xxiv
    Castlereagh, Viscount, xix
    Gray, Sir George, 156
    Milner, Viscount, xxii, xxiii
    Rhodes, Cecil, 174
    Somerset, Lord Charles, xix
  Common Law, 118
  Doctrine of Parliamentary Sovereignty, xxix, 117
  Imperial Conference (1926) 117
  Missionaries, xix, xxii
  Slave Emancipation Act (1833), xx
  South Africa Act (1910), xxiv, 117–120, 124–126
  Statute of Westminster, 117
Bunga (Transkeian Territories General Council), 16, 16n
Buthelezi, Chief Gasha, 52

Cape Town, *see under* Cities and Towns
Cape Town Agreement, 161
Cape Town City Hall, 192
Cape Town City Tramways Company, 193
Cape Town Railway Station, 90
Centlivres, Hon. A. van der Sandt, 69
Centralisation, increasing belief in of modern Nationalist policies, xxix

SUBJECT INDEX

Chamber of Commerce of Natal, 156
Chiefs, Tribal, 13, 16, 30
Christoforsen, Rev. A. F., 55
Churches, Christian
  Attitude generally to Apartheid, xxiii, xxx, xxxi, 33, 41, 73–85, 181
  Attitude of individual religious bodies
    Anglicans, xxx, 33, 74, 75, 181
    Apostolic Church, xxx
    Congregational Church and Union, 55, 85
    Dutch Reformed Church xxx, xxxi, 33, 181, 183
    Gereformeerde Kerk, xxx, 181
    Methodists, xxx, 33, 79–81
    Nederduits Gereformeerde Kerk, xxx, 76–79, 181
    Nederduits Hervormde Kerk, xxx, 181
    Presbyterians, xxx, 83–85
    Roman Catholics, xxx, 81–83, 181
    Seventh Day Adventists, xxx
  World Council of Churches, 85
Cities and Towns of South Africa
  Cape Town, 116, 164, 175, 177, 187, 192, 193
  Bonteheuwel, 176
  Kenilworth, 161
  Newlands, 90, 173–178, 191
  Westbrook, 175

Durban, 52, 116, 153, 156–158, 161, 162, 168, 193
East London, 115, 145
Johannesburg, 15, 23, 24, 56, 115, 166, 168, 187, 192, 193
Kimberley, 174
Klerksdorp, 168
Kroonstad, 78
Paarl, 192
Philippi, 192
Pietermaritzburg, 168
Port Elizabeth, 145, 159, 162
Potchefstroom, 78
Pretoria, 23, 24, 79, 119, 168, 193
Wynberg, 191, 192, 194
Civil Disobedience, penalties for, 208
Civil Service, xxxiii
Clayton, Archbishop Geoffrey, 74–76
Coloured Peoples Vigilance Committee, 164, 165
Commissions and Reports
  Broome Reports, 156
  Church and Nation Committee Report, 84, 85
  Commission of Enquiry into Mixed Marriages, 3, 4
  Eiselen Report, 41–47
  Fagan Commission, 94
  Health Commission, 151
  Joynt Report, 155–158
  Molteno Commission and Report, 36
  National Transport Commission, 193
  Native Affairs Commission, xxiii, 48, 49, 161

Commissions and Reports—*cont.*
 Native Education Commission, 48
Communism, 28, 185, 204
Congress of Vienna, xix
Convention of Coloured Organisations, 182
Coolies, 156, 157
Cottesloe Consultation, 85

De Villiers, Dr., 158
Dingane, xxi, xxii
Dutch East India Company, xvii, xix

Ecumenical Synod of the Reformed Church, 78, 79
Education
 Bantu, 41–60
 Colleges, *see* Universities and Colleges
 Criticism of Government—a Dismissible Offence for Academic Staff, 61
 Educational Policy, 13, 25, 37, 38, 41–60, 79, 90, 98, 100, 115
 Eiselen Report on Native Education, 41–47
 English Language, Teaching of, 58, 59
 Expenditure on, 57
 Gardening, 60
 Handwork, 60
 Indoctrination, 51
 Intelligence Tests, 50
 Literacy, 37, 46, 84
 Mathematics, 50
 Native Education Commission, 48
 Native Poll Tax, 41
 Qualities to be inculcated in Native Education, 46
 Religious Knowledge, 46
 Schools
  Curricula, 43, 44, 46, 50
  Inspection of, 44
  Meal System in, 58
  Primary, 43, 44, 58, 60
  Registration of, 48
  Secondary, 43
  Technical, 43
 Teachers
  Pensions for, 58
  Training of, 23, 25, 43, 52, 54, 58
 Trilingual in Native Primary Schools, 59
 Universities, *see also* Universities and Colleges
  Curricula, 66
  'Open', 67, 71
  Policy Regarding, 61–71
  White Persons, Excluded from University Colleges for Bantu or other Non-White Persons, 62, 66
Eiselen, Dr. W. W. M., 41
Electoral Roll, *see under* Franchise
Employment, Classification of, 105, 106, 112, 113
Equal Rights, 51, 57
Ethnic Classification, 19, 24
Eve Boswell, 191

Fear, Influence of, 34, 35
Franchise, xxii, xxiv, xxvi, xxix, xxxvi, 20, 29–31, 34–37, 39, 116–129, 164 (*see also* Voting Rights)
Freedom of Worship, 75

Geneva, 115

SUBJECT INDEX

Glendower Golf Course (Johannesburg), 193
Government Departments and Ministers (by function) and Other Officers
  Attorney-General, 207
  Bantu Administration, Department of, 42, 188, 189
  Bantu Affairs, Division of, 42, 47
  Bantu Development Authority, 42
  Bantu Education, Department of, 42, 43
  Bantu Technical Services, Department of, 42
  Bureau of Census and Statistics, Census, Director of, 24
  Community Development, Minister of, 186-191
  Deeds Registry, 141
  Education, Arts and Science, Minister of, 63-68, 90, 91
  Finance, Minister of, 61
  Indian Affairs, Department of, 189
  Interior, Minister of the, 21, 23, 24, 117, 119, 137-164, 171, 172, 181, 185, 195
  Justice, Minister of, 204
  Labour, Minister of, 113, 114, 116
  Lands, Minister of, 8, 10
  Mines, Minister of, 134, 143
  Native Affairs, Department of, 41, 43, 48, 49, 51
  Native Affairs, Minister of, 7, 48-52, 75, 76, 91-93, 122
  Planning, Minister of, 188

Government Gazette Extraordinary of 3 December 1965, 97-112
Grant, Mr. G. C., 55
Great Trek, The, xx
Group Areas, Demarcation of, 137, 138

'Halfbreed' Poster, 3
Hansard 4, 21, 23n, 91, 136, 186
Harris and others vs. the Minister of the Interior and another, 117, 119
Headmen, Tribal, 30
Henochsberg, Mr. Justice E. S., 55
Hepple, Mr. A., 114
Hillcrest Swimming Pool (Pretoria), 193
House of Assembly, xxvi, 21, 23n, 29, 48, 87, 91, 113, 114, 117, 121, 123, 127, 143, 155, 166, 198, 201-203

Imperial Conference (1926), 117
Independence (U.S. Aircraft Carrier), Visit to Cape Town cancelled, 192
India, Government of, 156
'Informers', 24, 183
Institute of Race Relations, 23-25, 112, 158
International Labour Organization, 115
Intimidation, Effect of on Opposition to Apartheid, 209
Italian Labourers in France, 14, 17

Jameson Raid, xxii
'Janey, Mr. and Mrs.', 173-178

SUBJECT INDEX

Judiciary
    Appeal Court, 117, 118, 119, 121, 124
    Chief Justice, 124, 125
    Common Law, 118
    Counsel for the Government, 117, 118
    Judiciary, Independence of the, 124, 162
    Law, Respect for the, xxix, 11, 30, 81, 92, 117, 118, 124, 207, 208
    Parliament, Sovereignty of, xxix, 117, 118, 120
    Privy Council, 120
    Supreme Court, xxix, 24, 39, 117, 119, 124, 171, 172, 203

Karroo, xvii
Khama, Sir Seretse, 52, 183, 184

Labour
    Aid Centres (for unemployed), 101
    Ambulance Drivers, 193
    Bantu Labour Board, 116
    Closed Shop Occupations, 115
    Collective Bargaining, 115
    Employment, Classification of, 105, 106, 112, 113
    Factories, 8, 9, 16
    Firemen, 193
    International Labour Organization, 115, 116
    Labour Bureaux, 97, 98, 101, 102, 109, 111
    Labour Disputes, 116
    Labour Regulations, 91–116
    Municipal Labour Officers, 98–102, 104–111
    Regional Labour Commissioners, 105–107
    Seasonal Labour, 14, 16, 82
    Slave Labour, xvii, 179
    Trade Unions, *see* Trade Unions
    Trading Areas, 168, 169
    Trading Licences, 149, 171, 172
    Traffic Constables, 193

Land and Property
    Communal Reserves, 134
    Controlled Areas, 138–148
    Expropriation, 138, 154
    Group Areas, 131–178
    Housing, 152, 166
    Land Policy, 2, 8, 13, 31, 38, 127, 128, 133–178
    National Parks Act (1926), 134
    Native Reserves, xxii, xxiv, 8, 13–16, 29–33, 42, 57, 134
    Open Areas, 138–148
    Partition, xxxv, xxxvi
    Property, Acquisition and Holding of, 135, 136, 145, 146, 169, 170, 190
    Residential Areas, 8, 9, 11, 14, 17, 22, 73, 110, 190
    Specified Areas, 138–148

Languages
    Afrikaans, xviii, xxiii, xxvi, xxx, 5, 6, 59, 164, 191
    Bantu, 44–46
    English, 58, 59
    Hottentot (or Hotnot), xvii

SUBJECT INDEX

Leisure, Restraints on Use of, 189
Lobengula, xxii
Local Preachers, 80
Lockat v. the Minister of the Interior, 171
Louis Armstrong, 193

Macdonald, Mr. D. C., 55
Manifestoes, Religious and Political
  Biblical Principles affecting Race Attitudes, 80
  Digest of Protest against University Apartheid Legislation, 68–71
  Education in Race Relations, 79, 80
  Handbook for Better Race Relations, 27–34
  Implications of Christian Race Attitudes, The, 80
  Methodist Attitude to Race, The, 80
  Safeguard your Future, 34–37
  Statement on Apartheid, 81
  We Dare not Remain Silent, 82
  Why the Methodist Church Rejects Apartheid, 80
Matthews, Dr. Z. K., 52
Medical Services
  Ambulance Drivers, 193
  Health Commission, 151
  Hospitals, 9, 81, 135, 192
  Hospitals, Emergency Treatment at, 74
  Hygiene, 46
  Medical School, Natal 62, 67
  Medical Services, 9
  Red Cross Pageant, 192

Welfare, 16
Missionaries, xix, xxii, xxxi, 41, 54, 55, 77
Mixed Audiences, 187
Mixed Marriages
  Commission of Enquiry into Mixed Marriages, 3, 4
  Nationalist Party emphatically opposed to, 11
  Prohibition of Mixed Marriages Act (1949), 166, 179–184
Mokitimi, Rev. Seth, 81
Mpande, xxi
M'Timkulu, Dr. D. G. S., 52
Municipal Amending Ordinance (Transvaal) (1905), 133

'National Convention' (Liberal Party), 39
National Days, 192
National Union of South African Students, 68
Natives (*see also* Bantu)
  Native Administration Act (1927), 30
  Native Affairs Act (1920), 48
  Native Affairs Commission, xxiii, 48, 49, 161
  Native Affairs, Dept. of, 41, 43, 48, 49, 51
  Native Affairs, Minister of, 7, 48–52, 53, 75, 76, 91–93, 122
  Native Education Commission, 48
  Natives Land Act (1913), xxiii, xxiv
  Native Laws Amendment Act (1937), 74

Natives (*see also* Bantu)—*cont.*
Native Laws Amendment Act (1957), 73–75
Native Poll Tax, 41
Natives (Prohibition of Interdicts) Act, 28
Natives Representative Council, xxvi, 16, 33
Native Reserves, xxii, xxiv, 8, 13–16, 29–33, 42, 57, 134
'Native Reserves of Natal', 111, 112
Native Trust and Land Act (1936), xxv, xxvi, 127, 134
Natives (Urban Areas) Consolidated Act (1945), 134
Nazism, xxviii
Ndlwana vs. Hofmeyr (1937), 117, 119
Negro Slaves, xvii
Newlands Rugby Field, 90, 191
Newspapers and Periodicals, referred to or quoted
Black Sash, 112
Bantu, 116, 187
Bantu World, 184
Cape Argus, 183
Cape Times, 90, 173–178, 183, 186, 191, 194
Daily Despatch, 183
Die Burger, 1, 183
Die Transvaler, 183
Die Vaderland, 183
Friend, 183
Forum, 184
Iso Lomuzi, 52, 53
Natal Daily News, 55–60, 182

Natal Mercury, 52, 54, 55, 157
Natal Witness, 182
Rand Daily Mail, 24, 115
Star, The, 167, 183
New Delhi, 158
'Ninety-Day Clause', 207
Nkomo, Joshua, 52
Nomvete, Rev. B. G. M., 55

Pan-Africanism, xvi, xxxii, xxxiii, 210
Parliamentary Acts and Bills
Appellate Division Quorum Act, 120, 121
Asiatic Land Tenure and Indian Representation Act (1946), 128, 140–44, 149
Asiatic Laws Amendment Act (1948), 128, 129
Bantu Authorities Act (1951), 126
Bantu Education Act (1953), 47–48, 52, 54
Bethalsdorp Settlement Act (1921), 137
Coloured Mission Stations and Reserves Act (1949), 134
Coloured Persons Representative Council Act (1964), 199
Coloured Persons Settlement Act (1946), 134
Criminal Law Amendment Act (1953), 208
Criminal Procedure Amendment Act (1965), 207
Electoral Consolidation Act (1946), 20, 194, 199

SUBJECT INDEX

Extension of University Education Act (1959), 61–68
General Law Amendment Act (1963), 28, 207
Group Areas Act (1950), 22, 24, 28, 29, 131–178, 188n.
Group Areas Act (1966), 198
High Court of Parliament Bill, 119
Immorality Act (1927), 28, 166, 179, 184
Immorality Act of 1927, Amendment to (1950), 180, 184–186
Industrial Conciliation Act, 28
Land Act (1946), 163
Land Tenure Act, 144
Liquor Act (1927), 180
Mission Stations and Communal Reserves Act (1909), 134, 137
National Parks Act (1926), 134
Native Administration Act (1927), 30
Native Affairs Act (1920), 48
Native Laws Amendment Act (1937), 74
Native Laws Amendment Act (1957), 73–75
Native Trust and Land Act (1936), xxv, xxvi, 127, 134
Natives Land Act (1913), xxiii, xxiv
Natives (Prohibition of Interdicts) Act, 28

Natural Resources Development Act (1947), 134
Newspaper and Imprint Act (1934), 197
Population Registration Act (1950), 19–25, 28, 139, 180, 195
Population Registration Amendment Act, 25
Precious and Base Metals Act (1908), 133, 137
Prohibition of Improper, Interference Bill, 1966, 194–203
Prohibition of Mixed Marriages Act (1949), 166, 179–184
Promotion of Bantu Self-Government Act (1959), 126, 127
Railways and Harbours Regulation, Control, and Management Act (1916), 88
Representation of Natives Act (1936), xxv, xxvi, 127
Reservation of Separate Amenities Act (1953), 87–91
Senate Act (1955), 121–126
Separate Representation of Voters Act (1951), 116–123, 194, 197, 199
Separate Universities Act 28, 64
Slave Emancipation Act (1833), xx
Slum Clearance Act, 166
South Africa Act (1910), xxiv, 117–120, 124–126

SUBJECT INDEX

Parliamentary Acts and Bills—
cont.
  Status Act, 117
  Statute of Westminster, 117
  Suppression of Communism
    Act (1950), 28, 204
  Unlawful Organisations Act
    (1960), 204
  Urban Areas Act, 94, 98–
    111
  'Viljoen Bill' (1957), 63
Paton, Alan, 37–39
Peoples
  Afrikaners, xvi–xxxiii
  Asiatics, 112, 113, 128, 129,
    140, 141, 159, 180, 182
  Bamangwato, 183
  Bantu, see Bantu
  Basuto, xxi
  British, see British
  Bushmen, xvii, xviii
  Chinese, 192
  Coloured Population, xxiv,
    xxxii–xxxvi, 8, 11, 12, 19,
    22–25, 29, 31, 35, 61, 77,
    79, 81, 83, 85, 112–114,
    117, 118, 122, 131, 132,
    139, 157–159, 161, 163–
    165, 173, 179, 180, 182,
    184–186, 190–192, 195,
    196
  Dutch, xvii, xxvi
  Europeans, 6–9, 11, 13, 22,
    24, 46, 75, 77, 79, 81, 83,
    85, 117, 137, 138, 141,
    144–148, 153–161, 179,
    180, 184–186
  Germans, xvii
  Grensboere, xvii, xviii
  Griqua, xxi, 195
  Hottentots, xvii, xviii, xxvi
  Indians, xxiv, xxxii–xxxvi,
    11, 12, 22, 29, 61, 77, 79,
    81, 83, 85, 128, 140, 144,
    152, 153, 156–161, 164,
    167, 169, 170, 172, 184,
    192–195, 204
  Japanese, 193
  Jews, 128
  Malays, 128, 195
  Syrians, 128
  Turks, 128
  Xhosa, xix
  Zulus, xxi, 54, 55
'Petty Apartheid', 186–194
Pogrund, Mr., 115
Police, 92, 94, 96, 114, 207–209
Political Parties and Associations
  African National Congress,
    204
  Afrikaner Bond, 164n.
  Congress Alliance, 35
  Congress Group, 114
  Congress of Democrats, 204
  Labour Party, 185
  Liberal Party, 35, 37–39
  Nationalist Party, xviii, xxvi,
    xxx, 3, 8, 12, 14, 35, 122,
    158, 180–186
  Pan-African Congress, 204
  Progressive Party, 34–37,
    115, 155
  South African Indian Congress, 184, 204
  Transvaal Nationalists,
    xviii
  United Party, 3, 27–35, 63,
    90, 95, 120, 122, 137,
    180–186
Political Parties and Associations, Assistance for or against, 195–203

SUBJECT INDEX

Population-Movement Control
  Banishment of Individuals, 205, 206
  Bantu Reference Book (or Passport), 99, 100, 102–105, 107, 108, 110, 111
  Deportation, 206, 208
  Detention without Trial, 207
  Finger Prints, 21
  'Freezing', 15
  Identity Numbers, 20, 21
  Immigration, 11, 28, 156, 157, 181
  Influx Control, 30, 91, 109–111
  Pass Exemptions, 30
  Pass Laws, 28, 30
  Photographs, 21
  Population Register, 19–22
  Public Meetings, 208
  Seasonal Labour, 14, 16, 82
  Voluntary Expatriation, 206
Proclamation R., 26, 188, 189
Provinces, Countries and South West Africa
  Basutoland, xxi
  Bechuanaland, 183
  Cape Colony, xxii–xxix, 164n.
  Cape Province, xvii, 3, 29, 30, 78, 89, 90, 117, 118, 122, 127, 133, 134, 143, 144, 145, 151, 154, 158, 159, 161, 163, 179, 180, 201, 203
  Congo, xxxiv, 210
  Natal, xxi, xxii, xxv, 29, 55, 112, 122, 128, 129, 133, 137, 143, 144, 149, 151, 152, 156, 179
  Nyasaland, 32
  Orange Free State, xxi, xxiv, 29, 122, 184
  Rhodesia, xxii, xxxi, 32, 183, 209, 210
  South West Africa, 123
  Transvaal, xxi–xxv, xxvii, xxix, 8, 11, 23, 29, 122, 129, 133, 143, 144
Punctuality, Desirable that Native Education should inculcate, 46

Race Federation, 31–34
Racial Riots, *see* Riots, Racial
Rand Stadium, 189
Register of Population, 19–25, 180
Retief, Piet, xxi
Riots, Racial at
  Cato Manor, 153
  Durban (Grey Street), 153
  Langa, 78
  Newclare, 153
  Sharpeville, 78

Sammy Davis, Junr., 193
Sanctions, xxxv
Schools, *see* Education
Schreiner, Mr. Justice, 125, 126
Scientific Societies, 90, 91, 193
Security Police, *see* Police
Segregation
  of Asiatics, 11
  on Beaches, 89, 90
  at Church Services, 73
  in Convents, 81
  Political, 9, 11
  in Seminaries, 81
  Territorial, 9–11, 13, 70

SUBJECT INDEX

Segregation—*cont.*
  Total, 7–10
  at Universities, 61–67
Senate, xxvi, 29, 87, 121–128, 136, 137, 143, 155, 198, 201, 202
Sewgolum, 'Papwa', 193
'Skollies', 177
Slave Labour, xvii, xx, 179
Slave Trade, xix
South African Presidents, Ministers, Senators and M.Ps
  Abraham, J. H., 181
  Ballinger, Mrs. Margaret, 91, 94–97, 181, 185
  Barlow, Mr., 93
  Basson, J. A. L., 90, 91
  Botha, General, xxiv, xxv
  Botha, P. A., 185
  Brookes, Senator Dr. Edgar H., xv, 2, 54, 55, 143, 144, 149, 150, 155–165
  Byron, Senator, 144, 149
  Clarkson, Senator, 142, 144, 148, 152, 153
  Conradie, Senator, 147
  Conroy, Senator, 3, 4, 15, 137, 139, 141, 143, 146, 147
  De Klerk, Senator, 90, 91
  Dönges, Dr. T. E. 21, 22, 180–184
  Eaton, N. G., 182
  Hertzog, General, xxiii, xxv xxix, 179
  Hofmeyr, Jan Hendrik, Senior, 164, 164n., 165
  Hofmeyr, Jan Hendrik, Junior, 3, 41, 164, 164n.
  Hosking, Senator, 149
  Jackson, Senator, 13, 137, 140, 149, 153
  Kotzé, Mr., 166
  Kruger, President, 160
  Lawrence, Mr. Harry, 51, 121
  Loubser, Mr. S. M., 185, 186
  Malan, Dr., 1, 166, 184
  Marais, Mr. J. A., 166
  Maree, Mr. W. A., 182
  Nicholls, Senator, Heaton, 49, 137, 139, 147, 151, 153
  'Onze Jan', *see* Hofmeyr, J. H., Senior
  Robinson, Mr., 94
  Shepstone, Sir Theophilus, xxi, xxii
  Smit, Dr. D. L., 49
  Smuts, Field-Marshal, xxiv, xxvi, xxix, 4, 5, 33, 34, 164n, 174, 181, 184
  Steyn, A., 182
  Steyn, Colin, 184
  Steyn, Dr. J. H., 182
  Steyn, Mr. Marais, 33
  Steytler, Dr. Jan, 36
  Strydom, Mr., 9
  Suzman, Mrs. Helen, 114, 115, 155, 166–172, 186–191
  Swart, Mr. C. R., 181
  Van Der Walt, Mr., 166
  Van Niekerk, Senator P. W. Le Roux, 146
  Van Ryneveld, Mr., 168
  Verwoerd, Dr., xxviii–xxxii, 2–17, 57
  Viljoen, Senator, 159, 162
  Waring, Mr. F. W., 186

SUBJECT INDEX

Sports and Entertainments, Apartheid Effect on
  Anglers at Knysna Lagoon, 90, 192
  Ballet, 191
  Basketball, Chinese, 192
  Beauty Contests, 192
  Boxing, 193
  Cinemas, 189
  Football, 189, 193
  Gardening, 60
  Golf, 193
  Music
    Handel's 'Messiah', xxviii, xxix, 187
    Symphony Concert, 192
  Pageant, Red Cross, 192
  Rugby, 90, 189, 191
  South African Bird-Watchers Society, 90, 193
  Swimming, 193
  Theatre at Wynberg, 191
Student Organizations, 68
Students, South African, National Union of, 6

Taxation, 38, 42, 57
Trade Unions
  Confederation of Labour, 113
  Congress of Trade Unions (Sactu), 114
  Federation of Free African Trade Unions (Fofatusa), 114
  Mine Workers' Union, 113
  National Union of Clothing Workers, 114
  Railway Staff Associations, 113

Trade Union Council of South Africa (Tucsa), 113–116
Trade Unions, Registration of, 112–115
Trade Unions, Statistics Relating to, 112–116
Transkei, xxxi, 32
Transkeian Territories General Council (Bunga), 16n.
Trekkers, xvii–xx
Tribal Affiliations, 14, 29, 56–59, 66, 132

Union Council for Coloured Affairs, 121
United States Ambassador to South Africa, 56
Universities and Colleges
  Adams College:
    Closing of, 52–55
    Mission Church of, 54
  Amansimtoti Zulu College, 54
  Bantu University Colleges 61
  Cape Town University, 68–70, 116
    Council of, 69, 70
    Senate of, 70
  Fort Hare University College, 68, 70
  Medical School, Natal, 62, 67
  Natal University, 67
  Rhodes University, 70
  South Africa, University of, 63, 67
  Stellenbosch University, 68, 70
  Witwatersrand, University of the, 68–70
    Council of, 70

SUBJECT INDEX

Urban Aspects
  Buses, 193, 194
  Counter, Bench, Seat or Other Amenity or Contrivance— Reservation of, 87–89
  Housing, 152, 166
  Libraries, 192
  Public Meetings, 208
  Public Premises and Vehicles, Reservation of, 87–90
  Shops, 9
  Slums, 166
  Taxis, 90, 193
  Toilets, 191, 192
  Urban Areas Act, 94, 98–111
  Urban Policy, 13–15, 30, 73, 77, 91–111, 134
  Wedding Receptions, 188, 191

Van Riebeeck, Jan, xv, xvii, xxvi
Voortrekkers, xxi, xxii
Voting Rights
  Cape Coloured Voters, 116–127
  Common Voters' Roll, 29, 122–124
  Conveyance to Polling Stations, 196
  Franchise, xxii, xxiv, xxvi, xxix, xxxvi, 20, 29–31, 34–36, 39, 116–129, 164
  Parliament, Abolition of African and Indian Representation in, 126–129
  Provincial Electoral Colleges, 122
  Proportional Representation, 122
  Separate Representation of Voters Act (1951), 199
  Special Roll, 36, 37

Wanderers Stadium, 189
Waterboer, Andries, xxi
'White Peril', 5
Wilcox, Dr., 158
Witwatersrand, 15, 68–70
Women's Church Associations
  European Women's Associations, 84
  Women's Auxiliaries, 80
  Women's Manyanos, 80
World Council of Churches, 85
Writers, referred to or quoted
  Barrow, Brian, 173–178
  Breytenbach, Breyten, 191, 192
  Brookes, Senator Dr. E. H., 75n.
  Carter, Gwendolen M., 179–186
  Cawood, Lesley, 76–85
  Horrell, Muriel, 112–116
  Hurwitz, N., 112
  Louw, Louis, 1, 2
  Macaulay, J. B., 75n.
  McConkey, Dr. W. C., 55–60
  Paton, Alan, 37–39
  Robertson, Prof. H. M., 116–126

For Product Safety Concerns and Information please contact our EU representative GPSR@taylorandfrancis.com
Taylor & Francis Verlag GmbH, Kaufingerstraße 24, 80331 München, Germany

www.ingramcontent.com/pod-product-compliance
Lightning Source LLC
Chambersburg PA
CBHW062127300426
44115CB00012BA/1842